The
Horse
Behavior
Problem Solver

**YOUR QUESTIONS ANSWERED ABOUT
HOW HORSES THINK, LEARN, AND REACT**

JESSICA JAHIEL

Illustrations by Claudia Coleman

 Storey Publishing

The mission of Storey Publishing is to serve our customers by publishing practical information that encourages personal independence in harmony with the environment.

Edited by Deborah Burns
Art direction by Lisa Clark and Meredith Maker
Cover design by Kent Lew
Cover photograph ©Adam Jahiel
Text design and production by Cynthia McFarland
Indexed by Susan Olason

Printed in the United States by Versa Press

10 9 8 7 6 5 4 3

LIBRARY OF CONGRESS CATALOGING-IN-PUBLICATION DATA

Jahiel, Jessica.
  The horse behavior problem solver : your questions answered about how horses think, learn, and react / Jessica Jahiel.
      p. cm.
  Includes bibliographical references and index.
  ISBN-13: 978-1-58017-525-8; ISBN-10: 1-58017-525-2 (alk. paper)
  ISBN-13: 978-1-58017-524-1; ISBN-10: 1-58017-524-4 (pbk. : alk.paper)
  1. Horses—Behavior—Miscellanea. 2. Horsemanship—Miscellanea. I.
Title.
SF281 .J35 2004
636.1'0835—dc22
                                                                    2003021733

Contents

ACKNOWLEDGMENTS

No book is ever the creation of a single individual.
In this case, several people (and one particular group of people)
stand out for their special contributions:

Madelyn Larsen, agent and friend,
who found the ideal publisher for this book.

Deb Burns, Lisa Clark, Cynthia McFarland, and Ilona Sherratt,
the Storey "dream team" that gave the book its form.

Claudia Coleman, the extraordinary artist who created the detailed,
accurate, and absolutely charming illustrations.

Karen Fletcher, "Web Goddess", without whom the HORSE-SENSE
mailing list and website would never have become a reality.

Last but not least: the HORSE-SENSE readers who have been
asking questions and telling their stories over the last eight years.

They are all constantly struggling with the difficulty
of matching theory to practice and applying horse management
concepts and general training principles to the individual animals
that they love, care for, and try so hard to understand.
Without them, this book would not exist.

DEDICATION

To the readers!

Horsemen around the world share certain qualities: a genuine affection for horses, an honest desire to learn, a willingness to listen to their horses, a willingness to look at the world around them and ask questions, and, above all, a willingness to give their horses the benefit of the doubt at all times.

Horsemanship doesn't mean learning lists and memorizing the "right" answers. It means watching, listening, reading, and learning. It means thinking about what you've learned, relating it to things you've seen and perhaps to things you've done, and applying your new understanding to your daily interactions with horses. Horsemanship means keeping your interest and curiosity alive, taking joy in learning and discovery, and always striving to learn more.

My goal is to help you understand how to figure things out for yourself by helping you to understand your horses. Most "behavior problems" in horses are nothing more or less than horses reacting to something in their environment. Most problems between humans and horses are the result of human actions — actions of a human involved in the present situation or in the past. Either way, the person who is in the best position to analyze and solve the problem is the current human in the horse's life — *you!*

My overall ambition, in my writing as well as in my clinics, has always been to enable horses and riders to understand each other better and enjoy each other more. Life is too short for any of us to make all the possible mistakes and discoveries on our own. It's essential for us to learn from other people's experiences — and that's what this book is all about.

FOREWORD

IN PAST CENTURIES, directions on how to partner with horses were few and far between. Horses had a purpose — to serve us — and we needed them to do so without complaint. Whether laboring in the fields, carrying soldiers to battle, or serving as transportation, equines were seen as utilitarian in nature.

But today's horses are so much more. Yes, some still toil for humankind, but today it's more of a partnership. Remote farms often find horses the ideal workmates. They protect and serve cities working with mounted police, and in the wilderness on park patrol. They partner with us in sport, from the racetrack to international Olympic events. They serve as friend, as mentor, as psychologist, and soulmate. For many of us, horses are our first love.

We owe it to them, then, to become educated, to find that "manual" that helps us understand the wonderful possibilities that exist between horse and rider. Jessica Jahiel has masterfully created one such book. In these pages, she examines our training and riding relationships, and provides valuable insight on how to solve the challenges that inevitably come our way.

So read on. And remember that in the chapters of your own horse life, the training issues you solve become footnotes on your way to a true union.

— MOIRA C. HARRIS
Editor, *Horse Illustrated*

PREFACE

"Why is my horse doing this, and what can I do about it?"

DURING THE THIRTY-PLUS YEARS since I began teaching riders and horse owners to understand their horses better, I've seen an encouraging trend: Horse owners are learning to ask much better questions. Instead of, "Is there a gadget/drug/punishment that will make my horse stop doing this?" today's horse owners are asking, "Why is my horse doing this, and what can I do about it?" The difference is huge and positive.

Even those who still think in terms of punishing their horses' misbehavior by mechanical or chemical means are often happy to find that all they really need is a greater awareness of their horses' feelings and a deeper understanding of the reasons behind their horses' actions. With very few exceptions, horse "misbehavior" is either normal horse behavior misinterpreted by humans, or behavior developed by the horses in response to mishandling by humans.

If you are a typical horse owner, you sometimes find yourself frustrated and baffled by the behavior exhibited by your horse. The problem may be new, or it may date to long before you acquired the horse. You may be alone on an isolated farm with no one to advise you, or at a busy suburban boarding or training stable where everyone is offering you advice — good, bad, and conflicting. You've resisted suggestions to "beat the behavior out of that horse," but you're still hoping for practical advice about what else you can do.

There are more than a few riders and horse owners who rarely see their horses, riding only in shows and meeting their trainers and horses on the show grounds. This book is aimed at another kind of person: you, the hands-on rider and horse owner. You care more about good horsemanship than ribbons, and you want to have a happy, trusting relationship with your horse.

Most behavior problems in horses can be managed, eliminated, or avoided entirely, provided that horse owners learn to understand and communicate clearly with their horses and manage them in a way that meets their needs. Many books indicate that there are simple generic formulas for problem solving with horses, but horse owners tend to find that there is a large gap between reading theory and actually putting it into practice. They buy books and videos, attend lectures, sign up for clinics, all in the hope of getting help with *their* horses and *their* situations.

If you're this kind of horse owner, you want to know how horses think, how they learn, how they develop behaviors and habits, and why they act the way they do. You want to know which behaviors are instinctive and which are learned, and you want to know what you can do to encourage, discourage, modify, or eliminate specific behaviors. You want to know how to prevent the development of bad habits in your young horses, and how to take appropriate corrective action to change or eliminate those habits in your older horses.

It is my hope that this book will help you understand your horses and enable you to put theory into practice. The issues discussed are common to all horses and horse owners, but they are presented here in a unique format: as a series of specific case studies — questions and answers — based on individual horses, people, and situations. The titles of the chapters are simple and self-explanatory; the questions are real and from ordinary riders and horse owners around the world.

For the last eight years, owners around the globe have been sending me their questions about horses, horse behavior, riding and training, and all other horse-related subjects, and I have answered several each week in the form of an on-line Q&A newsletter, *Jessica Jahiel's HORSE-SENSE: the Newsletter of Holistic Horsemanship*. The ever-increasing stream of questions, and the volume and intensity of reader responses, have made it clear that the world is full of riders and horse owners who need, want, and appreciate sensible, coherent, personalized information.

This book is a response to those questions and to reader preferences and needs. It is not a "cookbook"; you won't find a listing such as Rearing or Biting followed by a two-line formula for solving the problem. Instead, you'll find letters written by horse owners about their own horses and answers that combine general information about the problem and what probably caused it, as well as advice on what they can do for the specific horse in its specific situation.

Most of the answers are complex and demand that you think, consider, and ask yourself more questions. Don't worry if you end up with more questions than answers — a lifetime of horsemanship means a lifetime of asking questions, and your questions should become more complex and difficult as you grow in experience and understanding. As a wise old horseman once said, "The more I know, the more I know I don't know."

Each horse, owner, and situation is unique, which is why two questions about rearing or biting horses may have two different answers. Each answer is based on the question itself and on my assessment of the situation; the horse; and the experience, attitude, and abilities of the questioner. If a novice rider needs help to keep his horse from running back to the barn, I won't suggest that he perform a series of shallow serpentines in shoulder-in. In *every* answer, the emphasis is on the importance of understanding the nature of horses and knowing why horses act and react the way they do.

Can every problem be eliminated through simple changes in management and handling techniques? Not always. Most of the time, management changes are all that are needed, but sometimes discipline is required. If physical safety is an issue, discipline may be essential, but even necessary discipline must be done in accordance with the horse's nature so that the horse will understand and learn. Discipline must be clear, memorable, and make sense to the horse. Appropriate discipline, whether given by another member of the herd or by a human, is educational and leaves the horse feeling *more* secure. Lacking those two qualities is not discipline; it's either punishment or abuse, and neither has any place in horsemanship. Discipline must be educational, appropriate, performed promptly and swiftly and without anger, and then it must end, with no hard feelings on either side.

The best horse owners and riders are those who understand horse behavior in general, have a clear idea of what causes or provokes certain behaviors in horses, and are able to stand back and look at their own specific situations objectively. They analyze situations and act on the probabilities instead of guessing or assuming that their horses are bad, ornery, or resistant.

A good vet, a good riding instructor, and a good trainer are your best sources of immediate information and suggestions about a specific situation involving your horse. This book is not meant to replace any of those people; on the contrary, it is meant to add depth, clarity, and insight to the conversations you should have on a regular basis with your own equine professionals.

I hope that this book will help you achieve a better understanding of the nature of horses and the ways in which horses respond to different forms of management and handling. By better understanding your own horses, learning to look more closely at the situations and conditions to which their horses may be reacting, and understanding situations and events from the horses' points of view, you will be better prepared to have meaningful discussions with your vets, instructors, and trainers.

This is not intended to be a how-to book on the training of horses, but some discussion of training philosophies and techniques is inevitably included in the answers to most of the questions. Management, training, and riding are inextricably linked. Training a horse means teaching the horse, and every interaction you have with your horse teaches it *something*, even if all it learns is what kind of person you are and what kind of behavior it can expect from you.

All of the time, all over the world, I see riders and horse owners who want very much to do what's right and be good to their horses. The questions in this book come from just such riders and horse owners — real people like you with real horses, real situations, and real concerns. The answers address the ways in which they and you can do what's right and work with the horse to solve specific problems while building a strong, trusting relationship between horse and rider.

— JESSICA JAHIEL, *Summerwood Farm*

CHAPTER 1

Humans and Horses

IN RECENT YEARS, riders and horse owners have become increasingly interested in understanding more about the interactions between humans and horses. One of today's most popular concepts is that of the human exercising dominance over the horse by effectively becoming the "alpha horse" in the herd — even if the "herd" in question consists of only two beings. This is a useful concept as far as it goes, but all too often it is misunderstood and taken to extremes. Being chased and shouted at by a human doesn't make the horse think of that human as a trusted leader. Humans can become their horses' trusted leaders if they are willing to learn how horses think and what sort of leadership they want, and if they are willing to listen to their horses.

Being the "Alpha Horse"

Q I'm relatively new to horses, but my wife and daughter love them and have been riding for several years. We've recently bought a small farm, I'm retired from the military, and our horses are at home with us. My gals go to shows most weekends; I usually stay at home with the other horses.

My problem is establishing my authority with the horses. I don't like being crowded by large animals, and I find myself swatting them or yelling at them to get them to move back. My gals say I shouldn't have to do that. If I'm the "alpha horse" the others will step back and get out of my way to show respect.

First, do horses really recognize this kind of status? Second, if they do, how should I establish my alpha status? Third, how important is it that I become the "alpha horse"? When I was in the service, I never did like generals all that much.

A Relax. You don't actually have to play a general. You need to establish a superior status, but horse herds are hierarchical, not groups of omegas all bowing to the will of the single alpha. You don't have to overawe your horses — you need to outrank them, and you need to convince them that they can trust you.

Horses and riders should be happy to see each other
and should enjoy their time together.

Since you're ex-military, here is a question that will make sense to you: With whom does an enlisted man have regular contact? Whom is an enlisted man in the daily habit of noticing, paying attention to, staying out of the way of, obeying? Not the commander-in-chief, not a five-star general, but the person one or two ranks above him.

If your horse is a second-in-command type, then yes, you'll need to be the "alpha horse" — the general, so to speak. But if your horse, like most, would be more comfortable in the ranks of the herd hierarchy, all you need to do is show that you're one or two ranks above him. If he's a private, be a sergeant — you don't have to be a full-bird colonel.

To ask a horse to respect your space, make yourself larger. Inhale, lift your head and chest, square your shoulders, and raise your arms slightly from your sides. Imagine that you're walking down the sidewalk in a not-so-nice neighborhood and want the oncoming walkers to move out of your way. If you cringe, fold up, drop your head, and generally make yourself smaller, you're likely to get run over by humans and equines, because you're sending the message that it is *your* job to get out of *their* way.

Once you've established yourself as someone who outranks the horse, be clear, kind, and absolutely consistent. When you've gained the horse's respectful attention, you're well on your way to earning its trust.

Teaching Respect or Fear?

Q I have a wonderful six-month-old colt, Max. He is always happy to see me. We walk around and explore new things. When something scares him, I let him explore it. When he is ready, we move on. Sometimes he pulls back a little at a strange sound, as I'm sure most colts do.

My farrier is a great guy, seems to know a lot, and is well respected. A few months ago when he came out, he entered the pen before I had Max caught and haltered. I couldn't catch Max or even get close. I was frustrated but remained cool. My farrier said Max was defiant and needed to be caught on my terms. I never had a problem catching him before. The farrier ended up lassoing him. Max eventually calmed down, but was afraid of the lead rope for two weeks. Every time I walked up with the lead he would jump and sometimes run off. I wondered, What did he learn?

My farrier came back yesterday. I had Max caught and ready. He accepts having his hooves handled and doesn't mind the farrier's tools. The farrier walked up to Max, and suddenly Max reared and pulled away from me. I caught him and calmed him down. When the farrier approached, Max reared and pulled back again. He tried to get away every time the farrier approached. My farrier took the lead. Whenever Max pulled or reared, my farrier pulled him back. Max's halter had a chain under the chin, and Max was bleeding (slightly) from the chain. I changed the halter, but he kept rearing. My farrier got kicked a few times. I'm sure they will both hurt for a few days.

This horse's apprehension shows in his high head, wide eyes, flared nostrils, and tight mouth.

This is my dilemma: I was taught that horses should do what you want them to when you ask them. I agree, but I take a gentle, positive approach with horses. Once Max bit me, and I used the three-second rule and gave him a good smack to the ribs. He has never bitten again. Today Max let me go up to him, but jumped at other things (like the hose).

I think Max remembers the tight rope around his neck and remembers the farrier doing it to him. My farrier said, "Now he has learned that he can't push people around and act crazy." I'm not sure he learned that. I wonder if he has learned fear. Or am I too soft because I hate seeing my baby go through that? My farrier says I should get him gelded. What does that have to do with their relationship and the way Max acted around him? He is no problem with me or the gelding that is with him.

I like this farrier, and he is willing to come to my farm regularly. Should I let them work it out or find someone else to work with Max? I'm afraid that this will happen every time.

A You can force a horse into submission *once* just by overpowering him, whether you want him to be caught, stand for the farrier, get into a trailer, or just about anything else. But that's not good training. Instead of making the horse more familiar and comfortable with the situation, it teaches the horse to fear you and avoid that situation.

Every lesson should build *on* the previous lesson, *for* the next lesson. Loading a horse in a trailer, for instance, might take an hour the first time, but if you use that time to teach the horse that there is no pain involved and no need for fear, then the next time it might take half an hour — and so on, until he loads quickly and calmly. Similarly, when getting a horse accustomed to the sound and feel of clippers, using more time and patience in the beginning means needing less time and effort later.

Training is teaching. Time and patience are essential if you're going to teach horses. Whenever you work with a horse on anything, the next session should be easier and faster. Teach your horse for the future; don't try to show him that you're tougher and meaner and can force him to do something *right now*.

Max learned that he doesn't like to be roped, that he doesn't like the farrier, and that the farrier hurts him. These are not useful lessons. What he needed to learn was that he must allow himself to be caught when you want to catch him, and that he must stand reasonably still and allow his feet to be trimmed.

You may need a different farrier — not because yours is a bad farrier, but because he is a bad trainer. He created a violent, angry, adversarial situation with Max, and even if he is willing to be careful and patient from now on, it may be too late. A young horse that has been frightened, restrained, and hurt by someone may decide never to go near that particular person again. It's the risk you take when you opt for violent, forceful methods of dealing with horses.

A 10-year-old gelding that has a cranky day and doesn't want to stand for the farrier won't be injured, physically or mentally, if he gets a slap on the shoulder and is told, "Stand!" He has 10 years of experience with farriers and handling, and he knows what is expected of him. He knows that one yell and one slap mean, "You're out of line, now stand still," and that it's discipline, not abuse; thus he won't be afraid or feel that he must fight for his own survival. But without those years of experience, he might react just like Max.

Max has been frightened and hurt twice, as a suckling and as a young weanling. With no backlog of experience to tell him, "Stand quietly, this is not dangerous," he believes he's in danger and reacts by fighting for his life.

Horses react to fear and pain by running away — the flight response. When flight is impossible, they may fight. Holding a horse in one place and frightening or hurting him is, in effect, asking him to fight. Some "trainers" do this deliberately to force the horse into doing what they want. This practice is effective only if you are willing to take it to the limit and really break the horse — crushing his spirit and his mind to create a completely quiet, inert, resigned animal.

If an untrained or partially trained horse must stand still — say, for an emergency medical procedure — a calm handler with a twitch will get better results than will an angry handler with a rope or a chain.

That said, consider the farrier's viewpoint. Farriers don't like difficult horses or horses that bounce around; such horses may injure the farrier, and injured farriers can't make a living. A young colt is a baby, but even a baby horse can cause a severe injury. Your farrier is paid to trim your horse's hooves, not to train the horse — that is your job. If you put the farrier in a position where he has to do some "training" to ensure his own safety, that training is unlikely to be kind, slow, systematic, or progressive.

Teach your horse for the future. Don't try to show him that you're tougher and meaner and can force him to do something right now.

Your farrier wants to come in, do his job, and leave. He doesn't want to have to chase, catch, or subdue the horse to get the job done, and he doesn't want to put himself at unnecessary risk. There are enough physical risks in his job; even if no horse ever kicks him, bites him, steps on him, or jerks him around, he will probably end up with back trouble eventually. Furthermore, like our horses and ourselves, farriers can have bad days. If your bouncy baby horse happens to kick a farrier who is tired, sore, and has already been nailed by another horse, the farrier's reaction may not be pleasant or patient.

If you keep this particular farrier, then you, not the farrier, will have to work things out with Max. At six months, he can and must learn basic ground manners. Standing and leading are essential skills, and they aren't as simple as they seem. Standing means that your colt will stop and stay in one place when he is asked to stop and stay in one place. Leading means that he will go forward when you ask him to go forward, whether in the pen, in the pasture, in the barn aisle, through the woods, through a puddle, into a stall, or into a trailer. These lessons — "whoa" and "go" — are crucial. All of your horse's training will be based on those two concepts.

Max must stand calmly for the farrier — for his sake, for the farrier's sake, for your sake, and for the sake of all of his future training. In the two months before your farrier returns, you'll need to work with Max. Remember to wear your helmet while working with him: Rearing, striking, and kicking are normal colt behaviors, and they're dangerous. Don't take unnecessary chances.

Make leading, standing, and "farrier work" part of Max's daily routine. If he doesn't tie yet, run a long lead rope from his halter through a ring on the wall and back to your hand. This gives you the ability to be flexible without allowing him to pull back and run away. Ask him to stand, walk around him, touch him everywhere, run your hands down his legs, and pick up each foot in turn. Lift the foot and move it in different directions (without unbalancing or hurting Max), and tap the bottom of the hoof with the back of your hoof pick. Praise him for standing quietly, and put each hoof down carefully — never drop a foot — when you are ready. Practice until you can move his legs around and hold them up as the farrier will do, until you can hold each foot and tap it for as long as the farrier will. Take your time.

> *Max must stand calmly for the farrier — for his sake, for the farrier's sake, for your sake, and for the sake of all of his future training.*

When Max accepts this routine calmly, bring in a male friend (wearing a helmet) to watch while you go through the process with Max. Then hold Max while your friend repeats the routine — possibly a shorter version at first, picking up Max's feet for briefer periods and holding them closer to the ground and to his body.

When Max does something you like, praise him. When he doesn't, don't respond at all — pause and start again. Save the thumps and yelling "No!" for occasions when his actions are totally unacceptable. (Biting is one such behavior, and kicking is another.) But remember that a frightened horse, especially a colt, that can't pull away is very likely to rear, so set Max up for success by teaching him to stand calmly with his feet on the ground. If he is thinking about rearing, lead him forward into a turn. If he is moving forward on a slight curve, he won't be able to rear, and you can then praise him for coming forward when asked. This is setting him up for success. If you wait until he rears and then try to pull him down or punish him, that's setting him up for failure.

Do your leg-handling routine often, and make the experience as pleasant as possible. You want Max to develop the habit of standing quietly with you holding him while someone else handles his feet. When your farrier returns, talk with him before he approaches Max. Explain what you've been doing and exactly what you want him to do. If you want him to put Max's foot down and stand back if Max gets agitated, tell him. If you want him to wait while you lead Max in a circle and reposition him when you say, "Time out," tell him. If he understands that you are teaching Max to remain calm and under control, that you have a plan, and that you are counting on him to help implement that plan, he will be much more likely to follow your suggestions and much less likely to jump in and punish Max.

You have two long-term goals: You want Max to learn to stand calmly and quietly while his feet are trimmed, and you want your farrier to be willing to come out to your farm, knowing that your horses are easy to work with.

On the subject of gelding, your farrier is probably quite right. Six months is certainly old enough to geld a colt. Many breeders geld their colts at a few weeks old, and some even geld at a few days old. The earlier Max is gelded, the easier the process will be, and the more quickly he will recover. In another few months, Max will become "hormones with hooves." The sooner he is gelded, the sooner you can both relax and focus on his education.

Head Rubbing as a Sign of Dominance?

Q I've been told that horses should not be allowed to rub their heads on humans, that this is a dominance behavior and that riders should actively discourage it.

The school horse I ride regularly, Bubbles, was mistreated before he came to the school, and although he's a lovely, responsive horse to ride, as a consequence of the abuse he is very nervous around people and other horses. If you approach him or just put your hand out to him, he will pin his ears back and try to nip you. I always feed him treats when I go for lessons, so he is pleased to see me and whickers, and if he tries to nip me, a firm "No!" sorts him out and he looks sorry. He's never bitten me, so I think he's mostly bluff.

Lately when we are waiting to enter the arena or when we have finished a class, he will rub his head on me, and I've been pleased that Bubbles is seeking some human contact. But is this something I should let him do?

A No, you do not want to encourage this behavior. You should eliminate it, but in a nice way.

You are right to want your horse to trust you and be relaxed around you. He has obviously had hard times with previous riders and owners. The rubbing shows that he feels confident with you. He has accepted you as a friend and herd member and may be trying to initiate a mutual grooming session. Nonetheless, it's a good idea to discourage this practice in any horse.

Rubbing against you is an invasion of your personal space, and for horses, the right to invade another horse's personal space means that the invading horse is ranked higher in the herd than the horse whose space is being invaded.

Simple head rubbing can quickly escalate to pushing and shoving.

Personal space is a key concept in herd dynamics: The dominant individual can enter, or threaten to enter, the personal space of the others. Don't do things that will eventually convince your horse that he is the dominant one in this "herd." He'll be happier and more secure if you make it clear that he isn't to rub against you. It's different, however, if you initiate a scratching session; you have entered into his space to do something that he likes, and when you stop, that's that.

Rubbing may begin when a horse is trying to relieve an itch, but if you don't stop the practice, light rubbing can become hard rubbing, and hard rubbing can become pushing and shoving. If you don't say, "Stop that, I'm the dominant one here!" what began with an itch can indeed become an expression of dominance.

A horse testing to determine who is dominant is *not* being aggressive; this is normal horse behavior. Horses don't mind being number two or number ten, or even number one, in the herd. Knowing their rank makes them feel secure. What they dislike is not knowing where they stand in the ranking. Such horses are insecure and need to constantly test to see where they rank at any given moment.

There are other considerations, as well. A horse that rubs hard can knock you off your feet. Even if the rub expresses pure affection, you can still fall or get pushed into a gate or wall or another horse. Horses have no way of knowing that they may rub against your shoulder or back if you are wearing scruffy stable clothing, but not if you are wearing show clothes. They have no way of knowing that they may rub against some humans but not others (small ones, scared ones, clean ones). Horses need consistency. They can't have two sets of manners — barn manners and "party manners" (for shows and such). They simply don't know when something "doesn't count."

Teach this horse to wait for you to move into his space to pet him. In the long run, you'll be keeping him out of trouble with other people. Some people will hit out of fear if a horse leans into them or rubs against them; others feel that as a matter of principle, they must slap or punch the horse. By teaching the horse that rubbing is unacceptable, you'll save him from a lot of angry reactions, including smacks and slaps that he won't understand.

You have done good things with this horse. You've gained his confidence, and he feels safe with you. Let him feel safe and secure because he trusts you — and because *you* are in charge. Since you can stop him with a spoken "No," say that when he begins to rub against you. Then when he stands quietly, you can reach over and give him a scratch or a cuddle, and step back when you have finished. You won't frighten him or upset him; he'll feel much more secure because he'll know exactly what he can and can't do.

Developing a Relationship

Q My first horse, Guy, was my very best friend. I trusted him implicitly because he was always right! He was my best friend on the ground and cared for me in the saddle. His ears were always turned directly toward me. (I wish my husband listened as well or as willingly!) We had to put him down three years ago, just two weeks before his forty-eighth birthday. He was the truest friend and best possible horse and will always be missed.

When you and your horse are friends, you'll find that you can enjoy your time together even if you're just "doing nothing."

My new horse, Red, has come along beautifully in all the training that my husband has put him through: He stands perfectly still at the mounting stairs and is very safe, dependable, and trail-smart. I have no trouble with our riding relationship, as he inspires no fear in me. I cannot seem to establish the same relationship on the ground that I had with Guy. He and I spent many enjoyable, comfortable hours in each other's company. Perhaps we'd walk along in the hay pastures, munching grass and talking, or he would stand behind me looking at the pictures in a book I'd read to him. Guy was a wonderful companion.

Red is insecure in my presence, as I'm not there regularly enough because of work. He is often head shy (from mistreatment before we bought him), nervous, and very concerned about our other horses. Sharing is unknown to him, whether it's carrots or companionship.

Here is where the trouble lies: I don't know how to teach him what I like, or if I try to discover what he likes, such as massage or touch, there is no feedback from him. Most other horses talk with their ears (forward for positive, backward for negative, and so on) or body language, and Red seems to have never learned this. He speaks another language than what I'm used to, so we don't communicate well.

I'm at a loss to find ways to "get together" with this horse. He's kind and gentle and willing to please, and I feel clueless around him. Can you help me learn how to communicate with a very different kind of horse? I want to develop into his friend and for him to become my friend.

A Your new horse obviously wants to please you, and that's always a good sign. He carries some emotional baggage, but what horse doesn't?

This horse was probably raised in a stall or in isolation, and that makes his life, and your job, quite difficult. Horses learn to speak "horse" by growing up and interacting with other horses. Good trainers speak "horse" and can deal effectively with most horses — but not with horses that don't speak the language themselves.

Red is making progress; he's learning "horse" from the others in the pasture, which is wonderful, and he's obviously smart enough to learn it, which is even more wonderful. And he has learned to be a riding horse — more proof that he is teachable! He doesn't yet understand that there's more to life with humans than simply obeying them when under saddle. He doesn't yet realize that humans can make very good friends. You can teach him that.

For your first step in building an understanding with your horse, spend a day with him — not riding or grooming him, just watching him. This is a very old, tried-and-true method of getting to know a horse. A full day may seem like a long time, but it's an excellent investment in understanding. Observe what he does, how he eats, when he naps, what his actions and reactions are when he deals with other horses, where he grazes, what kind of grass he prefers, whether he likes to roll, and so forth. If he indicates to another horses that he likes to be scratched somewhere, you can scratch those same spots later. If he is more nervous when another horse comes up behind him from the left than from the right, or vice versa, remember that when you handle him.

Meanwhile, approach him with an open mind. Watch and wait, be patient, and be kind. It took years for you and Guy to develop your relationship. It'll take time for you and Red to develop a relationship, and the abuse/mishandling in Red's background will make the process longer, but you'll get there.

Horses perceive you not through your words or intentions, but through your actions. Horse language is very physical, although there are verbal components, and horses can learn to understand many words and tones. But in the beginning, which is where you are with Red, think physical language.

Every movement you make tells your horse something, either about what you expect from him or about what kind of person you are. So be aware of how you move, and *think* before you move. Be careful, deliberate, precise, and slow in whatever you do — changing a water bucket, putting grain in the manger, putting on a halter, stroking a neck, picking out hooves, combing a mane. Sudden, jerky, fast, or uncoordinated movements will startle and frighten a horse; try to move as though you were moving through water. Make all your movements deliberate, slow, and large. You want to be very clear so that your horse can relax and learn to trust you.

As Red becomes more relaxed, trusting, and confident in your company, you won't have to move so slowly. You'll find that as time goes by you can make smaller movements. When Red is relaxed, attentive, and focused on you, he will notice and respond to smaller signals.

Talk to him! Don't expect him to understand the words, but use your voice. The human voice can be wonderfully soothing to a horse. Keep it low and slow. High squeaky sounds, shallow breathing, and sudden noises create fear and apprehension, while low, soft sounds; slow, deep breathing; and quiet talking promote relaxation.

With horses, the more slowly you proceed, the more quickly you will get where you want to go.

CHAPTER 2

Catching and Leading

No MATTER what you want to do with a horse, you have to catch it first. Many long-time horse owners take it for granted that their horses will come up to them, stand quietly while halters are put on or lead ropes are attached, and then walk quietly with them, putting no pressure on the lead rope, turning when the owner turns, and even stopping when the owner stops.

It isn't always this way. Some horses are difficult to catch in the field; others are even difficult to catch in the stall. Owners are frustrated by horses that avoid capture or that pull back when led. Owners are endangered by horses that kick or rear on the way to the barn and by horses that pull away or whirl and kick when they're returned to the pasture.

Horse That Pulls Back

Q My wife and I purchased a 15.2 hh, 12-year-old gelding from a local youth ranch. Socks is a great horse: responsive, affectionate (really, he's a "lap horse"), intelligent, well-mannered on the ground, a good mover, and well-schooled under saddle.

Socks has only one behavior problem, and it's why the ranch sold him. He is spooky and pulls back on occasion when standing tied. Under saddle, he spooks in place rather than spinning, running, or rearing, so he seems a good prospect.

With consistent handling, he has gotten much better during the past ten months. However, he has suddenly begun to pull back again.

With the warmer weather, there is more activity at the stable — including kids and other people who are quick and boisterous. A few Sundays ago, Socks was tied in the grooming area. My wife was by him. An adolescent visitor with baggy, flapping clothing threw down his bicycle 25 feet from Socks. Socks startled and pulled back, the slipknot on the lead rope gave out, and he backed through an insubstantial fence (1" x 8" rails). He flipped over backward on the breaking rails; fortunately, neither he nor any people were hurt. Socks is now jumpy in the grooming area. My wife and I find that he is comforted by our

When a horse is suddenly frightened, his natural reaction is to try to escape.

presence, so one of us stands by him when he is tied. I have insisted on tying him so he does not learn he can pull back and get away. If he were to pull back and get in trouble, one of us would be in a position to pull the quick-release knot loose. We have made a point to take him to the farthest part of the grooming area, away from other people and horses. We tie him next to our other horse, who is fairly bombproof and is his trail buddy.

After the grooming incident, when I approach with Socks's saddle, he tenses and may jig a step but usually lets me continue to put on his tack. A few times he has pulled back. When he does, he recovers quickly with my calm voice and deliberate, slow movements. All the "giving to the halter" work may be paying off, also. I talk to him when approaching and rub him with the saddle blanket before putting it on him. We have a cue — I touch his elbow firmly with mine — that the saddle is next, and he accepts it calmly, even if he has just pulled back.

At the ranch where Socks previously lived, the procedure was for the nearest wrangler to kick him in the rear when he pulled back and make a disapproving sound. Another stable patron has suggested that we are being too easy and Socks is training us to get attention. I do not think such advice is well founded and have avoided kicking him, trying to build trust instead. While I see progress, I'm concerned about his apparent reversion in a higher-excitement environment.

Are we doing the right thing? Is his behavior to be expected with more people and activity? Should we continue on as we have, calmly building trust? Should we become more actively disapproving when he pulls back by kicking him in the rear with a sharp "buzzer" sound? If we did that, wouldn't the kick and sound just confirm that he has something to be afraid of?

A In this instance, you've done most of my work for me. As I read through your account of the last ten months with Socks, it was clear that you had already done almost everything I would have suggested that you do. Socks is a lucky horse.

In reply to your specific questions: Yes, you are doing the right things. His behavior is an understandable reaction, considering the increased number of people and activities. You could try to teach him something in the back pasture at home with no other horses or humans around, then bring him into the arena and teach it to him again. Next, add a few more people and another horse or two, or perhaps some music, and teach it to him again. It will get easier each time, but teaching your horse when there are no distractions, and teaching him in the presence of distractions are two different things. You should continue calmly building trust; you're in this for the long haul. Begin as you mean to go on, and then continue in the same way.

Disapproval and reprimands, such as the buzzer sound, are not appropriate actions as long as you perceive him to be frightened, which seems to be the case. It will simply frighten him more, which will make him sit back, hit the rope, and panic. Your goal is to make him feel *less* threatened, not more. It would be a good idea to teach him a signal that means, "Stand up straight, drop your head, relax"; it's a great "default" command for a horse, just as "Down" or "Stay" is for a dog. You can use it whenever the situation calls for the animal *not* to do what he's doing (or what he's thinking about doing). Take every opportunity to tell the horse what you do want, instead of yelling at him for doing something you didn't want him to do.

It may take only a few repetitions to help a horse catch on to an idea, but it will take many, many repetitions to turn the new behavior into a habit.

Don't kick or hit your horse. I have yet to meet a horse or human that has learned to feel trusting and secure as a result of being hit or kicked. However, a buzzer signal is useful under certain circumstances, and you may find it to be a good "Freeze, don't move a muscle, don't even think about moving!" signal. There's nothing quite like it if your horse ever gets caught in wire, for instance.

In your case, though, I would suggest that you teach Socks a signal that means, "Yes, good boy, you're doing what I asked." Clicker training would be an excellent choice for Socks, as it's clear and will allow you to register your approval while he is in mid-behavior. You'll be able to reward such behaviors as standing quietly and dropping his head; by rewarding them, you'll be able to reinforce them. Eventually, you'll even be able to request and expect those behaviors.

It's an entirely natural horse reaction to startle and run when suddenly frightened, especially when the horse is tied (that's already a frightening situation for a horse). Staying with Socks when he's tied should be routine, not a special treat. Leaving a horse alone and tied in the aisle of a busy barn is asking for trouble.

You've done a great job for the amount of time you've had, and for the amount of emotional baggage that Socks is carrying.

Successful training (and retraining) is gradual and progressive. The first step is to introduce a concept at home, set the scene so that everything will go well with as few distractions as possible so the horse can learn what you want him to learn — or better yet, he can teach himself what you want him to learn. Then, when he's mastered the concept or the skill, you do it repeatedly over weeks and months. It may take only a few repetitions to help a horse catch on to an idea, but it will take many, many repetitions to turn the new behavior into a habit.

Step two of training isn't to move on to the next subject, it's to repeat the same material *with distractions.* Add another horse in the arena or people talking next to the arena or someone playing basketball against the side of the barn. Your horse will regress a little or a lot. *That's normal.* What he's learned isn't yet part of him — at least not to the point at which he can do it on autopilot.

The horse that can walk, trot, canter, stop, turn, and back up without distractions can learn to do all of those things in the presence of a few distractions at home, and then in the presence of more distractions at home, and then away from home with few distractions, and then away from home with more distractions. Take it a little at a time, and expect some regression whenever you change the venue and/or add more distractions. The overall picture will show an upward trend, but if you look closely, you'll see that the line is actually a series of small zigzags: three steps forward, two steps back (with added distractions), then three steps forward, and so on. That's how progress works; it's not strictly uphill and linear.

You're making good progress and doing well. Don't be in a hurry, and don't let anyone push you. You're not training Socks for today, you're training him for next month and next year and the year after, and all the years after that.

Ears Forward, Ears Back

Q I've been trying to watch horses and find out more about how they signal how they're feeling. I never really noticed what horses do with their ears until I got a horse of my own. Now I want to understand his ear signals, and I'm not sure if I'm getting it right. I've been told that he will keep his ears forward if he is friendly and respectful of me, but that if his ears go back, he

On high alert

Angry and threatening

Calm and aware

Listening to the rider

Relaxed and secure

A horse's ears speak volumes.

is about to misbehave. When I ride him, he usually has one ear forward and one back, and he moves them around a lot. He hardly ever puts both ears forward. I guess this means he is not paying very much attention to me, probably because he knows I'm not a very good rider. Or does it mean that he doesn't like me? How can I get him to like and respect me so that he will put his ears forward and keep them there? I would like him to be like one of the show horses I see in magazines that always have their ears forward.

A You may be a better rider than you think. When you see your horse's ears swiveling, or see one ear coming back toward you and the other pointing ahead, this is good. It doesn't mean that your horse has a problem with you or your riding, it means that your horse is exactly what you want him to be during a ride: relaxed and attentive.

When a horse is concerned or nervous about something he sees or hears, he will become very alert. He will look directly at the source of his concern, and his ears will point in that direction. Horses' eyes and ears work together. A horse with his ears rigidly forward has all his attention on something — but that something isn't the rider.

If one of your horse's ears turns back toward you during a ride, that's normal and positive; it means he's listening to you. Don't worry about "ears back" unless you see *both* ears back, as far back as they can go, flattened along the horse's neck. Both ears in that position mean that the horse is very afraid or very angry.

Don't worry, you won't confuse the two positions. The difference is very clear, like the difference between a person raising his arm and waving at you and a person pulling back his arm and making a threatening fist. And there are other signs that will accompany an angry or frightened ear position: The horse's body will typically become rigid and unmoving and will feel as though it's suddenly grown much larger.

The magazine photos with the alert-looking horses are pretty, but they're not easy to take. Attend a few shows and watch carefully when the winners' photos are taken. You'll see photographers' assistants, trainers, and even helpful spectators waving hats, making funny sounds, rattling their change or their car keys, and generally doing anything and everything they can to persuade the horse to become alert and put both ears forward, even for an instant. When the horse is relaxed and a little bored, this can be quite a challenge.

Be glad that your horse is comfortable and relaxed when you're riding him. A nervous, frightened, ultra-alert horse with his ears up and forward all the time might be a photographer's dream, but it would be a rider's nightmare.

Kicking Habit

Q I bought my first horse two years ago and after four months discovered she was pregnant. Her filly is such a good girl: She leads well, and we can clean her stall with her in it. She has about an acre to run in and two other horses to keep her company.

The problem is that when she is in the stall and we want to open the door, or when she wants her back scratched and I don't have the time, I give her butt a soft push. She pins her ears back and turns around and kicks out. When she does that, I go to her head and walk her around. I do not want to hit her because I believe she is doing it because she feels threatened. I talk to her when I am coming in and when I'm in the stall. I do not want her to develop the habit of kicking around people, but I know what my riding instructor would say: Give her a kick. Please help.

A I won't say, "Give her a kick," but she does need to learn good stall man-ners and she can't be allowed to kick at humans. Kicking isn't acceptable behavior; sooner or later she's going to hurt a human, another horse, or herself.

First, I'll remind you that at her age, she really should be outdoors all the time, exercising freely, and not standing in a stall. Outdoor foals can work off their energy the way they're designed to — it's good for their bodies and their minds. Too much time in a stall is bad for any horse, and even worse for a foal.

I understand that you don't want to hit your filly, but by going around to her head and leading her when she kicks at you, you've taught her that you *want* her to kick. Kicking is a great attention-getting behavior; after all, whenever she does it, you come in and walk her around.

It's safest for both handlers and horses if the horses learn to turn and face the handlers whenever they enter the stall or paddock. Among horses, getting out of the way is a sign of respect. Kicking, or threatening to kick, when touched is horse language for "Move it, soldier, you're in the officer's way!" In other words, your filly thinks that she outranks you, and that she doesn't need to get out of your way — *you* need to get out of *her* way.

You need to convince her that you outrank her. Right now she's nine or ten months old and furry and cute, but she still outweighs you and has hard little hooves and plenty of muscle. She needs to learn who is "boss mare" soon, so that by the time she is fully-grown, she won't even think about challenging you.

Don't hit her, but do give her some leading lessons. She needs to move smoothly and quietly in whatever direction you indicate: forward, backward, turning to the left and to the right. She needs to learn to stand, tied or untied, and to move her hindquarters away from you when you tap her with a finger and say, "Over." This is a very important lesson, not just for your convenience in getting into her stall, but for everything you will do with her on the ground and under saddle in the future. For example, she'll need to learn to move away from your leg under saddle, and this is where it begins.

Horses are born with an instinct to move into pressure, not away from it, so this is indeed something that you need to teach her. Use your voice. A calm, soothing tone tells her that she is a good girl; if you calmly say, "Ow, sweetie, that really hurt me a lot when you kicked me in the leg just now," she will regis-ter only the calm tone and think that everything is just fine — and see no reason to change anything she is doing. If, on the other hand, you save the calm, sweet, slow, soft voice for praise and make a loud, rude noise to indicate that you are displeased, your communication with her will be much clearer. Try my patented game-show-buzzer sound — you know, the one you hear on just about every show when someone gets a wrong answer. That sudden, loud, nasal, *naaaaaah* sound is very effective with horses. Horses have excellent hearing and dislike loud, rude noises. The buzzer sound makes the point clearly, effectively, and immediately. Yelling "No!" can also be quite effective, but since *no* sounds very similar to *whoa*, I prefer to use my buzzer noise whenever I want to tell the horses, "Wrong answer!" The important thing is to make the noise, or the word, stand on its own. Don't try to slip a command or a reprimand into the middle of a long sentence; you'll only confuse the horse.

When you've used your buzzer noise in response to her ears-back, kick-threat action, just wait. Don't go around to her head, don't talk to her soothingly, don't reward her in any way — until she turns toward you, even slightly, even just bending her neck. Then praise her and wait. Most youngsters are clever enough to figure out what you like and don't like if you make your feelings clear, and that

Problem behaviors left uncorrected in a foal will become more dangerous as the horse matures.

means encouraging the behavior you want, actively discouraging any completely unacceptable behaviors, and saying and doing *nothing* in response to any wrong guess that isn't actively dangerous. When she takes a step toward you, praise her and scratch her neck or withers. You want to create a new habit in her: that of watching you, paying attention to you, and approaching you with her *front* end.

Don't do too much at one time; young horses have short attention spans. Short, clear lessons repeated daily will have the effect you want. A few minutes at a time is all you can ask of a filly this age. If she kicks and you have to smack the offending leg with a whip, do it — and make the buzzer noise — and remember that you are friends again as soon as her foot touches the ground. This is horse discipline, and she'll understand it. If she kicked her mother, the reaction would be instantaneous: a sharp squeal and a sharp nip, with no hard feelings afterward.

Foals are sweet and cute, but remember that everything you do with them in their first year will either save you time and trouble later or cause you trouble and force you to take much more time in the future. Firmness now will eliminate a lot of resistance later.

You'll find that being firm and clear with your filly won't make her cranky or resentful. On the contrary, she will feel much more secure and happy once she realizes that she isn't the leader after all.

Hard-to-Catch Horse

Q I have two horses, a gelding and a mare, and my problem is a common one. I can catch my gelding with little difficulty, but I always end up working twice as hard to catch my mare. I have tried a number of things, like taking feed in with me, going to my gelding and waiting till the mare comes to me, and separating the two. I've even tried catching her, taking her out to eat grass or a treat, and then letting her go, but nothing seems to help. I've run out of ideas and I am at my wits' end here. What can I do to make it a little easier to catch my mare?

A This is a common problem, and it's a very annoying one. You're on the right track, though. Your idea of catching her, taking her for a treat, and then letting her go is a good one. Your mare needs to associate getting caught with something pleasant.

The best way to convince a horse that something is pleasant is to make it true. This doesn't just mean treats, although going into the field and giving the mare a treat when she comes up to you, then turning and walking away, can be a very effective method of creating interest. It means creating a positive expectation in your mare so that she actually looks forward to those times when you come to take her out of the field.

When your mare leaves the field with you, what happens? A horse that enjoys its work is always easier to catch than a horse that dislikes the time it spends under saddle. If your horse nickers and comes toward you when she sees you coming with a saddle on your arm, that's a very good sign. If she comes to you when you have a treat but won't get near you when you have a halter, lead rope, or tack, that's not such a good sign.

*With patience and persistence, even the most confirmed evasion
artist can be taught to be caught easily.*

You need to teach your mare that it's quite safe to approach you in the pasture, because nine times out of ten, she will just get a treat and a scratch and you won't try to hold her — in fact, you'll walk away. The tenth time, when you *do* take her in, give her a small feeding while you groom her and make the entire experience — grooming, tacking up, and riding — as pleasant and positive as you can. Then take her back to the field and give her another small treat just before you turn her out.

Double-check everything that could make her uncomfortable while she's working — her teeth, her back, her feet, her bit, and the fit of her saddle and bridle. When you ride her, talk to her and encourage her so that she enjoys the experience. Praise her when she does well, when she tries, and when she seems to be thinking about trying. Keep her comfortable, make her work easy, and take every opportunity to praise her. Making the work fun can effect a huge change in a horse's attitude about being caught.

Take your time, be patient, and realize that no two horses are exactly alike. Your mare may always be a little harder to catch than your gelding, just as some horses will always stand for a moment and look into a trailer before loading, while others will walk right in. The important part is for you to be able to catch your mare without having to follow her around the pasture for an hour until she gets bored enough to stand in one place — although that too can work.

Rearing While Being Led

Q I have a 16.2 hh, five-year-old Thoroughbred gelding. He has recently been off work for three weeks due to an injury, and he has started rearing and pawing the air as he is being led. He is right up in the air, and the hooves come increasingly close to me. I have tried snapping his lead rope tight as immediate discipline. Is there anything else that I can do to prevent this from turning into a habit? He has also reared up when being ridden and fallen over backward. Luckily, no serious injury was incurred.

A Rearing is perhaps the single most dangerous behavior that a horse can exhibit. If it becomes a confirmed habit, the only safe course is to get rid of the horse.

Your horse is young and energetic, and it's understandable if he reacts badly to being confined. But horses must learn that rearing, like biting, is not acceptable under any circumstances. In this situation, particularly if the initial injury was to a hind leg, the act of rearing, with the extra stress it imposes on the hind legs, could compromise your horse's healing. Because of the risk of damage, you should mention this new habit to your vet, ask for suggestions, and perhaps ask him to come out and examine the horse closely.

When he was injured and confined to his stall, did you reduce or eliminate his concentrates and offer him only grass hay, or a mixture of grass and alfalfa? Thoroughbreds — like horses of any breed — become agitated in confinement if they are fed as though they were in full work mode. (Don't assume that an overfed horse will become fat. Some confined horses remain at the same weight, but become nervous and aggressive.) In any case, confined horses tend to develop "stall courage," since they have no outlet for their energy. Now that he is rearing, you must try to eliminate this habit as quickly as possible, so that it will be safe for you to keep the horse.

First, *never* handle this horse unless you are wearing your safety helmet. This is one of the best moves you can make to ensure your own safety while you retrain your horse.

If your horse rears while you are leading him, you may be able to shift his balance in that moment just before the rear, when his weight begins to go back onto his hind legs. There is always a brief pause before this happens — perhaps just a fraction of one second — but if you are very attentive, this is enough

Rearing is dangerous to horse and human alike and needs to be corrected promptly.

warning for you to snap the lead and take him not just forward (this could become a pulling contest, and he would surely win), but *sideways* and forward.

This has three effects: First, it shifts the weight of the horse's forehand to one side, and he will naturally try to put his front feet down to balance his weight. Second, it puts his attention on you, because you are telling him to do something; "Come over this way and come along" is a much more effective command than "Don't rear!" Third, it's a distraction. Often a horse taken sharply sideways and forward will forget that he was thinking about rearing. This works quite well with overeager young horses being turned out into their fields in the morning. When they try to rear, it's comparatively easy to break the habit by taking them sideways each time they think about going up.

Whenever you train a horse to do (or to stop doing) anything at all, you must always make it easy and pleasant for the horse to do what you want him to do and difficult and unpleasant for the horse to do what you do not want him to do. But you have to be careful and think about exactly what you are doing with the horse and why, and what the effect is likely to be.

Standing, yelling, and jerking the lead will not help — it will make matters worse, as the horse will react by coming to a complete stop, then pulling back and up. This will put him in an even better position to rear. If, on the other hand, you take advantage of the moment to shift his balance sideways and put more weight on his front end, he will have to rebalance and move forward, and rearing will become much more difficult.

Don't try to lead him from the bridle or from the bit, and don't try to use a bit to "cure" the rearing. You will only make it worse, as a horse with a sore mouth will often rear higher and even go over backward. Instead, lead him from a longeing cavesson, which will give you much more authority without causing him pain. Some people will tell you to use a chain over the horse's nose, but there are several disadvantages to this. One is that it inflicts severe pain, which is just as likely to cause the horse to rear and go over; another is that the chain will tighten when you jerk the lead, but will not necessarily loosen afterward. And a third disadvantage, in the long term, is that punishment is not your goal — retraining is your goal, and you can do that much more effectively with a longeing cavesson. Use a properly designed and properly fitted one with hinged steel plates on the noseband, not a head collar with rings sewn onto the nosepiece.

Whatever you do, do not sit back, lift your hands, or pull on both reins. These actions encourage your horse to rear.

Rearing under saddle is also extremely dangerous. Before you do anything else, have the horse's teeth checked, just in case there might be a sharp edge somewhere contributing to mouth pain. Check his bit as well for fit and suitability; *any* mouth pain can provoke a rear.

For a horse to rear under saddle, he must stop and shift his balance back onto his hind legs. If this happens while you are riding, you can do exactly what you did on the ground: take the horse forward and lead him into a turn. Lean forward, loosen your outside rein, and take your inside rein hand quite low, bringing his nose toward your knee (not as far as your knee, just in that direction). At the same time, use your legs strongly to send the horse forward. The result should be a circle in the direction of your low inside hand. By putting weight (yours and his) onto his forehand and taking his head and neck to the side while sending him forward, you make it easier for him to keep his feet on the ground. He can't rear until he has both hind legs together underneath him, and he can't stop and rebalance them there if he is moving forward in a circle.

If you aren't paying close attention and the moment of hesitation passes without any action on your part, immediately lean forward when the horse rears, loosening the reins and stretching your arms around his neck. Weighting his forehand like this may send him down and forward, or it may not, but at least it will make it more difficult for him to rear high and very difficult for him to go over backward.

Whatever you do, do *not* sit back, lift your hands, or pull on both reins; those actions make it easy for the horse to rear, even *encourage* him to rear, and make it more likely that he will go over backward. Riders have been killed this way. If you feel the horse going up high enough that he is likely to go over backward, take your feet out of the stirrups immediately, lean forward with both arms around his neck, and slide off, landing feet first. Sometimes bailing out is necessary just for survival. If he does go over backward, you do not want your body to be between the horse and the ground.

Preventing rearing requires knowledge, planning, and focus. You must know what is involved in a rear and in what position the horse must place himself in order to rear. You must also have a plan so that you can react without hesitation at the very moment that the idea of rearing comes into the horse's mind. If you are sensitive to what the horse is doing and thinking and keep your focus on him and on the information he is giving you, you will sense that tiny hesitation and send him forward and sideways before the rear actually happens. It's much easier to prevent rearing than to deal with it.

Horse Whirls and Kicks When Turned Out

Q My horse is well behaved most of the time. My only real problem is when I turn him out. He gets turned out every day in a pasture with five other horses. After I ride him, I always take off his tack and put on his halter and lead rope and walk him down to the pasture and turn him out with his friends. When we get near the gate he starts to dance a little, and by the time I open it and he goes through, he is really excited. He starts shaking his head and pulling on the lead, and I have to keep pulling back on the lead and yelling, "Whoa!" just to get his attention. When I undo the lead rope, he rips away from me and runs to the other horses, but sometimes he gives a big buck first. Last night he hit my arm with one of his hind feet. He doesn't wear shoes but it hurt anyway, and I have a big bruise. It hurts my feelings that he is in such a hurry to get away from me, and now it hurts physically too. He is so easy to catch in the pasture, so why is he such a problem when I turn him back out?

A Turning out a horse can indeed be dangerous, as you've found out. Your horse isn't desperate to get away from you, and he isn't kicking at you because he dislikes you. If he didn't want to be with you, you wouldn't find it so easy to catch him and take him out of the pasture when you want to ride him.

By the time the ride is over, your horse is thinking about being out with his friends, free to eat and move around and play games without interference from any human. After a ride, he's warmed up and feeling good. He's happy to see his friends and happy to be turned out — and he's not paying much attention to you at all. You need to get his attention on you and keep it there, but yelling at him and jerking the lead rope aren't the best techniques.

In addition, some horse owners like to slap their horses on the haunches and yell when they turn them out, just for the fun of watching them wheel and run away. This is not a good or safe practice, but it's common, and it's possible that a

It's worth the time to train a horse to stand quietly when you turn him loose.

previous owner or handler taught your horse to expect this. But whether he's kicking and running out of habit or out of joy, you can focus his attention on you and keep it there — and teach him to stand and wait until you're ready for him to run away and join his friends.

Spend some time practicing and perfecting your leading skills. Your horse should pay close attention to you and should walk forward, turn in either direction, and back up for as many steps as you ask, and he should halt and stand quietly when you ask.

In the short term, treats can be helpful. Don't use a bucket of grain — it will only attract the other horses to the gate. Carry a few peppermint candies (preferably ones in noisy plastic wrappers) in your pocket. Unwrap one before you open the pasture gate. When you reach the gate, instead of pulling and yelling to get your horse's attention, ask him to stop and stand, praise him, crinkle the wrapper, and give him his treat. When he has eaten it, take out a second treat (be obvious about it; you *want* your horse to notice), open the gate, walk through with your horse, and turn him around so that

> *If he knows that he might get a treat but he isn't sure, he'll be very interested in pleasing you.*

he is facing the gate. Ask him to stop and stand, close the gate, praise him, crinkle the paper again, and give him his treat. Talk to him quietly for a moment, then unfasten the lead rope, but keep one hand on his halter. Stand with your back to the gate and your horse facing you, pull out one more treat, praise your horse for standing, and give him the treat. Then take your hand off the halter and step back. *Never* turn your back on the horse, and never take your attention off the horse — if he does whirl and buck for the sheer joy of it, you can get hurt.

Once you've gotten your horse to the point that he is calmly standing and waiting for his treat, you can begin offering the treats less often — perhaps every third or fourth time you turn him out. This will reinforce his new behavior. If he comes to expect treats every time he's turned out, he may begin to pester you for treats, which will cause other problems. If he knows that he *might* get a treat but he isn't sure whether this will be the time, he'll be very interested in pleasing you, and you'll be able to use verbal cues and the treats to reinforce and shape the behavior you want.

Frightened Untrained Horse

Q I just bought a mare. She is about five years old, has never been broke, and I am sure she has been abused. I have had her and been working with her for a month. I now have her in a small pasture and can get her to come up for feed, but not when I'm anywhere close. When I make the slightest move or noise she panics.

Is there a way that I can give her a drug to help calm her down so that I can get a halter on her and show her that all humankind is not cruel? I have other horses around that I love and give affection to in front of her, trying to show her that no one will hurt her.

A What you need in this situation is goodwill and patience. If this horse is five years old and has been abused, there's a good chance that all she knows about people is that she would prefer to stay away from them. Even if she hasn't been abused, she may have no reason to like or enjoy human company. You're going to have to convince her otherwise, but you can't force her to trust you. You're going to have to spend time showing her that you can be trusted.

First, check her diet. If she's in a good pasture, she may not need more than grazing, a salt block, and water. If the pasture isn't adequate, you may need to supplement with hay, but I'd suggest using grass hay or a grass mix, not alfalfa. Talk to your vet about a suitable feeding program.

Second, get her used to your presence. Take a lawn chair, a book, and a "boom-box" out to the pasture, sit down, start playing some soft music, and settle in. Don't chase her, don't try to catch her, don't even stare at her; just sit. For the first few days, she may stay as far from you as she can get. But horses are sociable animals, and when she becomes less afraid, she will become curious, and she'll want to see what you are doing.

When she starts to work her way closer to where you are sitting, it'll be harder for you to just go on sitting, reading, and listening to music, but do it anyway. Again, don't try to chase or catch her; she needs to learn that she can come near you, run away, and come back, and you'll still be doing whatever you were doing. Do homework if you have homework, write letters if you want, but books are always handy. The "boom-box" will help her get used to voices and music. If she comes nearby, talk to her if you like, but don't get up and don't stare.

The most important first lesson for the untrained, abused horse is that humans are harmless, even boring.

This may go on for *weeks*. It's worth taking the time to do it, because if she's already been abused and you have someone rope her for you and snub her down so that you can force a halter onto her head, it may be months before you can get close enough to get that halter off again. Don't be in a hurry.

Let her learn about you — what you look and sound and smell like, how you move when you pick up your book or put it down or get up and stretch and walk around the edge of the pasture. Let *her* approach *you*.

When she finally approaches — and she will — don't grab her; let her sniff you and run off. She'll come back. If you grab, it will take a lot longer for her to come back. Just smile, and the next day, bring a nice, scratchy brush out with you.

When she comes back and stands, you can pet her, but do it in a way that will feel good to her: Stroke her neck and scratch her withers; don't try to pat her nose or stroke her forehead. If you get a chance to use the brush, use it in the same areas. Most horses, even nervous ones, get itchy in those places and really enjoy a scratchy brushing.

If your other horse is turned out with her, she can learn from that horse too. When your other horse approaches you, talk to him, pat him, use the scratchy brush, and then go back to your book. Don't use treats at this point, because you may create a situation you don't want. You are trying to help your young mare learn to relax and trust you, and having another horse mugging you for treats will only interfere with this lesson. Let the mare see that the other horse can come to you, get scratched, and go away when he wants to, without being caught or chased. And let her see that you can get up, sit down, cough, sneeze, talk, sing, walk the fence line, or whatever, and that none of this behavior is dangerous to her.

Even the most nervous mistreated horses will usually respond to this routine. Drugs aren't the answer — talk to your vet about this. Anyone who has ever tried to inject a frightened, nervous horse with a tranquilizer can tell you that a horse with surging adrenaline may become more instead of less agitated. And in any case, you have to keep thinking ahead; your goal is not to get your hands on her today; your goal is to sit down in your chair today, watch her run away, and then have her run away less enthusiastically tomorrow when you sit down again.

> *Don't use treats at this point, because you may create a situation you don't want.*

You can't say: "Mare, come here. Let me catch you and put a halter on you and force you to learn that I am a nice person." But you *can* say: "I'm just part of this pasture and part of your life and I'm here all day (or for a few hours a day). I won't try to chase you or harm you; I'm just sitting here reading my book and listening to my music, and when my other horse comes over, he gets his itchy neck scratched." Then let her make the decision; let her be in control. She can decide when to come to you, how near to come, and when to leave again.

When she understands that it's up to her, she'll be able to relax, and then she'll be ready for more grooming — and eventually for the halter, the lead rope, and all the rest. At that point you'll be ready for some professional help, perhaps in the form of a good natural horsemanship clinic by a reputable trainer such as Harry Whitney or Mark Rashid. Round-pen work can be useful if it's done well, and it would almost certainly benefit this mare. Whether you get help or continue to work on your own, don't rush. Take the time you and your mare need to create a lasting bond. It will be the basis for the rest of your lives together.

CHAPTER 3

Grooming and Handling

IT'S A SHAME that so many horses are fearful and resentful of what should be a pleasant experience. In nature, horses groom themselves and each other and enjoy the process greatly. With the right approach and some well-chosen grooming tools, horse owners can teach their horses to relax and enjoy being groomed by humans.

Moving Away from Pressure

Q My four-year-old gelding was a rescue horse. He was with a lot of other horses that were never handled or trained until they were rescued and sold. He is friendly and I can catch him and lead him, but it is always a struggle when I need him to take a step backward or sideways. Backward is his worst direction; he just pushes right back when I push on his nose. Sideways isn't a lot better. Sometimes he will take a step over when I just poke him with a finger, but

Horses should be taught to move away from gentle pressure and to know the verbal cue "Over".

other times he won't, and when I push hard with my hand and even lean on him, he just stands there or pushes back. I thought horses were born knowing to move away from pressure. Did his bad situation make him forget, and is it too late for him to learn it again?

A   Horses are born with an instinct to move *into* pressure, not away from it, so don't worry: Your gelding hasn't forgotten anything. Moving away from pressure is something he just hasn't learned yet, and it's certainly not too late for him to learn. You can teach him yourself.

His first reaction to a push on the nose or a pull on the halter will be to push back and lift his head. In the early stages of his education, don't push on his nose — he'll respond better to a more natural signal. Use your fingers to poke (not push) him in the chest while you tell him, "Back". Once he's learned what you expect and learned to associate the word *back* with stepping back, you'll eventually be able to point at his chest and ask him to step back.

It is a good idea to teach him to move sideways, away from pressure, but again, don't push him, and don't use your hand. Position him so that stepping away from you will be natural and easy. If you turn his nose slightly toward you, it will be easier for him to shift his haunches away. Use your finger to tap him near his hip, say, "Over," and then pause. Don't push, and don't lean on him; he will just do what comes naturally, which is to push back.

Be sure he is calm, relaxed, and balanced when you begin this lesson. If he's standing with his legs sprawled or with his front or hind feet together or crossed, it will be difficult and frightening for him when he's asked to step sideways. If he's standing balanced, he'll be able to step sideways with relative ease.

Head-Shy Horse

Q My two-year-old filly will not let me comb out her forelock. She raises her head high in the air and shies away. Can you help me teach her how to lower her head for grooming and haltering purposes?

A Go slowly, and take all the time your filly needs. Many horses are head shy for a variety of reasons. Since your filly is only two, you need to teach her to trust you now so that this will never be a problem again — for you or for anyone else.

Horses see very well, but have two blind spots: They cannot see something coming up directly behind them, which is why we speak to them and touch them when we walk up behind them, and they cannot see something that is coming toward them from directly in front, right between the eyes. This is why horses do not like strange people who march up to them and try to pat them between the eyes or stroke their noses. Unless you know a horse very well, and she knows you very well, always approach quietly from the side, and always stroke the horse low on the neck, toward the shoulder.

It isn't really important for you to comb out your filly's forelock this week or next week or even next month. But it's important for her to learn to relax around you, and for you to be able to put a halter on her.

Be aware of the horse's blind spots when grooming.

Some people make horses head shy by hurting their ears. For instance, some people don't want to go through the trouble of unfastening and fastening a halter properly, so they undo the throat snap and push the halter up over the horse's forehead and ears. This is often the case with head-shy and halter-shy horses, so it's important to take the trouble to put the halter on properly.

Any change you make in her behavior will have to be gradual and incremental; don't expect too much at once. Instead of using a comb on her forelock, just rub the base of her ears for a week or two. Stand next to her, not in front of her, and rub her ears gently, from the side. Keep calm, stay quiet, and let her put her head down instead of you reaching up. If she gets nervous or worried, step back and stroke her neck instead. When she relaxes, move slowly back up to the base of the ears. Your aim is not to grab her ears or her forelock; you want to teach your filly that having her head handled by you is pleasant and comfortable. Use treats, use patience, and try to make every experience pleasant, not painful. Your filly will come around.

Horse Frightened of Clippers

Q I own a nine-and-a-half-year-old Quarter Horse–Arabian named Jet. He is the sweetest horse in the world and I love him so much. You would never think that he has any vices. Not long ago, before a small barn show, I got out the clippers to trim his whiskers, and he was totally terrified! We tried calming him and soothing him, but nothing would calm him down. I tried to get a more experienced rider in the area to help groom, but Jet reared about six times. I had no idea what to do and we were shocked, knowing what a good boy he is. The next day, I tried to use the scissors instead. He was not as scared as he was of the clippers, but he was pretty nervous. I asked the previous owner how they had clipped his whiskers and she said they had used drugs. Is there any way to clip him or get him used to the clippers without the injection?

A Fear is not a vice; being worried about clippers isn't a moral failing on the horse's part. You've owned this horse for just a few months, and he's almost 10 years old. A lot has happened to him in those years, including, no doubt, some unpleasant experiences involving clippers. Retraining him is going to take a little time, but it will be worth the effort.

Allow the horse time to become accustomed to the clippers' noise and vibration.

He has probably been tied short, held by a twitch, or even held by an ear while someone clipped his face, and now he is very frightened of the whole process. You can't change what's been done to him before, but you can teach him that things are different now. Allow plenty of time for the process, listen to your horse every step of the way, and let him set the pace. What matters is process and progress. It takes time to introduce a green horse to clippers and let him feel secure in spite of the noise and vibration; it takes much more time to reintroduce a fearful horse to clippers. Don't let anyone push you into hurrying.

Your first job will be to accustom the horse to the sight and sound of the clippers, so that he will accept them as harmless when they aren't touching him. One of the easiest ways to do this is to hang them outside his stall and turn them on at feeding time; just let them hang there and run quietly, then feed him. You may need to do this for a few weeks, depending on how bad his past experiences were, but he will eventually accept the sound and learn to associate it with something good (food) instead of with something bad (being held and frightened and/or hurt).

Once he's used to the clipper sounds and doesn't worry about them anymore, you can move on to the next phase: holding the clippers, letting him see them, and touching him with them. Make them part of your grooming routine — but don't plug them in or turn them on. After you've used your dandy brush, go over the horse with the clippers. Touch only his neck, chest, and shoulders; stay away from his face, flanks, and belly. Use the back of the clippers rather than the blades; you're not clipping him, you're just rubbing the clippers against him to show that they are harmless. Use a little pressure, just as you would with a brush. If you touch him too lightly and tickle him, he won't like it. If he gets worried, back off, brush him a little more, then start again.

If you get tense whenever you pick up the clippers, your horse will quickly figure out that he was right to worry.

Keep your own attitude very casual — sing along with the radio! If you hold your breath and get tense whenever you pick up the clippers, your horse will quickly figure out that he was right to worry, because obviously clippers *are* scary. After all, you're afraid of them, too.

When he's quite relaxed about being touched with the clippers, plug them in and turn them on. Use them the same way for another week or so, rubbing the back of the clippers over the less sensitive parts of his body. This is good for both of you — it teaches the horse that the clippers won't hurt him, and it teaches you how much pressure is right to keep your horse comfortable. When he's at ease with the clippers on his neck, you can begin to rub the back of the clippers against his cheeks, his jaw, and so forth.

When he's at ease with both the sensation and the sound, turn the clippers around and start to use them. Again, start small: Clip a few hairs under the jaw, then go back to the brush or do something else for a moment. If he begins to worry, dance, or get anxious, move the clippers and hold the back of them against his neck or shoulder. The idea isn't to get it all done quickly the first time; the idea is to do a very little and keep the horse calm and relaxed, so that the next time you can do a little more.

Horses often worry about having clippers vibrating against their faces. It's not always because of previous bad experiences. Although that's quite common, it can be a simple matter of unpleasant vibrations and noises. Horses have enormous sinus cavities, and clipper vibrations can send horrid sounds *inside* the horse's head. Some horses simply hate this and can eventually learn to tolerate it, but will never be happy about it.

Your horse can learn to relax and accept the clippers, but it's going to depend on your patience and your close observation of his reactions. Be quiet, calm, and cheerful, and don't frighten your horse. Take as much time as he needs. If it takes a week, a month, or three months to get him comfortable with clippers, it doesn't matter. What's important isn't how fast you get the job done, it's how well you do it. Clipping three hairs, praising the horse, and coming back a minute later to clip three more may seem like a lengthy process, but the more time you take and the more careful you are now, the better off you and the horse will be.

Biting: Prevention Is Best

Q I'm worried that my sweet new horse could turn into a biter. His last owner was a 10-year-old girl who taught him to "kiss," and he always wants to nuzzle people in the face. It's very annoying when he does it to me, and it scares other people when he does it to them. My instructor says I should hit him on the head whenever he does it, but all my books say never hit a horse on the head. I can't let him bump himself into something hard because he's trying to nuzzle my face, and I never have anything in the right position to put between him and my face. My instructor's other idea is that I should poke him hard in the nose whenever he does this, but that doesn't seem right either.

A It's very irresponsible to teach a horse to "kiss" and nuzzle humans in the face. Unfortunately, you are stuck with the habit created by your horse's previous owner. Fortunately, you are obviously sensible and kind, and you aren't going to punish your horse for doing what he was taught to do.

Hitting a horse on the head is not the way to end this behavior, and it's never acceptable. You don't want to make your horse confused, upset, and head shy, and you don't want to risk harming his eyes. Both of these are common results of hitting a horse on the head.

Poking him in the nose isn't the answer either. Hitting, slapping, and poking will typically have one of two effects, and neither is good. Your horse may

Pressure on a sore spot may provoke a reflexive bite.

become frightened and head shy, or he may try to nip instead of nuzzle, not out of meanness, but because he'll interpret the slap or poke as an invitation to play.

Horses, especially colts and geldings, play biting games. Watch two geldings playing together in a field — you'll see a lot of nipping, biting, and halter grabbing. If they aren't wearing halters, you'll see the same behavior, but with lips and teeth closing on skin. "Nip your buddy's face" is a perfectly normal horse game, but it's not one that any human can afford to play. That's why slapping your horse on the head or poking him in the nose won't stop his head from coming into your personal space. You will mean, "Stop that — get away," but he will hear, "Yes! Let's play this game, and let's play harder. This is fun!"

Your horse needs to learn to keep his face away from your face. He isn't biting yet, and he isn't doing this out of anger or aggression, so punishment, even the self-inflicted kind, isn't appropriate here. Your horse needs to be taught a new habit to replace his old one. The new habit will be keeping his mouth to himself and staying out of your personal space.

The method I've found to be most successful is mouth rubbing. If your horse's muzzle appears in your personal space, don't hit it but immediately put your hand on it and rub it. Rub his lips, his mouth, and the end of his nose. Rub fairly hard, and keep rubbing for fifteen or twenty seconds, a minute, or even longer — as long as it takes for him to decide that enough is enough. The idea is not to hurt him, but to annoy him by giving his muzzle much more attention than he wanted. When he begins to find the process unpleasant, let him take his head away and stand quietly with his face out of your personal space. Talk to him, praise him, and wait.

You shouldn't have to do this more than four or five times. If he's like most horses, he will quickly figure out that trying to nuzzle your face doesn't result in praise or treats, and that you won't play the nipping game with him. He will realize that the annoying muzzle rubbing happens every time he puts his face in your face and at no other time. He'll quickly learn to avoid performing the action that creates this consequence; instead, he will stand without moving his head into your space.

This method of discouraging biting is excellent as both prevention and cure. It will work with the inquisitive, mouthy young foal and with the old trooper who's just trying to get a treat by doing what he's been taught or encouraged to do. Both you and your horse will remain calm and friendly, and you'll get the behavior change you want.

Horse That Bites

Q In August, I purchased Chewey, a 10-year-old Thoroughbred gelding, after having ridden him three or four times for lessons. I knew he was what the people at the barn call cranky (grinds his teeth, swings his head to bite, sometimes stamps his feet), but I attributed it to being very ticklish or sensitive, because he is really puppylike when he's not being groomed. He was in full training with my instructor when I bought him, and I left him in the same situation for two months until I would have time to ride him frequently.

Since the beginning of October, I have been riding Chewey six days a week. Now that we are bonding, he has really cut down on all of the antics, but yesterday while I was sponging him off after our ride, he bit me hard. I usually have him cross-tied so that he can't reach me, but yesterday there wasn't enough space for him in the cross-ties. I didn't actually think he'd bite me; I thought it was theatrics to get me to stop sponging him. What do I do with that kind of behavior? Is he possibly just very sensitive, or is he being aggressive/dominant?

What can I do to fix it? I grew up with horses, but none of them ever were biters or especially ticklish, so I am at a loss for experience in this situation.

A There's a lot you can do in terms of teaching and training and even changing some of your grooming techniques, but the first priority has to be safety, and that means that sore or not, sensitive or not, your horse can't be permitted to bite you under *any* circumstances.

Horses are not given to "theatrics" — if he wants you to stop brushing or toweling or sponging, he probably has a reason. Either you've reached a sore area or you've reached a ticklish area, and he's trying to tell you that he's not very happy.

Have your vet take a look at Chewey and check for sore areas; if you're brushing/sponging over a deep bruise, for instance, it will hurt. Check your saddle for fit, and check your own riding position. Is the saddle rubbing him anywhere, at a standstill or in motion? Are you using a mounting block so that you don't pull the saddle onto his spine during mounting and dismounting? Does the saddle fit *both* of you, or is it an old saddle that one or both of you may have outgrown? If the saddle is too small for you, your weight will be concentrated in one area, just under the cantle, and that will make a horse very sore in no time at all. Since you've been riding him six days a week, he's had plenty of time to develop a sore back from any saddle or riding problem.

Some horses can't tolerate really hard, stiff brushes in certain areas, notably the flank and belly. Other horses are truly ticklish and find light touches with soft brushes extremely irritating.

If you and your vet don't find anything painful, remember that sensitiveness and ticklishness are possibilities too. Some horses can't tolerate really hard, stiff brushes in certain areas, notably the flank and belly. Other horses are truly ticklish and find light touches with soft brushes extremely irritating. These horses prefer harder brushes and more pressure.

Another possibility is that your horse may be expecting trouble. Not all grooms, at the racetrack or elsewhere, are always perfectly gentle and kind with the horses. A horse that expects to be hit while being groomed is likely to get anxious and unhappy during the grooming process.

In addition to having the horse checked out, you are going to have to do two things that may at first seem contradictory. One is to show the horse — by doing it over and over and making it pleasant — that you are not going to beat him up during grooming. To make it really pleasant for him, though, you're going to have to pay attention to what he is saying to you, and when you get to an area that is sensitive, ticklish, or sore, listen to him when he says, "Don't brush me that way," or, "Don't rub me there."

The other action you need to take is to make it clear to your horse that although you are listening to him and you are trying to do what feels good to him, he is not permitted to bite — ever. Be ready to make a very loud, rude sound if he so much as swings his head toward you; that will let him know what you think of the idea. If he swings his head with serious intent, be sure that what he runs into is either your elbow or the wooden back of the brush — you aren't going to hit him, you're just going to be sure that if he swings into you, he encounters something hard. Be very aware of where he is at all times. It's your job to keep the bite from happening in the first place, and if you can do that you'll never have to deal with the consequences of being bitten.

Show the horse that he doesn't need to escalate his behavior because you're paying attention and responding to his body language at a much earlier point, when it's still at the twitching-skin and ears-slightly-back stage. If we'll listen when our horses whisper, they'll never feel that they need to shout to get our attention.

Filly Fights Bath and Fly Spray

Q Salsa is an 11-month-old paint filly. She is quite a sweet horse and seems to be learning everything well, but at bath and fly-spray time she rears, strikes, pulls, and fights. My husband can't even keep hold of her! When bathing her, I start slowly at her legs and talk gently to her the whole time. Should I tie her for this? I'm worried about her slipping and falling if she fights and tries to get loose.

For the last fly spraying, my husband held her on the lead with a stud chain while I sprayed, and that was even worse. She still managed to pull free and it took me a few minutes to calm her down. It was very scary because she was running with the lead dragging. We put her in her stall and sprayed her from the

It's hard to bathe a moving target.

outside. She didn't like it, but fly spray is a must in our area because we have a lot of mosquitoes. Salsa has had a mind of her own on other things I've taught her, but with persistence she has learned quite well. With this issue, I am not sure if it's just my approach.

A My advice would be to change your approach completely. First, give this filly *no* excuse to get spooky. Horses are instinctively frightened of strange sounds and sensations — anything unfamiliar is a potential danger until proven otherwise. Most horses are initially nervous and worried about fly or other spray, and most horses that have been brought up in stalls or stalls and paddocks, away from natural sources of water, are equally nervous of water. They are especially nervous of the sensation of spray hitting their legs and bodies, and the noise frightens them as well.

You must think about what your long-term goals are in this situation, and then you will need to adjust your short-term goals accordingly. If you use chains and leverage to force your filly to stand while you spray her or bathe her, you will probably manage to spray or bathe her *on that occasion.* But you will also convince her that spraying and bathing, in addition to being strange and nerve-racking activities, are actually painful and unpleasant experiences.

Horses are much more nervous than humans, and humans can get very nervous in certain situations. Imagine yourself at the doctor's office, getting ready for a shot. If you are held down by several people who yell at you, you will become tense and fearful and the shot will be much more painful. It will then be difficult for anyone to get you near that office again.

Your filly can't intellectualize any of this, much less understand that spraying and bathing are good for her; from her point of view, she's being forced (painfully) to stay in one place while unpleasant things are being done to her. So forcing the issue may make her stand still today, but she will be more frightened the next time it happens and even more frightened the time after that, and it will take more force and more pain to keep her still. Eventually, you won't be able to keep her still. In other words, if you insist on winning the battle, you will eventually lose the war.

Change your tactics. Take the time and make the effort to make spraying and bathing nonthreatening, nonscary activities — even pleasant ones — for your filly. This will be less traumatic and dangerous for all of you. Horses in a panic can run over humans, and horses in a panic can slip and slide and fall on a wash rack. The key is to make the experience positive.

In the short run, if fly spray is necessary, take some old soft rags to the barn, wet them with the fly spray, and wipe the filly down. Give her the insect protection she needs without fighting about it. That will allow you to separate the fly-spray issue from the learning-to-stand-for-spraying issue.

Before she can learn to stand quietly for spraying or bathing, she needs to learn that she is safe while being sprayed or bathed. A horse's natural safety depends on movement, and your filly's anxiety level will be much lower if she's allowed to move. When she's less worried, she'll be able to relax — and she'll be able to learn.

Take your filly out on the grass or somewhere with wide-open spaces and good footing. Wear gloves, and tie a knot at the end of your lead rope. Carry a spray bottle loaded with water (or mild saline, in case it gets in her eyes or yours); during training, this is a good alternative to expensive fly spray. When working with any horse that rears or strikes, be extra careful and wear your ASTM/SEI helmet while you work with her. Be safe, not sorry.

Begin by spraying the ground, then her feet, then her lower legs, and work your way up slowly. Talk to her while you do it. When she moves, shifts, dances, or jumps, let her — as long as she jumps away from you and not on top of you.

Allow her to move around, but don't say anything at all. React as little as you possibly can — no jerks on the rope, no screaming, no hitting. Stand quietly until she calms down, then talk to her and spray again. Make this part of the daily routine. Don't spray near her neck or face; be happy if you can do legs and body after a few days.

If she knows that she can get away and that you aren't going to chase her, hurt her, or yell at her, she will eventually calm down because you will no longer be confirming her fears. While being trapped or held in one place is extremely frightening to horses, being allowed to move around is calming. It's the reason that nervous horses become much less afraid of trailers if they are trained to relax and stop thinking of the trailer as a trap. If such horses are loaded into the trailer and allowed to get out again when they like, ten or even twenty times, after a while they realize that they can get out of that box, that they aren't trapped forever, and they stop worrying.

Bath time should be similar. Take a hose and a bucket outside with you and put the filly on a long lead rope. Start doing the same thing you did with the fly spray. If you need to put the chain over her nose once to convince her that rearing is absolutely not allowed, do it, but adjust it so that it loosens as soon as she comes down, and don't pull on it yourself. Let the filly teach herself; she'll learn faster that way.

Cold water can be quite a shock — don't try to train a baby to love baths by tying her up and hitting her with a cold-water spray. Instead, use a sponge and bucket of warm water (leaving a black rubber bucket full of water in the sun for a few hours will work), and sponge her with the warm water while talking to her. If she pulls away, let her walk around and move away from you, as long as she doesn't go too far. Just stop talking and stand quietly. When she quiets down, start talking again, and go back to your sponge and bucket. Eventually, she will figure out that it isn't going to kill her, it doesn't even hurt, and it may even feel good.

My preference for teaching young horses about bath time is to wait until it's a hot, humid day and the horses are sweaty, sticky, and uncomfortable. On days like that, they learn very quickly that water makes them less itchy, gets rid of flies, and feels good.

An 11-month-old filly is big enough to do a lot of damage, but she is still a baby. You aren't just teaching her skills, but you are also teaching her attitudes about learning, dealing with people, and new things. Try to keep her confident and happy. She's still a couple of years away from riding age, so you have plenty of time.

If you don't feel confident of your own ability to train your young filly (not an easy task for a first-timer!) you won't be able to convince her. Do you have a good trainer in your area — someone who trains with a brain instead of a two-by-four? Ask her or him to come out and help you with the filly for a few sessions. It can make all the difference in the world, and some good help will be worth the investment. As someone once said, "Education is expensive, but ignorance is *more* expensive."

The hose isn't cause for alarm if you take your time and use some psychology. My horses are always easy to hose down because they are introduced to the hose gradually and gently, in a field or arena where there is plenty of room to move around. I hold them loosely on a lead rope and show them the hose and the water, then begin by wetting their feet and the area just above their feet. They can move anywhere they like — as far as the lead rope will allow — and they do move around, but not for long. If I tried to force them to stand stock-still while I used the hose on their legs, they would become frightened and stop thinking. This way, they are free to move their feet and step away from the water if they choose. Since they are not being forced to stay in one place, they don't worry about being unable to get away, and since the hose isn't hurting them and the water finds them wherever they go, they soon stop worrying about it. (I use the same approach to get them comfortable with spray bottles.)

My preference for teaching horses about bath time is to wait until it's a hot, humid day and the horses are sweaty and uncomfortable. On days like that, they learn very quickly that water gets rid of flies and feels good.

It also helps to introduce the hose and water at a good time. I wouldn't introduce a horse to a hose bath on a cold or a windy day, when the horse is nervous or agitated or when the water might feel unpleasant. I usually wait until a very hot, sunny summer day, and I "forget" to put fly spray on the horses' legs. When the flies are biting and the horses are unhappy with the sensation, I bring out the hose, and most horses quickly figure out that the sensation of cold water on their lower legs is a welcome, pleasant alternative to the sensation of biting flies. Once they've learned to associate the water with relief and comfort, they will always have a good attitude about the hose. Then I can begin to teach them how nice the water feels everywhere else (except their ears or eyes; *never* put the hose in a position where it can spray water into these areas). As a result, my horses never worry about the hose, and one of them will actually come up and ask for a shower whenever she sees someone using the hose to fill the water tank.

Do Treats Spoil a Horse?

Q My question involves a six-year-old Thoroughbred gelding. What do you think of using treats as positive reinforcement in training? I can get my horse to bow and go in-hand over a practice wooden bridge, and he knows what "Good boy" means because I give him a carrot or piece of peppermint candy when I say it. I understand that he is not a dog, but he seems to respond with this method. For example, after one very rotten training ride he did not get his reward. The next day he was much better and got his "Good boy" and his treat.

I also noticed that he gets tense and grinds his teeth if my instructor rides him, but he doesn't do that when I ride him. I take that as my horse thinking, "She really makes me work," and, "My mommy is a pushover." Does that mean he can reason between work and reward when it comes to different riders? Or does that mean he just doesn't like to have to honestly work under someone who can make him?

I'm new to English riding and have owned my horse for almost a year. I bought him from the owner of the barn in which I work. He is a retired racehorse, so we are both green. He has never bucked or reared, he is an honest jumper, and he is doing quite well with dressage when he wants to work. I do not jump him, but a young, experienced rider schooled him over jumps during the summer, and now he has a new rider for jumping (both my horse and the rider jump under lessons only).

I feel we started him fairly for coming off the track. He got three months rest, then another three months working only on the ground, then very light saddle work, and then progressed to light jumping and dressage. Rewarding him with treats started even before I bought him last February; I've been voice- and treat-rewarding him since he came from the track last October. Did I do wrong? Am I spoiling my horse? He doesn't get pushy or bite, and he never knows for sure if he will get a treat unless he worked well under saddle or on the ground.

Just as people need to learn how to offer a treat, horses need to learn how to accept a treat.

A There is nothing wrong with giving a horse treats, just as there is nothing wrong with giving a dog or a child treats — if you are sensible about the treats and how you give them.

Horses can and should be trained to accept treats gently and politely, without pushing, shoving, grabbing, or biting. Most horses will quickly learn what sort of treat-taking behavior is acceptable. A few horses do not seem to be able to understand or remember that pushing and grabbing are unacceptable, and those horses should not be hand-fed treats. It doesn't mean that you can't give such a horse a treat, but if your horse tends to "mug" you for treats, it's wiser and safer to drop the carrot, apple, or sugar into the horse's feed bucket and let him retrieve it.

Treats can be a part of training. Treats aren't bribes; you have to remember that horses, unlike children, cannot be told, "You will get a treat provided that you do this." Instead, you can teach a horse, through consistent rewarding, to expect a treat after performing a certain action. A horse with good manners about accepting treats won't understand that the treat is connected to whatever she did, but she will understand that the treat implies that you are pleased with her. It's a very important difference.

A horse that understands that she must not crowd your space and body-search you but must wait politely to be given a treat is a horse that can be hand-fed treats. A horse with poor treat-taking manners is usually a horse that has been hand-fed treats by someone who didn't understand horses very well and who allowed the horse to pester, to push, to poke at pockets and hands, and to "find" the treat and demand it. That's a very effective way to create a horse that crowds, bites, and loses respect for the personal space of humans, and that's not a good thing.

One reason to teach a horse how to accept treats politely is that, humans being humans, someone is bound to offer your horse a treat at some point during his life. When that happens, the human and your horse will both be safer and happier if your horse has learned "treat etiquette."

The "treat training" you've described is basic operant conditioning based on learning by association. You've used a treat (something your horse likes very much) to teach your horse that "Good boy," the words you use when you offer the treat, means, "I am showing goodwill." It doesn't necessarily convey "I am pleased with you," and it does not convey "I enjoyed our ride."

A reward after a ride isn't very meaningful. To you it may mean, "I liked my ride." To the horse, it may simply mean, "Yes, the ride really is over now," or even more simply, "Here is something good to eat." By the time a ride is over, the horse won't connect the treat with anything that happened on the ride. If you gave the horse a smack instead of a treat, he wouldn't connect the smack with anything that happened on the ride either. He would instead connect the smack to whatever he happened to be doing when you gave him the smack.

If your horse is trying to rub his itchy head on your arm, and you give him a whack on the neck, he will think, "Ow, rubbing caused a bad noise and a bad feeling in my neck." If he could intellectualize it, he would think, "This action had unpleasant consequences." If your horse is trying to rub his itchy head on the side of your arm and you give him a treat, he will think, "This is a great thing to do, I must do it again right now," or in other words, "This action has enjoyable consequences."

If you want to refine the action-consequence or action-reward sequence, you might want to try clicker training with your horse. Clicker training can help you refine your communication and your timing so that you make it very clear to your horse exactly which of his actions you like. By teaching the horse that the click sound means, "Good, you're doing well; I approve," you can help your horse understand exactly what you want him to do.

For instance, you mentioned crossing a practice wooden bridge. Most horses, when first introduced to such a bridge, will stop and stare, reach out their necks and heads to sniff the bridge, put one foot on it, take the foot off again, stand for a moment, put the foot back on, and then — if all is calm and the bridge doesn't sound or feel too scary — put a second foot on it. At that point, the horse may or may not go across the bridge. All of this will typically happen within a minute or less. Even if you have wonderful timing, it's likely that you won't be indicating your approval at exactly the right moments.

If the horse knows that the click sound (or your voice saying "Good boy") means approval, then you can click when he reaches toward the bridge, when he puts his nose on it, when he puts his foot on it, and so on. When he moves backward or hesitates, you can simply wait and do nothing. Since a well-timed click (or "Good boy") is both informative and reassuring, a horse trained this way will typically go over the bridge fairly quickly and very calmly — and be perfectly happy to do it again.

Clicker training may make use of treats in the beginning just to create an association between praise (or a click) and something the horse likes very much (the treat).

Clicker training, like all good training, may make use of treats in the beginning just to create an association between praise (or a click) and something the horse likes very much (the treat). As training progresses, the "Good boy" or the "click" becomes a reward in itself, and the treats can be eliminated altogether. A well-trained horse, attuned to his handler or rider, wants to please and will gladly accept praise as a reward.

Your other question is more difficult to answer. Your horse should not be tense or grinding his teeth during any lesson or riding session. Horses, like humans, need to be relaxed and feel secure to learn their lessons well, and a horse or a human that is tense, irritated, annoyed, or frightened is not going to learn or develop in a useful way.

Horses are quite happy to work if the work is understandable and doesn't hurt them and if the person asking them to work is nice about it, even if the work is hard. Horses are not happy to work if they are uncomfortable or frightened, and anyone who thinks that training consists of forcing a horse to work needs to take up another hobby, preferably one involving inanimate objects rather than living creatures.

"Honest work" isn't something horses avoid; it's something they enjoy. When they don't enjoy it, something is wrong with the trainer, with the conditions of work, or with the work itself. Horses respond differently to different riders because each rider will provoke different reactions. But horses' reactions don't have anything to do with work-reward issues; riders who understand horses and are reassuring and fair will almost invariably elicit positive responses from horses. Treats, a kind word, and a pat can make horses' work more pleasant — just as appreciation can make any individual's job more pleasant — and there is nothing at all wrong with making work pleasant. After all, a horse's job can be complicated, difficult, and physically demanding. But whether the job is carrying handicapped riders in an arena, participating in 100-mile endurance rides, or doing a third-level dressage test, the work should always be enjoyable.

You've answered your own final question. Your horse doesn't bite, isn't pushy, doesn't demand treats, and doesn't even expect to get treats all the time, so you've just described a horse that is definitely *not* spoiled. Stop worrying. You're doing a good job.

Horse Won't Hold Up Foot for Cleaning

Q I am 13 years old and have been riding all my life. Right now, I am riding a 15.2-hh Anglo-Arab mare. I have one question: When I am picking out her feet, she doesn't want to hold her foot up for me. I try to rest it on my leg, but then she just leans on me! How can I get her to hold up her own foot and stop leaning on me?

A Here's the best way to keep a horse from leaning on you when you're cleaning her feet: First, be sure that the horse is well balanced on the other three feet, so that she doesn't need to lean on you for support. Second, stay very close to her body, and when you're holding her foot, don't pull the foot or leg out away from her body, or she'll tend to follow it — and lean on you. Third, while you're holding each foot to clean it, tip the toe *up* so that the bottom of the foot is facing the ceiling. The hoof will be in a better position for you to clean it effectively and quickly, and with the fetlock joint bent, the mare is much less likely to lean on you.

With the foot in this position, you can see exactly why it's so important to clean from the heel toward the toe and not the other way around. If you clean from toe to heel, a small slip of your hand could push the sharp end of the hoof

Be sure that the horse is well-balanced and standing on secure,
level footing before you lift his leg.

pick into the horse's fetlock.

When you've cleaned the hoof, let the joint straighten and the toe point down before you tell the mare, "Foot down," and put her foot on the ground. Horses sometimes lean on you in an effort to get their feet near the ground, because they're anticipating the discomfort of having you suddenly drop the foot when you've finished cleaning it. If you always tell the horse when you're about to put a foot down, she won't worry about getting an unpleasant surprise, and that will eliminate one more reason for leaning on you.

CHAPTER 4

Medicating

MEDICATING HORSES can be difficult if the horses are nervous about the handler's actions. Many horses have learned to fear the sight of a syringe, not because it is intrinsically frightening or because its contents are so distasteful, but because they associate it with being handled in an angry and forceful way. But if horses are relaxed and confident and trust their handlers, it isn't difficult to administer medications orally or by injection. Horses can learn to trust their handlers and to accept and even welcome the syringe. As always, sneaking up on the horse is bad; calm, quiet persistence is good. Even "problem horses" can become easy to medicate if you take the time to let them become comfortable with the entire process.

Giving Oral Medications

Q My horse has been "eared down" to give him shots and paste wormer. This happened before I bought him. It's been six months now and he's better about shots, but he still begins to move around and toss his head when he sees a worming syringe. Then he puts his head up so high I can barely reach his mouth, and even if I get the paste in there, he spits most of it out. I don't want to let the barn owner twitch his ear. Is there a way I can change his behavior, should I have the vet worm him, or should I just avoid the issue and use the daily feed supplement wormer?

A Don't let anyone twist his ear or put a twitch on it. That kind of human impatience is what caused this problem in the first place. Horses have delicate ears. The cartilage is breakable and the ear can be torn. Keep standing up for your horse and don't let anyone hurt his ears.

Rough, forceful handling is only a onetime solution, because even though the horse may be forced to submit once, he will put up more of a fight the next time and will object even more strongly to the idea of having anything pushed into his mouth. Instead, use a gentle strategy that teaches the horse to accept the worming syringe.

Horses dislike feeling trapped, and when a horse is being held while someone is shoving a metal or plastic tube into his mouth, he will naturally try to avoid the situation by running away or, if he can't run away, by lifting his head high or shaking it vigorously. A lot of the things we do with horses go against their nature, but with time and patient kindness, we can help them learn to relax and accept our ministrations.

The way to teach your horse to accept an oral syringe is to practice using it. For this lesson, which may take one day, ten days, three weeks, or three months, you'll need patience, an old shirt, a clean oral syringe (a carefully washed wormer syringe is ideal), and a large container of something that tastes good to your horse. Applesauce works well; so does fruit-flavored yogurt, although not the kind with fruit pieces that can block the syringe. Whatever you use should be tasty, reasonably smooth, and not too thick or too cold. Water is too thin — it will soak your shirt and run into your armpit when the horse lifts his head (and at first he *will* lift his head). Molasses is too thick, sticky, and messy.

For example, start by filling the syringe with applesauce. Some applesauce will stick to the outside of the syringe; that's fine. It will interest your horse and make it more likely that you can get the syringe into his mouth.

For the first time, only insert the tip and squirt a little bit of applesauce; the idea is to reduce the horse's resistance gradually by giving him nothing to resist. Most horses will drop their heads and look for more applesauce. When you use the syringe next time, your horse's head will go up again, but probably not as far, and as soon as he figures out that the syringe isn't going to hurt him and that applesauce comes out of it, he'll become easier and easier to treat.

Keep repeating the process, twenty or thirty times if necessary, every day for three or four weeks. Most horses get the idea within a day or two; traumatized horses take longer, so allow as much time as your horse needs. You'll find with every try that the horse is more interested in opening his mouth and less interested in pulling away. You'll barely have to hold the horse — one hand resting lightly on his nose will be enough. As the horse learns to lower his head and open his mouth, you can start to dispense more and more applesauce, and you can put the applesauce farther back in the horse's mouth. Aim for the very back, on top of the tongue. When the horse feels something there, he automatically swallows. It doesn't matter if he spits or dribbles applesauce, but by the time you bring out the expensive worming paste, you'll want to be able to place it where the horse will swallow all of it automatically and quickly.

Aim for the very back, on top of the tongue. When the horse feels something there, he automatically swallows.

If you're planning to train your horse in order to prepare for giving him worming paste, start early. Practice several days or weeks beforehand with applesauce, and on worming day give the horse several syringes full of applesauce, the last one on the very back of his tongue. As soon as he swallows, administer the worming paste in the same spot. When the horse has swallowed the paste, give him a few more syringes of applesauce nearer the front of his mouth, where the taste and smell will be appreciated.

The feed-through worming products seem to be quite effective when they are fed to all the horses in the barn and when paddocks and pastures are cleaned frequently. Ask your vet whether this would be a good way to protect your horse from parasites. But don't use it merely as a way to avoid dealing with the oral-syringe issue, because at some point in your horse's life, you or someone else may need to give him medicine with an oral syringe. It will be much better if your horse is familiar with the process and accepts it calmly.

Injections

Q My horse was sick, and my veterinarian says that she will need to have a shot every day for two weeks. I can't afford to have the vet come out every day to do this. He showed me how to give the shot in my horse's rear end, but I'm so afraid that I'll do it wrong and hurt her. When I did it the first time, my horse switched her tail and put her ears back, and I felt horrible and guilty for hurting her. I am worried that she will not like me if I give her shots for two weeks. What will a horse think about a person who stabs her with a sharp needle every day?

A If you own horses, it's useful to know how to give injections. Intravenous (into a vein) and intradermal (between layers of skin) injections are more complicated than subcutaneous (just under the skin) and intramuscular (deep into a large muscle) injections.

If your vet has shown you how to give an intramuscular injection, you know the routine; here are a few reminders that will make the process a little easier on you and your horse.

Use a new needle and syringe for each injection. The individually packaged sterile needles and syringes are practical and very convenient. Have a container handy in which to put the discarded needles and syringes immediately after you've given the injection.

If you've been given different sizes of needles and syringes for various medications, be sure that you know which

If the needle is inserted quickly and smoothly, it will feel like a fly bite.

drug goes with each size; don't mix and match. Some medications — penicillin, for instance — are in a thick solution that require a larger-diameter needle. It's nearly impossible to push a thick solution through a small-diameter needle.

Before you give the injection, get your horse accustomed to being tapped several times at the injection site, then pinched or poked — these are sensations associated with injections, and you want to teach the horse to accept those sensations calmly. Don't wait until you have a syringe in your hand — practice the tap-tap-tap-poke maneuver when you're grooming your horse, long before the injection is scheduled.

If a horse's familiar, trusted handler approaches calmly, perhaps while the horse is eating, taps her a few times on the large muscle of the buttock, and then pops the needle in decisively, the horse is unlikely to become frightened and may not react at all.

When it's time to give the injection, don't hunch and worry and try to sneak up on your horse. That behavior will make her nervous, and that's just what you want to avoid. You want to be quiet and relaxed, just like your horse, and you want to put the needle in quickly. It's actually the needle going through the skin that hurts, not the needle being pushed into position, deep in the large muscle.

When you're ready, speak to your horse in a calm voice, tap her several times just where you're about to insert the needle, and then insert the needle quickly and firmly — pop it all the way in, right to the hub. Don't try to push it in slowly and gradually; slow is painful. Be definite, not tentative, and your horse will experience only a split-second sensation like a quick fly bite — not pleasant, but not exciting either. Your horse won't react strongly or become agitated as long as the "bite" is quick and as long as you remain calm.

Once the needle is in, attach the syringe and pull back on the plunger so that you can be sure the needle isn't in a blood vessel. If you see blood, remove the needle calmly and try again with a new needle. If you don't see blood, push down on the plunger. And that's it — you've done it. Now dispose of the used needle and syringe. The safest place to put them is in a "sharps" container, available at your local drugstore. Alternatively, you can put them into an empty coffee can and give them to your vet, who can dispose of them properly.

Remember, horses are grazing herd animals. They have a lot of experience with fly bites, and they don't have human-style "needle phobia." What they do have is the ability to register and reflect the feelings of their herd members. Your horse will register and reflect your feelings.

When horses react badly to the sight of a vet holding a hypodermic, it's usually not because they're afraid of the injection. Most horses barely notice the injection — they're reacting to other things, such as being held tightly, which makes them afraid, and being approached by an unfamiliar, strange-smelling human who seems to be trying to sneak up on them. If a horse's familiar, trusted handler approaches calmly, perhaps while the horse is eating, taps her a few times on the large muscle of the buttock, and then pops the needle in decisively, the horse is unlikely to become frightened and may not react at all.

If you do this every day for two weeks, your horse will simply accept it as part of her routine. She won't hate you for it, she won't be frightened, and she won't hold a grudge. Horses are incredibly accepting and forgiving animals, and your mare will still be your friend.

Treating an Eye Injury

Q One of my horses hurt his eye, and my vet gave me ointment to put in it four times a day. The first two days I managed to do this only twice, so now the barn manager is helping. She uses a twitch to keep my horse from moving, and then I put ointment on my finger and try to wipe it on his eye. I don't like this method, but it works. If we don't use the twitch, he puts his head up in the air and won't let us near his eye, but this way seems brutal.

It's also hard to get the ointment onto his eye. He starts blinking when my finger gets close, and sometimes all the ointment goes on the outside of his eyelid. Plus, I know this can't possibly be sterile since I'm using my finger. Should I wash my hands with alcohol? Is there any way to accustom a horse to having medicine put in his eye? If there is, I would like to practice with my other horse in case this ever happens to him.

A Horses are very curious animals that like to investigate things and they have large, delicate, protruding eyes. Eye injuries are common in horses, and you are sensible to think about preparing for such an eventuality.

You can certainly help your horse learn to accept much of the handling associated with administering eye medications. Teaching him to lower his head on cue is very helpful; so is teaching him to stand quietly for grooming, handling, having his bridle path clipped, and much more. To help a horse become relaxed about having his eyelids handled, just add an extra half-minute to your grooming routine, and make it part of your daily practice. Once your horse understands that part of his daily grooming involves having its eyelids and the area just around he eyes wiped gently with a soft, clean, damp, warm washcloth (or 4x4 gauze square), he won't become excited or frightened when you do the same thing as a prelude to medicating an eye.

Right now, you're dealing with a medical emergency (any eye injury requiring four-times-daily medication qualifies as that), and your top priorities are clear. You must get the right amount of the right medication into the horse's eye as often as necessary, and you must not create any new injuries in the process. A horse with an injured eye is likely to be in considerable pain, distracted, worried, and intolerant of new and frightening procedures. If using the twitch is the only way to get access to your horse's eye, and the only way to enable you to administer the ointment as prescribed, then use the twitch.

Sterility is not as high on your priority list. Just try to keep everything clean. Keep the tubes of ointment clean and dry, wash your hands before you put the ointment in your horse's eye, but don't use alcohol. Your horse probably won't like the smell, and he certainly won't enjoy the sensation if a drop of alcohol should come into contact with his eye.

The ointment-on-finger method is a perfectly good one, and much safer than trying to squeeze the meds directly into your horse's eye from the tube. If the horse jumps or jerks his head, the metal or plastic tip of the tube can cause great damage to his eye. The flat pad of your finger or thumb is far less likely to create an injury. Just be sure that only the ointment, not the tip of the tube, touches your finger.

And there is an easier way to apply the ointment — one that works *with* your horse's nature instead of *against* it. Your horse's blinking is his natural reaction to something approaching or contacting his eye. Instead of trying to make a sudden movement to pop the ointment into the horse's eye between blinks, you can hold his eye open with your hand, then allow him to use his natural blinking reflex to help distribute the medication.

When you medicate a horse's eye, wash his eyelids and the surrounding area as you usually do, then stand close to the horse and rest your hand against his face. Don't put it under the halter, but do support the hand against the horse's face, so that if he moves his head, your hand will go with it. Place your index finger on his upper lid and your thumb just at the very edge of his lower lid, and then use your thumb to pull the lower lid down. He can't blink while you're doing this, and your action will expose the inside of his lower lid, creating a little "shelf" that's the ideal place for you to wipe the short line of ointment that's on the index finger of your other hand. Then just remove your fingers from his eyelids. His normal reaction at this point will be to close his eye and blink, and that's good — it will distribute the ointment all over the surface of his eye.

Equine eyes are incredibly delicate, and your ability to keep medication in your horse's injured eye may well be the most important factor in the final outcome of the treatment. The twitch won't traumatize your horse if it's used calmly and briefly, as part of the medicating routine. Remember that your top priority is to get those meds into the horse's eye on schedule! The medication won't be effective if it stays in the tube, falls to the ground, or is smeared across the outside of the horse's eyelid.

Don't worry if you feel clumsy at first: That's normal. With practice, you'll quickly become more adept.

One last thought: The first days of treatment are very important. If you have difficulty administering the medications, don't wait two days or one day or even an extra hour before getting help. In extreme cases, a tube can be stitched into the horse's eyelid so that medications can be applied to the other end of the tube (usually halfway down the horse's neck) and will reach the eye on schedule.

Drugs for Behavior Control

Q Could you please give me some more information on reserpine? My Thoroughbred raced for six years. He is now twelve, and we have been working on dressage for the last five years. He is still very skittish. For example, he will spook at anything in the indoor arena he is ridden in every other day. He is very sweet, but I am very frustrated with his mental state.

A former trainer of mine suggested reserpine. Could you please give me the specific side effects associated with using the drug? How often does it need to be given, is it given orally or is it injected, how extreme is the mood change, and will he act lethargic like a horse that is on ace? Do you think that there can be a good reason or time to give such a drug?

A I won't go into the details of administering reserpine. Your vet can tell you all that: He, after all, will need to prescribe and purchase the drug, which is not available over the counter.

I will discuss its effects, but first, I *strongly* suggest that you look for an alternative method of calming your horse. Look to diet and exercise first. Many riding horses need much more turnout time and much less grain. Providing 24-hour turnout on pasture, with supplemental hay as needed, can create amazing changes in the behavior of overfed, underexecised horses.

After diet and turnout time, address all of the usual issues of comfort. Have your horse's back and feet and legs checked, have his teeth thoroughly floated, and evaluate your saddle and bit suitability, fit, and adjustment. It's usually a good idea to look at your riding, too. If you are both bored with your routine and not paying much attention to each other, he's more likely to spook and you're more likely to be surprised when he does.

If you have access to a qualified person who does equine massage, you may be able to help your horse a great deal by arranging for at least one evaluation session. Discomfort is a big factor in 99 percent of what riders think of as misbehaviors, including a lot of spooking.

And now, let's discuss drugs.

Reserpine is a useful drug for the human patients who are given it as part of the treatment they require for their blood-pressure problems.

For horses, it's often — far too often — used as a sedative. Some racehorse trainers use it to calm excitable youngsters just beginning their training. Some show-horse trainers use it to make their horses calm or dull.

Just to give you an idea of where reserpine fits into the life of a riding horse with no overt illness or injury, here's what the United States Equestrian Federation (USEF) has to say about the use of reserpine for horses in competition.

The Drugs and Medications rule classifies all drugs and medications as either *Permitted, Restricted,* or *Forbidden.* Permitted drugs are supposed to be used for therapeutic purposes, but even this category includes such misused substances as anabolic steroids. Restricted drugs are therapeutic drugs that are allowed to be used only up to certain limits (determined by the plasma concentration level in the horse's blood at the time of competition). Most of the NSAIDS (non-steroidal anti-inflammatory drugs), like Bute, fall into this category.

Then you have the Forbidden drugs — those that can affect the horse's performance. There are two groups of drugs in this category. One group consists of those forbidden drugs that can still be used under certain very specific circumstances: if it is used in a therapeutic way, if its use is properly reported, and if it is not administered to the horse during the 24 hours before competing. Those exceptions are made only for *therapeutic* drugs, though, and there has to be proof that there is a genuine reason to use them for their therapeutic effects.

> *Some racehorse trainers use reserpine to calm excitable youngsters just beginning their training. Some show-horse trainers use it to make their horses calm or dull.*

The second group of forbidden drugs consists of *nontherapeutic drugs:* in other words, drugs for which there is no legitimate therapeutic use in the competing horse. This means that there is *no* illness or injury that could possibly require the administration of the drug.

Reserpine is a forbidden, nontherapeutic drug.

The key word here is "competing." A substance that might possibly have a legitimate medical use under other circumstances (see below) has no place in the system of a horse that is being trained or competed. In my mind, this sort of drug also has no place in the system of a horse that's being ridden. If the horse cannot be ridden without being sedated, then something is wrong.

You ask whether there might be a good reason or time to use reserpine. My short answer is, "Not for training or riding!"

The drug is occasionally used in situations where a long-lasting sedative is deemed appropriate by the veterinarian in charge of a particular animal. Some mares are bad mothers, known for attacking and sometimes killing their newborn foals. In such cases, attending veterinarians may choose to administer reserpine to the mares for a few days before they foal, to make them less ferocious in their initial reaction to their foals. Under related circumstances, reserpine has also been used to help certain mares "let down" their milk.

Some trainers routinely administer it to nervous young stock when training begins, but I don't like to see this. I'm all in favor of drugs and medications that serve to treat illnesses or injuries, but when it comes to a horse's education, "better living through training" is always preferable to "better living through chemistry."

I suggest that you talk with your veterinarian about analyzing the horse's diet and comparing it to the animal's actual nutritional needs. If the horse is deficient in an element that cannot be met by diet alone, a supplemental vitamin or mineral may be indicated. But be aware of the difference between necessary dietary elements and drugs. It is possible for a horse to need more tryptophan in its diet. It is possible for a horse to have a magnesium deficiency. It is not possible for any horse to have a reserpine deficiency.

You asked about the side effects. Drowsiness and diarrhea, slow reaction time, fatigue, and dullness are common side effects in both humans and horses. Other side effects listed for humans include mental depression, dizziness, headache, arrhythmias, and edema. If horses are similarly affected, any one of these side effects could create great danger for both horse and rider.

There is simply no good reason to use any substance that can put both your horse and you at risk.

Reserpine may not be compatible with your horse's digestive health. In humans, gastric ulcers are a contraindication for reserpine. Before you allow anyone to administer reserpine to your horse, consider the fact that a very high percentage of horses, especially those that are confined and/or fed grain, suffer from gastric ulcers.

If a horse that requires surgery has reserpine in its system, the anesthetic given for the surgery can combine with the reserpine to cause the horse's blood pressure to fall, very suddenly, to a level at which he cannot survive.

This drug is also a long-acting, long-lasting one. Most drugs will clear a horse's blood or urine after a week or ten days, but the presence of reserpine can be detected at any time up to 45 days after administration.

Ask your vet to do a blood workup and find out whether there is anything unusual about your horse's blood profile. If there isn't, ask his opinion of administering reserpine to a 12-year-old riding horse to make it calm and quiet (and, if he is a good vet, stand back and be ready to say, "I was just kidding,

Doc!"). Then ask about the possibility of using tryptophan or magnesium instead. Both can be administered in the feed, neither will have a damaging effect on the horse's reflexes and motor coordination, and both can be discontinued without leaving a long-term residue.

When you're faced with a behavior problem, always begin with health and management. The effects of major changes in management can be very dramatic, even when an older horse is involved. Sometimes the answer is as simple as full-time turnout and work outdoors instead of confinement and work in an indoor school. Sometimes a simple diet change will do the trick, especially if an adult pleasure horse is being fed as if it were a young racehorse. If you are worried about keeping weight on the horse, talk to your vet about a feeding plan that will include more grass and hay, more fat, and a smaller amount of concentrates. If you simultaneously provide more, and more interesting, exercise for your horse, you may see a huge improvement in a relatively short time.

I hope that you will work with your vet and your present trainer/instructor, and disregard the advice of the person who suggested reserpine. There is simply no good reason to use any substance that can cause short- and long-term damage; that doesn't address, treat, or cure any real problems; and that can put both your horse and you at risk.

CHAPTER 5

Vet and Farrier Visits

It's IMPORTANT for horses to accept not just their owners, riders, and regular handlers, but also the professionals they see only occasionally: veterinarians and farriers. The way horse owners behave around their horses when those professionals are present will have a huge influence on the horses and their behavior. Horse owners need to work with, not against, the nature of the horse, and they need to direct and encourage their veterinarians and farriers to do the same.

Foal Meets Farrier

Q My mare's first foal was born at the end of February. He is so sweet and cute and just a total delight. On your advice from the *HORSE-SENSE* archives, I had him gelded when he was just a few weeks old. You and my vet both said the recovery would be fast, and it was so fast that it didn't seem to bother Gunner at all! Gunner is such a wonderful, laid-back little guy, and I've just been enjoying the heck out of him.

My vet said that I should plan to have the farrier come out and trim Gunner's little hooves before he is three months old, so I've called my farrier and made an appointment for Gunner and his mom to get trimmed at the same time. My vet also said to get him ready for the farrier, and I'm not sure what that means or how to do it. When I asked him, he just said, "You know, just handle him. Get him used to it." I thought if I started right now, we could be ready by the time the farrier comes out.

Here's what I've done with him so far: I touch him all over and run my hands down his legs whenever I'm in the pasture or shed with them. He's pretty good about it. I've picked up his front feet a couple of times, but I'm not sure if I'm doing it right. They're so little, and I don't want to hurt him. I haven't tried to pick up a back foot because he is pretty quick to kick out when he's not happy. How can I get him ready so that the farrier will like him and he will like the farrier?

A You've done very well with Gunner, and you still have plenty of time to get him ready for the farrier. By teaching him to accept handling all over, including his legs, you've taken the first step. Now you just need to continue.

When you work with Gunner, don't tie him up; he's far too young to be tied, and he could panic and hurt himself badly. Instead, ask someone else to hold him. You might want to tie up his mother nearby. If she's standing there calmly, he isn't likely to try to run away and he won't become worried about where she is. Letting her stand nearby without tying her is also a possibility, but it's riskier. If she decided to wander around the corner of the shed in search of a little wisp of hay that blew away, the foal might think that he needed to follow her, and if you said, "No," you could end up with an upset foal on your hands. Eventually, you'll be able to take Gunner off by himself to have the farrier or vet work on him, but for now, keep him calm and quiet and with his mother.

Standing next to Gunner, pet him, scratch his withers, and begin moving your hand slowly down his leg. Don't be tentative or too light — you don't want to tickle him or annoy him. Foals usually appreciate a good scratch on the withers and a good scratch just above the tail, so start with that and then work your way down the front and hind legs.

Practice ahead of time so that your foal's first farrier visit will go smoothly.

When you get to the foot, be sure that Gunner is standing in good enough balance that he won't fall over when you pick up a foot. Foals can place their legs in amazingly pretzel-like configurations, so begin your handling routine when he's reasonably balanced.

Move slowly and deliberately, and when you pick up each foot, talk to Gunner. Tell him what you're doing and why, and tell him when you're about to put his foot down. Don't drop the foot, and don't let him kick it out or down. Tell him, "Foot," pick up and hold the foot, then tell him, "Foot down," or, "Put it down," and place his foot on the ground.

With hind feet, do the same thing: Begin with a hand on his rump, take it down his leg slowly, and pick up the foot slowly. He needs to understand and accept that for the moment, you are in charge of that foot. He also needs to be relaxed about the process. Keep your hips and upper thigh close to his hindquarters, and keep his leg and foot right next to your leg. This will help him stay balanced and keep him from thinking about kicking out. If he does get worried and tries to kick out, you might get bumped, but you'll be too near him to get kicked. On the other hand, if you try to hold his hind foot high and far behind him, you'll be asking for a kick, and you'll be in a prime position to be kicked.

Here are a couple of don'ts: Don't take his foot up very high or try to pull it away from his body. The higher his foot is lifted, the more unsteady he will be, the more worried he will get, and the more likely it is that he will try to move. At first, lift the feet just barely off the ground. As he becomes more familiar with the routine, you can lift them a little higher and then a little higher. Keep expanding his comfort zone, but always stay within that zone.

The same idea applies to the length of time you hold each foot. Three or four seconds will do at first; the idea is to teach him that he has no reason *not* to cooperate. Pick up the foot, count to five, tell him, "Foot down," and then put it down. No worries, no fuss, no problem. As he becomes more familiar with the whole idea and learns how to balance his weight more easily on the other three legs, you'll be able to hold the foot up longer. Expand to 10 seconds, 20 seconds, then 30 seconds; take your time, slowly increasing the holding time. You could add five seconds each time, but the training will be more effective if you add two seconds each time and do the foot-holding exercise frequently.

Watch Gunner's reactions and let them tell you what you should do next. If he is clearly accepting and a little bored with having each foot held for 20 seconds, try 25, then 30, and so forth. If he is on the edge of becoming nervous and jerking his foot away from you when you hold it for twenty seconds, go back to fifteen seconds and build back up to twenty. "Bored but polite" is the reaction you want.

When you're able to hold his foot for twenty or thirty seconds, add the hoof pick to the routine. If he's calm, you'll be able to clean out his feet and get him in the habit of accepting the feel and sound of the pick. If you have one of those nifty hoof picks with the brush on one side, even better; you can get him used to both implements.

When picking up and cleaning all four of Gunner's feet is easy to do and he's learned to allow you to lift his feet higher and hold them long enough to clean them slowly and put them down gently, you can add still another sensation. Use the side or back of the hoof pick to tap the bottom and sides of his hooves. Gunner won't need shoes for years, and if he's lucky enough to have really good feet he might never need them at all, but it's still a good idea for him to learn that tapping sounds and vibrations won't hurt him. He can become what farriers like best, an "easy" horse.

Use a few gentle taps at first. Let him show you how he's going to react. Sometimes relaxed, sleepy foals that don't mind anything else will suddenly wake up and become agitated when you begin tapping their hooves, so do a little at a time, pay attention to his reaction, and increase the tapping when he's accepted the idea. By the time you're able to do this step, it should be easy for both of you.

Last but not least, when your farrier comes out, have him trim the mare's feet first so that your foal can watch and see for himself that Mom is fine with this whole process. Then remind him that it's Gunner's first time, and tell him and show him exactly what you've been doing with Gunner's feet. He'll probably want to see Gunner standing and perhaps walking around for a moment, and then he'll look at the feet. He may do nothing but give each hoof a few strokes with the rasp. Or if the ground has been very soft, Gunner may need to have a little bit of his hoof growth removed with small hoof nippers. Either way, your farrier is going to want to make the experience as gentle and pleasant as possible for the foal. After all, he's going to be trimming Gunner for years to come, and this first trim will help establish their relationship. If he gives Gunner a scratch on the withers and rump, or possibly a treat, that will also help begin a friendship.

Before your farrier leaves, ask him if there are other things you could be doing with Gunner to make him even better about standing to have his feet trimmed. He may have all sorts of useful suggestions, and he'll appreciate the fact that you are planning to train your young foal in a way that will make his job easier and more pleasant.

If Gunner's mother is calm and relaxed about all of this, she'll help you. If she is standing right there, calm and accepting, while the farrier works on her hooves and then on Gunner's hooves, you'll have an extra advantage in getting Gunner's relationship with the farrier off to a good start.

Mare Won't Stand for New Farrier

Q I have a Thoroughbred mare who normally is very quiet and has wonderful ground manners. She is a chronic founder case and is not sound, but gets around very well.

Last week a new farrier came to trim her, and she reared up on him when he

Always try to be present when the farrier is working on your horse. An attentive owner can often stop problems before they become serious.

tried to trim her back hooves. She has never done this before, and although I wasn't here, I was told she was kicking, rearing, and out of control. This doesn't sound like her at all.

The farrier said he would not come back and said she was not being worked. It is very hard to work her because of her feet, so what can I do? And what would have caused her to act this way?

A Horses always have a reason for their actions and reactions. Whenever a horse's behavior changes dramatically, I look for some corresponding change in the horse's physical condition, situation, or environment. Horses are reactive animals, and a horse with a history of standing quietly for the farrier isn't going to become violent and out of control for no reason.

In this case, you had one very significant and obvious change: a different farrier. It's always a good idea to be present when your horse is being handled by a new person, whether that person is a farrier or a vet or the person who leads the horses from stall to pasture in the morning and back again in the evening. Horses often get blamed for bad behavior when they are actually being asked to do things that they can't or don't know how to do, or that are physically painful for them.

Not all farriers are equally gentle and tactful with horses. The good ones are, of course. Bad farriers can be abusive and violent, and even the quietest horse will probably react badly to a chain over the nose and a rasp or a boot in the ribs, especially if the horse is used to quiet handling by another person. Sudden, abrupt, jerky movements will always cause problems.

A farrier who yanks a horse's leg out away from its body is going to provoke a strong reaction even in a young, sound, fit, flexible horse. In an older or sore horse, it may cause great pain as well as surprise and fear (more about this later).

It's not enough to know how to balance a hoof well; there's a lot of animal attached to those hooves, and the farrier, like the vet, has to deal with the whole horse.

I've been lucky enough to have a lot of very good farriers. I've also had a bad one, albeit very briefly. And I've seen a few bad ones, but usually those disappear over time, as they tend to lose customers quickly.

You're the one who knows the horses and has to explain how they have been moving, how comfortable they have been, what their previous trimming/shoeing has been like, what (if any) special trims or shoes are being used, and why. You're also the one who has to prepare the horses; reasonably clean, dry feet and legs are much easier to handle than soaking wet or mud- or manure-caked ones. You're also the one who needs to tell the farrier about any particular problems a horse may have.

Older horses, lame horses, and horses with chronic conditions such as arthritis, recurring abscesses, and certainly chronic founder cases like your mare require special handling during trimming and shoeing. Such horses may need to have their feet held much nearer to the ground, or their legs held nearer to their bodies. They may need to have the farrier work on one foot for a few minutes, then put the leg down and wait a moment or two before picking it up again. To work on such horses, a farrier must know horses well enough to read their body language, and a farrier must be sympathetic enough to realize that horses can be stiff, sore, frightened, and confused.

In your particular case, I can't speak about what the farrier did or didn't do, because you weren't there to see and describe his actions. But I can tell you that I would consider the following factors:

▶ **The farrier's horse-handling skills.** It's very, very important to know what these are. It's not enough to know how to balance a hoof well; there's a lot of animal attached to those hooves, and the farrier, like the vet, has to deal with the whole horse. An aggressive, violent, frightened human can provoke bad behavior in even the sweetest, quietest horse.

▶ **The ground manners of the horses at the barn.** Was the farrier happy with the behavior of the other fourteen horses? Did they stand quietly? And if they did not, was it because they always bounce around? If they're all usually quiet and cooperative for farriers, but weren't quiet or cooperative for this farrier, then the common denominator is number 1, the farrier's handling skills. If the farrier is unhappy with the other horses too, then perhaps they all need more training at home before the next visit from any farrier.

▶ **The soundness and physical condition of your mare.** I realize that a horse with chronic founder isn't going to be worked. But are you quite sure that your mare isn't in constant pain? The behavior you've described sounds like that of a horse that can't bear to put extra pressure on her front feet by lifting her back feet. If a horse is cooperative about having her front feet trimmed but goes into fits when a hind foot is lifted, I would consider the possibility that the front feet might be too painful to take the additional pressure. Horses with abscessed front feet will often behave like this; so will horses with laminitis. If your mare is having a flare-up in her front feet, that could explain her unwillingness to put even more weight on them and her rearing in reaction.

There are ways of making the process less painful for a horse like this. You can use thick mats in the aisle or wherever the horses stand for the farrier, instead of asking the horses to stand on an unforgiving concrete surface. If the horse is trimmed, not shod, you can even have her trimmed in her stall or on some other soft surface, perhaps in an arena. (This is not something you would do if the horse were being shod, because the nails could be accidentally dropped and left.) The trim will probably not be as precise and accurate as it would be on a hard surface, but that may not matter greatly, as you're not riding this horse. Standing the horse on rubber mats would be the best choice, as the mare would get the benefit of the cushioning and the farrier would have the flat surface he needs to do his best work. You can explain to the farrier exactly what is wrong with the horse and why she must be handled in a particular way, and then you can supervise and help, to ensure that the horse is handled appropriately.

If you aren't able to be there yourself, be sure that someone who knows your horse and handles her well is there to fill in for you. As for what you can do right now, here's what I suggest:

1. Have your vet come out to examine your mare. There is a possibility that her condition may have become worse, and that her pain has increased to the point where she cannot tolerate having her hind feet lifted. If this is the case, you and the vet will need to talk about your options. There's nothing wrong with keeping a much-loved but unsound horse as a pasture pet, provided that the horse can be kept comfortable and happy. There *is* something wrong with keeping a much-loved horse alive if she cannot be kept comfortable and happy.

2. Talk to the farrier yourself. Get his report on the situation. If he said that he won't come back, find out why. Was he unhappy with all the horses, or just with your mare?

3. Ask your vet and your previous farrier about this farrier. You didn't mention why your previous farrier wasn't available, but there can be a number of reasons for losing a blacksmith. Retirement, too much business in other counties or states, a change of specialty — I've lost good farriers for all of those reasons. But in every case, I was able to get recommendations and suggestions so that I didn't accidentally hire the wrong farrier as a replacement.

Frightened Horse Is Hard to Shoe

Q I half-lease a 13-year-old Quarter Horse mare, Daisy. She and I have been riding together (and learning together) for about 14 months — I just started riding again after about a 30-year hiatus. My trainer and I are working to develop Daisy as a hunter. She's very sweet and never mean, yet spirited, and she can be stubborn. Patience is the key with her. I'm always trying to figure out how to make things that I want her to do become *her* idea, so that she moves more willingly and happily. I try to reward even the smallest positives.

I have learned that Daisy has had some bad experiences, perhaps with previous leasers or before she arrived at this barn. When the farrier came (to help with her flat feet), she was again afraid and kept trying to pull away. Yet she was never vicious. The shoes eventually were put on. This farrier was great, but I learned later that a previous one hit her when she pulled away.

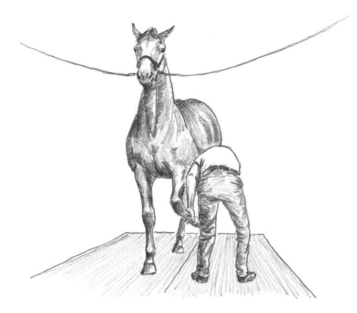

It will take time, patience, and a good farrier to overcome previous mishandling or abuse.

The farrier recommended that in order to help Daisy become more comfortable with the shoeing process, every time I pick her hooves I should tap her on the hoof (imitating a hammer) with increasing force over time so that she becomes accustomed to it. So I started doing that. I tap her until she pulls her foot away, then talk to her quietly to reassure her, then do it again until she accepts it. At first it seemed like it was working. Now, about two weeks later, she gets antsy when she knows I'm going to get near her hooves.

Should I keep doing this? Is this the best approach? I don't want her to lose trust in me, yet I'd love for her to learn that it won't hurt.

A Your farrier is on the right track and so are you, but you are going to have to be very sensitive to Daisy's reactions. This is a good way to train a horse to accept having something done to it, but you have to be careful to do it correctly, so that what you teach the horse is actually what you want it to learn.

Your goal is to desensitize Daisy to the shoeing process so that she can learn to accept it calmly. You'll do this by introducing the process gradually. Begin by tapping her hoof, do it until she becomes anxious, then back off. Wait a moment or two until she is relaxed again, then go back and repeat the process. Each time, take it a little farther, seeing how long you can tap before she gets worried. You should be able to do it a bit longer each time, as she gets more accustomed to the process.

I suggest that while you tap her foot, you also talk to her soothingly. When she pulls her foot away, place it on the ground, stand back, and say nothing. Don't pet her, don't talk, just stand there and wait until she becomes quiet again, and then start over. Pick up the foot, talk to her, and tap lightly, gradually making the taps harder. Again, as soon as she pulls away, gently place her foot on the ground, stand back, and do and say nothing until she's quiet. Again resume the process.

She's doing the best she can to learn, and she is learning, but she thinks like a horse, and you're going to have to think like a horse, too.

I think that what's happened is that you have inadvertently taught Daisy to get antsy. I know you were trying to do just the opposite, but look at the situation from her point of view: When she holds up her foot, you tap it, which may not be terrifying but isn't intrinsically enjoyable. When she begins to pull away and move around, you let go of her foot and you reassure her. To Daisy, this means that you want her to react this way — after all, whenever she does it, you reward her!

She's doing the best she can to learn, and she *is* learning, but she thinks like a horse and you're going to have to think like a horse, too. Horses don't associate what you're doing or saying with what they just did, as we humans do; they associate it with what they are doing at that moment. If you reassure her while you are tapping, then give her no input when her foot is on the ground, she will learn to associate the tapping with the reassurance. Right now, she associates your reassurance with her pulling away and getting her foot back on the ground.

Start over by just picking up the foot, talking to her, and putting it down. Then pick it up again, hold it a little longer, talk to her, and so on. But when you put the foot down, don't pet her and don't talk. Gradually work up to tapping. You don't have to tap very hard; simply tap her soles with the back of your hoof pick. It makes a bit of noise — not as loud a noise as the farrier's hammer will, but that's fine. It's really just the idea that she needs to get used to. Once she's accepted that you will sometimes hold her feet up for a short time to clean them and sometimes hold them up for a longer time to tap them, you won't have to do it every time you clean out her feet.

Your farrier sounds wonderful; be good to him (coffee on cold days, cold drinks on hot days, a well-behaved horse with clean feet, and a bottle of fly-spray handy). Try to be there to hold your horse while he works on her. You can also take a pocketful of treats and give them to her when she is standing quietly.

Another step you can take to increase Daisy's comfort level is to get to the barn before the farrier arrives and give her some exercise. Free-school her in the arena, longe her, or ride her. You don't want her to be tired, but you do want her muscles warm; even fifteen minutes of walking will make a big difference. When a horse comes out of her stall and is stiff, she can find it physically uncomfortable to have to hold up each leg for the farrier. If you can warm up Daisy and let her stretch and play a little, *then* ask her to stand for the farrier, she will be more comfortable, physically and mentally.

Yearling with Vet-Visit Trauma

Q I have a yearling Chincoteague pony, Cricket. She was totally wild for the first two months of her life before she came to live with me, and it took me more than six weeks to gain enough of her trust to be able to touch her. We've worked together every day for about eight months, and she has come to trust me. In fact, she is unquestionably the gentlest, kindest, least reactive yearling I've ever worked with. She happily stands in cross-ties, loves to be groomed, comes when called, is easy to lead, and enjoys being bathed. However, she still has issues with new people. She is visibly nervous around new people and prefers to have a little time to size them up before they approach her and attempt to touch her — unless they offer her a carrot, in which case she quickly overcomes her nervousness!

She has had regular farrier care since she came to me and had regular vet visits for her baby shots and boosters last fall. All of her previous vet visits had gone well. Three weeks ago, the vet came out to the farm to give the first of two West Nile virus (WNV) shots. Everything went fine.

Yesterday, the vet came to do the second WNV shot, some of her other regular spring shots, and a Coggins test. The doctor that came out yesterday is an experienced veterinarian, and she has worked on my other horse before. She's kind and efficient, but she'd never worked with Cricket before. For whatever reason, Cricket was not cooperating yesterday when it was time for shots. We usually do them out in the yard to prevent negative associations with the barn aisle, stall, or cross-ties (since she was a wild baby she has lingering discomfort with all confined spaces). The vet just couldn't get close to her for long enough to give an injection, and Cricket was really working herself up.

Against my better judgment, I finally gave in to the vet's suggestion of putting her on cross-ties to do her shots. As you can probably guess, it was a disaster. Cricket tried to kick the vet, ended up rearing and plunging in the cross-ties, and nearly knocked both of us down. (I was holding Cricket and attempting to hold a twitch on her as the vet did the shots.) After the vet had given her two shots, I came to my senses and insisted that we move her to another location to finish up. We ended up finishing in an outdoor sheep pen (about 5 feet per side), where we pushed her up against the wall. Once she figured out that she couldn't escape, she relaxed and we easily completed the last shot and the Coggins test.

After her shots, I put her back out in the paddock. When I went out later to groom and work with her, she was absolutely traumatized. She wouldn't let me catch her, she flinched when I touched her, and it took me over half an hour to coax her into the aisle of the barn — and another 15 minutes for her to relax. I gave her half a gram of bute to help with the physical discomfort she must have from the shots, but mentally, she's a mess.

Do you have any suggestions for helping Cricket relax and regain trust in me? What could I have done better to prevent this from happening? How should I handle subsequent vet visits so we can improve upon this experience, rather than have it degrade to the point that she can't be handled by a vet?

A I'm so sorry that you and Cricket had to go through this. It probably wasn't pleasant for the veterinarian either, if that's any comfort at all. I don't think that Cricket is likely to be emotionally scarred by this. Yes, there are some things that you could have done differently, some things you might not have done if you'd had time to think about them, and quite a lot of things you can still do. So please relax. Let's look closely at where you are now, and then go forward. You haven't wrecked your filly, and she doesn't have to have a lifetime aversion to veterinarians.

To help Cricket relax and regain trust in you, just handle her the way you always have. She was relaxed and trusting because you had taught her that she could relax and trust you, so do it again. It's that easy. Let's put this in perspective. Cricket's experience with you has meant eight months of good memories and good associations, set against probably half an hour of you trying to keep her quiet for the vet. As I tell my riders, you have eight months of substantial deposits in your "confidence account" against one (not really very impressive, although I know you were frightened at the time) withdrawal.

Now, stop thinking that you abused your horse. You didn't. Did you beat her or kick her or whip her or scream at her? Did you try to frighten her or hurt her? No. You asked her to hold still, you probably spoke sharply when she bounced around, and you used a twitch when it was necessary to keep her from trampling the vet and you. That's not abuse. It may not be the ideal form of training, but it's a very effective form of survival. If you or the vet or Cricket had sustained an injury while all this commotion was going on, *that* would have been bad and had lasting effects. One of the realities of working with horses is that even young ponies are generally significantly bigger and heavier than adult humans, and all horses and ponies react more quickly than humans. This is precisely why we need to train them to stand still when we ask, even if our request is, in their opinion, not entirely reasonable.

Even young, tiny, adorable ponies are stronger and faster than humans.

Cricket sounds like a sensible pony. Remember that she is still quite young, and she will probably demonstrate the same behavior pattern again if nothing is done differently. This can work *for* you. You realize now that cross-ties aren't ideal for medical procedures of any kind; never add swinging ropes, ties, or chains to a situation involving an agitated horse.

She didn't leap about and rear and try to run because she couldn't get away; she did those things because she thought that perhaps she *could* get away. Remember that after all of that, when Cricket had every excuse to behave badly in the sheep pen, she was quiet and still because she knew that she could *not* get away. That should tell you that your filly has all the normal horse reactions (fright leads to flight, which, if flight is impossible, then leads to fight), but she also has intelligence, good sense, and trust in you. When you were definite instead of tentative and told her, "Right, you're going up against the wall of this pen; now hold still for a moment and the shots will be over," she didn't explode or freeze; she calmed down. That's a sign of great intelligence and adaptability, and it shows that at that point, she accepted the fact that you were in charge.

If everyone is quiet and calm and very definite, if everyone moves slowly and talks to Cricket, and if the pockets of the lab coat contain carrot sticks, you have every chance of changing her attitude to "Oh, hurray, here's another vet. Now I'll get a treat!"

By the time you went to fetch her again, she had had a little time to think about what happened and quite naturally did not want a repeat of that particular adventure. That's understandable and normal. I don't think she was absolutely traumatized, but I do think that she was suspicious that you might be planning a repeat of the afternoon's events!

What might have helped prevent this from happening?

1. You could have turned Cricket out that morning or taken her out for exercise before the vet arrived, so that she would have been a more relaxed and peaceful pony.

2. You could have said to the vet: "This is my wild yearling filly. She's very good, but she's very timid with strangers. Here's my tactic for helping her make friends with new people: Please take these four carrot sticks and feed them to her and talk to her for few minutes so that she can register that you belong in the 'friend' category and not in the 'unknown, could be dangerous' category." Most vets are very willing to comply with such requests, even if they are in a hurry, for three reasons: good horse vets love horses; vets prefer to work with calm horses that aren't rearing and behaving dangerously; and good vets are always interested in doing things that will make the next visit easier, not more difficult. Like horses, vets are all individuals, and although Cricket had been quiet for a different vet three weeks earlier, that clearly didn't mean that she would always be quiet for every vet.

3. You could have said no to the cross-ties. Cross-ties are not inherently safe, and a lot of bad accidents occur when horses are on cross-ties. It's generally a much better idea to hold the horse for medical procedures than to tie it. If you know that your pony is not good on the cross-ties, you must say so and suggest taking her elsewhere for her shots. Otherwise, you end up with a situation like the one you've described, in which the pony, already anxious about the vet and the cross-ties, senses that you, too, are nervous and becomes frightened and tense, then gets shots that hurt because her muscles are tight. At this point, the pony decides that she was quite right to be afraid of the cross-ties and the vet, and she tries to get away by rearing, bucking, and leaping. She ends up making herself more frightened, and the tension escalates more and more rapidly.

So what should you do instead? Next time, go directly to the sheep pen. To make subsequent visits better than this one, practice. Cricket should practice all the skills she will need to be worked on by a vet or a farrier. She needs to know how to stand quietly, keep all four feet on the ground, and take a step forward or backward or sideways when asked. She needs to know how to lift her feet and to allow them to be held up and tapped. She needs to lower her head when asked. She needs to accept being poked and prodded here and there, so poke and prod her. Handle her everywhere; put your fingers in her mouth, touch her tongue, rub her gums. Let her know that you can do these things, that there is no danger, that she can almost sleep through them all.

Practice until Cricket is perfect at being handled and examined, until she is utterly bored with it. Then bring in a friend to do all the same things while you watch or hold Cricket, or do both. Then bring in another friend and begin again. Use a thermometer, use a stethoscope, wear a lab coat; then have your friends do the same. If everyone is quiet and calm and very definite, if everyone moves slowly and talks to Cricket, and if the pockets of the lab coat contain carrot sticks, you have every chance of changing Cricket's attitude to, "Oh, hurray, here's another vet. Now I'll get a treat and a cuddle!"

Remember, this was one vet visit out of all the ones she's had up until now, and although Cricket probably wouldn't care to be put on the cross-ties for that same veterinarian, she is not likely to have a fit the next time she needs medical attention. But do practice everything she needs to know, over and over — perhaps even in the cross-ties someday, maybe a year from now when calm obedience is such a habit that you can practice there, too. It's important to get her relaxed and calm, though, because up until now, all of her medical attention has been routine care, not emergency care. She needs to develop the habit of being a bored, peaceful horse for the vet — any vet — because someday a vet may need to treat her in an emergency when she is already in pain and actually has a good reason to be frightened. You want to have such an enormous confidence account and such a well-established habit of calm acceptance that Cricket will behave well even in an emergency situation.

CHAPTER 6

Tacking Up

MOST PROBLEMS involving tack have very simple causes. They are basically either handling problems or reactions to pain caused by tack that doesn't fit or suit the horse, isn't positioned correctly, or isn't fastened correctly. Horses have a limited number of ways to express their discomfort with their tack, and a horse that anticipates pain from a bit, bridle, or saddle is likely to try to avoid the tacking-up process. If tack is comfortable and fits the horse well and the rider tacks up slowly and gently, most tacking-up problems can be avoided. Removing tack should also be a slow, gentle process — a saddle that is hastily pulled off can jar the horse's spine, and a bridle that is pulled off too quickly can hurt the horse's ears and teeth.

Hard to Bridle

Q My mare hates having her mouth, chin, and nose areas touched. Taking the bit when she's being bridled can be a battle. She pulled back once when being bridled and snapped her halter in half. So I have two questions: one relative to the short term, and one relative to the long term.

What is the best approach to cure her of her dislike of being touched in those areas? I take fifteen to twenty minutes each day just to feel and stroke her nose, chin, and so forth, and she is praised when she does not yank her head up in the air or step backward to escape the "torture." I am trying to convince her to associate this experience with nice things such as verbal praise, cuddles, and treats such as pieces of apple. I do not do this with her tied; usually she is either in just a halter, loose in her stall, or ground-tied.

Bridling her causes me a lot of stress, as she just does not want to take the bit. I try to praise her and give treats like a sugar cube when she does accept it. I often have to plan an extra twenty minutes to get the bridle on. She is 15.3 hh and I am 5'3", so I have a terrible time when she sticks her nose in the air and does not want to bring it down. I understand that it's not something she likes and therefore wants to avoid; that's why I'm working with her to calm her fear. But in the meantime, I need an approach that will allow me to bridle her without a to-do. She is not just gritting her teeth; she is strong about not wanting the bit in the mouth or her mouth touched. Once bridled, she's as happy as a lark.

A In the long term, you are doing exactly the right thing: getting her used to having her mouth and chin area handled. Many mares become touchy about their muzzles when they are three or so, then are quite relaxed again a year or so later. If she's still a filly, she may outgrow the sensitivity. While she's still sensitive, though, be sure that you handle her mouth and nose area with enough pressure that you aren't just tickling her.

Take two fingers of one hand and make circles on your other arm with your fingertips. Vary the pressure from hard to barely discernable — you'll find that hard pressure hurts and very light touches can be incredibly annoying. Somewhere in between is a medium pressure that is comfortable. You need to experiment with your horse and find out where her comfort level is.

If she's an older mare and has been ridden or trained by someone else, she may have developed a behavior pattern based on the way she was handled. Some riders dance around their horses and make a huge fuss about bridling, and eventually the horses begin to react the way they think their owners want them to.

To teach her that bridling is no big deal, first approach her slowly and calmly, as though putting on the bridle is routine and you are going to do it smoothly and quietly while talking to her about other things. Try to think of this as a very minor part of the getting-ready-to-ride process, and believe that she will be quiet and put her head down for you. Wait for her head to come

Instead of getting involved in a "reach for the sky" session, teach your horse to lower her head for bridling.

down — if it goes up, stop talking, don't touch her, and just wait. When her head comes down, pat her and talk to her. She'll get the idea. I call this form of training "as if" — you treat her *as if* she has no problem with being bridled, and she responds *as if* she doesn't have a problem. Soon she will not have a problem.

But before you do that, keep in mind that pain can cause many misbehaviors. Since your horse objects so strongly to the process, it would be a good idea to eliminate physical causes first. Check her mouth for sores and have the vet check her teeth — perhaps they need floating. A few sharp edges can be excruciatingly painful to a horse, especially if they cut into the lips when her mouth and nose areas are handled or compressed. Tooth floating can eliminate an incredible number of mouth problems and behavior problems based on mouth pain.

You know how important it is that the horse wears a bit that fits properly, so check this, too. Also check the adjustment of the bit in her mouth. Is it hanging too high or too low? Check her halter and the cavesson of her bridle; both should be comfortably loose. Cranking a cavesson tight is a good way to make a horse fear and resent the bridle, the halter, or anything that goes around the face.

If her mouth and teeth are fine, the bit fits well and is adjusted properly, and the cavesson is fastened loosely, move up to check her ears and the area surrounding them. She may have an injury, a bruise, or a sore, or the problem may be more subtle. For instance, I was once presented with a horse that objected very strenuously to bridling, although his teeth were fine, he had no sores in his mouth, and the bit fit him well. I watched the owner bridle him, and she didn't bang the bit against his teeth or scrape the bridle over his eye — both of which can also cause a horse to dislike bridling. But what I did notice was that the browband was too short, so that it pulled tightly across the horse's forehead, rubbed against the base of his ears, and pulled the top of the crownpiece against the base of the ears from behind, causing him pain in all three places. The horse was miserable, and every time he looked at anything, he got more miserable, because the eyes and ears work together. Thus, when he looked in any direction, his ears tried to move and were pinched and rubbed by both the browband and crownpiece. This is not an uncommon problem.

Put the bit in your horse's mouth and attach it to the left cheekpiece. Since she isn't used to having her bridle put on this way, she hasn't established habits of avoidance.

The horse's owner went to the tack shop for a longer browband and the problem was solved. It did take several days to finally convince the horse that the bridle wouldn't hurt anymore, because he was expecting pain. His owner is still careful and slow when she bridles him — which is the right way to bridle any horse.

In the short term, here's my formula for easier bridling. Remove the cavesson from the bridle and ride without it for a few weeks. Strip the bridle down to the bare essentials: a well-fitting crownpiece, browband, cheekpieces, and bit. Unbuckle the bit from the near side (left), lift the bridle, and place the crownpiece gently over her ears. Ask your horse to open her mouth — you can put the fingers of your right hand lightly on her nose, and then slide your thumb into her mouth — and then put the bit into her mouth and attach it to the left cheekpiece. Since she isn't accustomed to having her bridle put on in this way, she won't have established habits of avoidance.

Do some practice sessions with her halter and a handful of treats. Hold up the halter so that she has to lower her head into it and put her nose through it to get her treat. Don't follow her head up — just keep your hand (and the treat and the halter) low and let her figure it out.

When she's quiet during this process, you can go back to "normal" bridling, but leave the cavesson off for a while. Hold the crownpiece and the throatlatch in your right hand, the bit in your left hand, and a treat in your left hand along with the bit. Your mare will quickly learn that she needs to lower her head to get the treat, just as she did with the halter. If the bridle goes on smoothly and quietly and doesn't hurt, she will think less and less about it as time goes by. When she is quiet and lowers her head readily, you'll be able to put the cavesson back on.

One more point about the cavesson: Be sure that you always unfasten it before putting on or taking off the bridle. Some riders forget to do this, and the result is that the horse can't open her mouth wide enough to accept or drop the bit. The bit hits the horse's teeth on the way in and on the way out of the mouth, and the horse quickly becomes difficult to bridle.

Problem Bridling a Young Horse

Q I've got a two-and-a-half-year-old Thoroughbred gelding, Woody, that I have just recently started under saddle. My vet did a thorough exam and felt there was no reason not to start him with slow and gentle under-saddle work. I am doing 90 percent of my riding at the walk and a tiny bit at the trot. I am still focusing on ground work and only ride two to three times a week. I have owned this horse since he was eight months old, and I'm trying my best to work slowly and carefully with him.

I have been riding him in a rope halter with clip-on reins, and he does great! He stops every time and is very responsive. I have put a bit and bridle on him about half a dozen times now, but I've never ridden in one. The first couple of times I used a D-ring, French-link snaffle and longed him in it. He tossed his head and chewed the bit a little, but had no major problems. (I leave a thin rope halter on under his bridle and longe him from that so there is no pressure on his mouth.) After just a couple of times, he wasn't fussing about the bit at all, but I started having trouble getting the bridle on him. I had my trainer check the fit of the bit, and I had my vet check his teeth. The vet said that Woody is the right age to be teething, but that there didn't seem to be any problems that would interfere with the bit. I switched to a Happy Mouth bit, a loose ring with a center roller. It is a nice, lightweight, hard plastic bit, and is even apple flavored. I longed him in this bit a couple of times, and he was great. I thought my problem was solved, but every time I tried to put the bridle on him it became more of a battle, and now it is almost impossible.

I have tried teaching him a cue for "head down," but it only works when there is no bridle in sight. I hid the bridle and snuck it up a couple of times without him seeing it, and gently rubbed it on his cheeks and face until I could slide it on, but then he caught on. Finally, I tried putting the bridle on with the bit attached on one side only, and then pulling the bit through his mouth and attaching it after the bridle was on. That worked twice, but not anymore.

I can't think of any kind of trauma that he has had related to the bit. The whole thing has been a very gradual and gentle process. Is this a common problem? Do you have any ideas? Everyone tells me he needs to get used to the bit and to stick him in his stall with a bridle on for a couple of hours. My feeling is that the bit is for working, and that is the only time I want the bridle on him. I did let him graze with the bit in his mouth on a lead line a few times because that seemed to help him relax and get used to the bit. My problem isn't when the bit is in his mouth; the problem is trying to get it in his mouth!

A Bridle problems aren't unusual with very young horses. I would look at the tooth issue first. As your vet mentioned, Woody may be teething, and this often causes bridle problems. When your vet comes back, ask him to check for retained caps and also for incipient wolf teeth.

Remember that the horse knows more than you or the vet about what hurts! A small sore spot or a tooth that "may need floating in six months" can cause a good deal of pain. Let the horse be the judge. Some horses, like some humans, have lower pain thresholds than others. A good vet will tell you that sometimes he or she can't find the source of a problem, but that doesn't mean that there isn't a source, or that the problem isn't real.

Some horses dislike their bridles because the rider takes off the bridle quickly, puts it on too quickly, or doesn't undo the cavesson, and the bit bangs the horse's teeth on the way in and out of the mouth. Be sure to watch your technique when bridling.

I also encourage you to look at the bit itself. Be sure that it fits Woody well, and double-check to be sure that you really do have a French-link. It's not easy to find a French-link D-ring snaffle, but D-ring Dr. Bristol snaffles are very common and sometimes the staff at the local tack shop or catalog outlet will mislabel or confuse the two. If you are using a Dr. Bristol mouthpiece in place of a French-link, the horse may react strongly to the severity of the bit. With a Dr. Bristol, the center link is long, thin, and flat; with a French-link, the center link

A thorough dental exam by a vet or equine dentist will help determine if tooth problems are causing bit problems.

is short, rounded, and shaped a little like a peanut or a fat figure-eight. There's an enormous difference in the action of these bits.

Also look at the headstall of the bridle. A horse doesn't have to have a single traumatic experience to become bridle shy; he can be reacting to a series of annoying discomforts. A horse that doesn't want to be bridled may have trouble with the bit itself or with his rider's hands. The horse may have sore or sensitive ears because of something inside an ear, such as an ear fungus, which can make him very head shy. Or he may have sore or sensitive ears because of something *outside* the ears, such as a browband that is too short.

Similarly, a cavesson or throatlatch that is too tight can interfere with a horse's mental and physical comfort. Keep both loose; you should be able to put several fingers under the cavesson, and your fist between the throatlatch and the horse's jaw.

Next, I would consider Woody's level of comprehension. He is a very young horse and is just being introduced to the bit. He doesn't know what the bit is for, and he doesn't understand how he is supposed to respond to it, although he most certainly does feel its action. Remember that no horse is born with an understanding of the bit or of any of the aids; he is born only with the capacity to learn to understand them. If he associates the bit with pain for any reason, he's going to be unwilling to accept the bridle.

After checking everything above, consider the possibility of riding him in a Bitless Bridle or a well-fitted headstall attached to an English jumping hackamore noseband (the kind made from leather-covered rope and ending in two rings for the reins — not to be confused with a mechanical hackamore, which can inflict damage).

One of the reasons against starting horses under saddle at this age is that this is precisely the age at which they are having tooth issues. When someone like yourself, a conscientious, caring rider, is being very careful with a homegrown horse of two-and-a-half, doing only short rides at the walk, I worry much less. But you won't lose any ground by riding him in a hackamore noseband for a few months. After the first few weeks, you can use a bradoon carrier attached to your hackamore headstall and just let him carry a bit without your putting any pressure on it.

When Woody is moving comfortably and is entirely responsive to the hackamore reins and not worried about the bit, you can add a second pair of reins attached to the bit and ride him with both reins, with most of the pressure on the reins attached to the noseband. This way, he will learn to associate light bit pressure with what he already understands about signals from the reins.

Over a few weeks or months, depending on his needs, you can make a gradual shift so that the pressure is equal on both reins. Shift the pressure to the bit rein slowly, and finally, when the noseband rein is just hanging there, you can take the noseband off and ride with your single rein attached to the bit. By then, your horse should be having fewer teething troubles, and he will have learned what he needs to know without pain or fear.

Horse Bites When the Girth Is Tightened

Q Most of the time, Precious, my horse, pins her ears and tries to bite when I saddle her and initially tighten the cinch/girth. This started about 18 months ago after she returned from two months with a trainer. I've been working on it — saddling slowly and gently, praising her a lot when she's good, stopping when she acts up — and it's helping some, but she almost always tries to bite. Last week, I let my guard down for a split second as I was checking the girth and she bit my arm. It happened so fast and I was so shocked that I didn't know what to do. By then, three seconds had passed, so I decided I had to let it go. I was very careful to not act angry, and I just continued tacking up. It felt like she was watching me and waiting for a reaction that never came. I'm afraid now she really thinks it's okay to do that.

A It sounds as though your mare had a hard time with the trainer — this behavior is typical of a horse that expects pain from a sudden yanking of the girth. You need to understand why she is doing it, but you also need to make her stop doing it. There's no harm if she makes faces, but she can't bite. It's too dangerous.

You were right not to punish her once you had let too much time go by. But the next time she bites — or better yet, the next time she puts her ears back and turns her head to bite, but *before* she bites — make a horrible noise at her and stamp your foot hard. If you were a horse and she tried to bite you, your reaction would be to squeal and kick her hard — don't kick, but if you're coordinated enough to tack up with a riding whip in your hand, you can certainly smack her solidly in the chest once while you shout, "No!" or make a loud "wrong answer" buzzer sound (my personal preference, because it doesn't sound like anything else and the horse can't possibly get confused). Then, after you've reacted vehemently and loudly, ignore any faces she makes and just continue tacking up calmly and quietly, always keeping an eye on her.

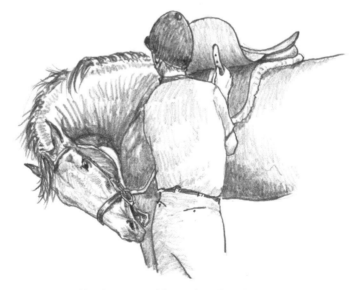

Biting is unacceptable, no ifs, ands, or buts.

When you first fasten the girth, always fasten it loosely. Then stretch each of her front legs forward, so that the skin behind the elbows is pulled tight. This will remove any wrinkles that could chafe if they were allowed to stay under the girth — one reason horses learn to hate having the girth tightened. It will also shift your saddle back into the correct position, if necessary.

After a few minutes, take the girth up by *one* hole. Then walk your horse into the arena. When you approach the mounting block, take up the girth another hole. After you've ridden for five or ten minutes, check your girth again; you may need to tighten it another hole. Don't overtighten the girth — it's miserably uncomfortable for the horse and teaches her to hate and resent the saddle and the saddling process.

Take your time; be clear about what behaviors you will and will not accept. Praise her when she is pleasant, and she should come around eventually, although she may always make faces when you saddle her.

Mare Dislikes Saddle

Q I have trained and retrained horses for a few years, but there is a particular case with which I am having trouble. This is a gorgeous nine-year-old Arabian mare with great conformation and good weight (although she is currently three months pregnant). She is very smart, but spooky at times. She has the attention span of a gnat, so whenever I longe her I have to constantly ask her to do different but simple things such as transitions, changes of directions, turns on the forehand and on the haunches, side passes, back-ups, and jumping obstacles. She is very responsive and most of the time has no trouble doing any of these things when I just use body language.

She used to hate to be caught, be led on the off side, be saddled, or have anything near her face, but now she comes to the gate when called, can be led and saddled from either side, and likes it when I massage her ears. Recently, she let me mount from each side. But whenever I walk her around saddled, whether she is mounted or unmounted, she tenses up and gets scared, apparently just by the squeak of the leather. I longe her while saddled for five minutes, and she bucks and tries to run off. When I take the saddle off her back she's fine again. The saddle fits, and several years ago she used to be ridden just fine.

This horse is reacting in anticipation of an unpleasant or painful event.

A It sounds to me as though you're doing a great job with this mare; the list of things you've accomplished with her is impressive. It also sounds to me as though there is a saddle-fit problem, probably deep under the saddle where you can't see or feel it, but where the mare can feel it. Yes, she could be reacting to the squeaky leather, but I'd bet that there's something more serious going on. Here are some suggestions you can use to find out what's happening.

First, try her in another saddle — one that fits her and doesn't squeak. See whether she is still frightened of it after the first five minutes. She'll probably run and jump around for a few minutes just because she's used to doing that whenever she's saddled, so don't take it seriously until five minutes have passed. Then try her in several other saddles, until you find one that lets her move comfortably on the longe. Then double- and triple-check the fit, because a saddle that seems to fit a horse that's standing still may not fit well enough to let her move freely on the longe; a saddle that seems to fit a horse on the longe may be very uncomfortable for the horse once a rider has been added to the equation. Horses are truthful animals, and they're usually quite specific about where their saddles hurt, so pay close attention to your mare.

Second, if you are comfortable riding her bareback, and if she is comfortable being ridden bareback, that might be a good way to determine whether it's a saddle, riding, or a squeaky-leather issue. If she doesn't get tense when she's ridden bareback, that will tell you quite a lot.

Third, you don't say what her previous experiences have been, other than the fact that she was ridden several years ago. It's possible that her saddle and riding experiences weren't happy ones, and that the squeaky saddle or the discomfort it causes brings back unpleasant memories. Don't assume that she has a lot of experience being ridden, and don't assume that her experiences under saddle were good ones. Either way, the best thing for you to do is to start her from the ground up, introducing the saddle slowly and teaching her to accept it calmly while she is standing, being led, being longed, and, finally, being ridden.

Saddle-fitting is as much art as science, and the only one who can truly say whether a saddle fits is the horse.

It's also entirely possible that she's not in the same shape she was in when she was ridden a few years ago. The back contours of a four-, five-, or six-year-old riding mare aren't necessarily the same as the back contours of that same mare three or four years later — especially if she hasn't been ridden as much or is pregnant. So even if you're using the same saddle that she was ridden in earlier in her life, it may not fit the same way or feel the same to her. If the saddle was wide enough to accommodate a wide, muscular Arabian back, it may be sitting on her spine now that she's out of (riding) shape. A saddle that's temporarily too wide can be "padded up" using big Kodel pads for a Western saddle and gel or inflatable pads for an English saddle. If you do this, be very careful, as it's surprisingly easy to make a bad fit worse with the use of pads.

If, on the other hand, the saddle fit her in her younger, thinner days and is now too narrow for a wider, older horse, then padding will only make the fit tighter and more painful, and any solution will have to begin with a wider saddle.

The squeak, as you guessed, may also play a part. Horses have very sensitive ears and acute hearing, and a squeak that merely annoys a human might be a sound that a horse would find frightening, highly irritating, or both. Some people can't bear to be in the same room with squeaky Styrofoam (have you ever had one of those cheap Styrofoam coolers in the back seat of your car?), and some can't stand the fingernails-on-a-blackboard noise. Some humans can even hear those high-frequency dog whistles.

If your mare reacts strongly to the squeaky leather, you'll need to know whether the problem is the sound itself or the fact that it's connected with an uncomfortable experience. If it's the sound, try oiling the saddle (or using baby powder, if it's synthetic) to eliminate the squeak. This also brings us back to trying other saddles.

This mare is three months along in her pregnancy, so you have another five or six months to figure out the saddle issue and do light work, including light riding. Make all of it as pleasant as possible, and then she'll have a set of new good memories to consider during the last few months of her pregnancy and during the half-year or so that she'll have her foal at foot.

Then, once you start her back into work, you'll have to begin again from the ground up, as her shape will have changed again. This isn't a bad thing, though; the entire process will be much easier, faster, and more pleasant the next time around.

Saddle-fitting is as much art as it is science, and the only one who can truly say whether a saddle fits is the horse that wears it. If your mare says that she's uncomfortable, believe her.

(The vast subject of saddle-fitting is too complex to address adequately here. See the Resources section for more on the topic.)

PART II

Under Saddle

CHAPTER 7

Moving While
the Rider Mounts

MANY OF THE UNWANTED BEHAVIORS exhibited by horses under saddle are reactions to tack, rider skills, and rider demands. Other behaviors are the results of the horses' expectations based on previous experiences or training. Riders should not take these behaviors personally or react with anger. They need to learn to evaluate the behaviors dispassionately and set about teaching the horses different behaviors. While doing so, it's important for them to keep the horses' comfort in mind. For example, it's much easier to teach a horse to stand for mounting if the horse is standing in balance, the tack fits well, and the rider is coordinated, considerate, and uses a mounting block to minimize the stress on the horse's back.

Standing during Mounting

Q I have recently bought a pinto, Danny, who is about 14 years old. Although I have had the good fortune to speak to two of Danny's previous owners, who reassure me that he is a "rock," I am finding him to be quite the opposite at the moment!

For example, Danny will move when I am trying to mount. We end up playing a game of "try if you can," and as I am not as nimble as I used to be, simply getting into the saddle is exhausting. Could you advise me on how to solve this problem?

In addition, Danny and I have only been a team for about four weeks, and I get the chance to ride only on the weekends. I am finding each ride to be a challenge, as he has a tendency to stop at various points along a trail and decide that he has had enough! My friends have said that he is testing his new owner to see what he can get away with. Would this be correct? I am keen for our time together to be a partnership, rather than a fight every step of the way.

A I like your attitude — you're right that your relationship with your horse should be a partnership. Give it time to develop, though; a relationship doesn't automatically get transferred along with the ownership papers. It will take time for your horse to get to know and trust you, and for you to get to know and trust him.

Standing during mounting seems like a simple thing to do, but horses must be taught to do it, and there are several components to it.

First, the horse must be comfortable. This means that the saddle shouldn't pinch and that the rider should get on from a mounting block, to spare the saddle, the horse's back, and the rider's own back. In addition, some saddles fit just fine until the rider is in them! Check yours; if the saddle is too tight or it digs into the horse's shoulders because it's placed too far forward (this is *very* common), the horse will anticipate pain whenever you are ready to mount, and will want to walk away. And who can blame him?

Another comfort component is the rider's toe. Be sure that you turn it into the girth when you get on, because if you don't, you may be giving your horse a dig in the belly while you mount. Again, a normal horse's response to this will be to try to avoid the discomfort, and that means that he will swing his hindquarters away or move forward.

Mounting blocks are good for both horse and rider. The horse must learn to stand quietly.

One very important component is whether the horse is trained to listen to the rider's leg. If your horse moves off while you are still adjusting your reins, the problem is *not* related to the reins; the problem is that the horse is not trained to the leg and is not waiting for your leg to say, "Okay, go." Many novice riders tend to think that a horse like this needs a jerk in the mouth, but that's wrong for two reasons. First, you never, ever, use the bit to punish a horse. Second, the horse is not disobeying or ignoring the bit; he's ignoring the rider's legs. He may be doing this because he has no idea that he's expected to wait for a signal to go. You'll have to teach him.

You can use verbal commands to reinforce your aids from the saddle. If your horse is used to being longed, long-lined, or free-schooled, he will know what "Whoa" and "Walk on" mean, and you will be able to teach him what your seat and leg aids mean by reinforcing them with the words.

Some horses are allowed to walk off while the rider is mounting — racehorses, in particular, are not made to stand still — and sometimes it's the third or fourth owner who needs to teach the horse to stand. But remember that you need to teach your horse to stand, not frighten him into temporary paralysis.

You want him to stand for mounting — not just for two seconds next to your mounting block, but for as long as you like, wherever you like, including next to a fence or a rock or a fire hydrant, anything you might need to use as a mounting block at home or on a trail ride. You want to be able to mount, adjust your position, adjust your stirrups, adjust your reins, zip up your jacket, and *then* ask the horse to move off. If you are patient and teach the horse gently, taking your time, you will get there.

The same is true when Danny stops to look at things on trails; he's ignoring the leg signal that tells him, "Okay, you've looked at it, now move along, please." My suggestion is that you arrange to take a few lessons with a good instructor in your area, so that you can get an objective evaluation of Danny's training and your own riding, and so that you can get some help in creating the relationship and trust you want.

There is always someone who will tell you, "Punish that horse — don't let him get away with that!" I say don't listen. Wait and find out what the horse can do, what he knows, and how well you two are communicating. Don't punish him for what may be a misunderstanding. But you're probably wondering, If the horse does something I don't want him to do or doesn't do something I do want him to do, should I punish him or not? Here's my checklist:

- Is the horse physically able to do what I'm asking?
- Does the horse understand what I'm asking and know the response that I want and expect?
- Did I ask correctly?
- Did I ask at the right moment, so that it was physically possible for the horse to respond appropriately?
- Did I stay out of the horse's way so that he could respond?
- Did I give him time to respond?

If you can say "no" to any of these, or if you are less than absolutely sure of *all* of these, then it's not appropriate to punish.

If I get all the way to the last question and I'm still saying "yes," then it may be appropriate to punish, but I probably won't because I'd rather try again, be more clear, and avoid creating an adversarial relationship with the horse. I never lose sight of the fact that I am the educator in this relationship, and that punishment has no place here.

There's an enormous difference between a horse trying to get away with something and a horse genuinely not understanding what you are asking, either because you are unclear or because he hasn't been taught all the things you think he already knows. The quickest way to ruin a relationship with any horse is to punish when punishment isn't appropriate. You're Danny's teacher now: Your job is to educate him so that he understands what you want and is able to do it when you ask. This may take some time and some help, but the effort will be worth it in the end. Be patient, get a little help to start you off correctly, and enjoy the process.

Mounting and Dismounting

Q I am a 46-year-old man who has ridden and owned horses for the past 15 years. Unfortunately, I suffered a mild traumatic brain injury (not horse related), and while I am not looking for sympathy, I do need some ideas in dealing with my horse, Caleb. Mounting and dismounting seem to be real problem areas for the horse and me as a team, and I understand the horse's reasoning. I had little time to get acquainted with him before I was injured, but there were no mounting or dismounting problems. I'm a big guy, and I learned to swing quickly and easily into the saddle and to ride lightly (make the horse's job easier through good riding techniques). The problem I have is that Caleb moves around during my slower and more uncoordinated mount and dismount. Once I'm in the saddle we communicate perfectly. Mounting aids are not the answer, because the real problem is that the right side of my body does not work like it used to, and it takes more time and a lot more effort to throw my leg over the saddle. I know he should stand, but I can't get angry at him for my disability, which I'm sure causes him extra discomfort.

A Your horse can certainly learn to stand quietly for mounting and dismounting. It will take some help and some practice, but it's entirely doable and will make both of your lives easier.

You're right to think in terms of how the horse is thinking and reacting, and you're also right to think that he's reacting to something that's uncomfortable for him. He's probably confused and physically uncomfortable if you aren't able to mount smoothly. The process isn't very comfortable for horses unless the saddle fits well, the rider is smooth and accomplished, and the rider's technique doesn't put extra strain on the horse's back. That's why savvy riders in all riding disciplines use a mounting block whenever they can — it takes strain off the horse's back and minimizes the twisting and pulling effect that, over time, will damage both the horse's back and the saddle tree. Using a mounting block also takes quite a bit of strain off the rider's back.

My best suggestion for you is to build a really wide, tall mounting block and teach Caleb to stand next to it. If you make it wide, stable, and solid, with several wide steps leading to a top platform, it will be easy for you to line up your horse next to the block and then walk up it yourself and get on from the top. It's truly amazing how quickly most horses learn to stand quietly during mounting. Once they know that the process won't hurt their backs anymore, they understand that they don't have any reason to move until the rider is settled in the saddle and asks for forward movement.

Here's a method that works well: Ask the horse to stand next to the block and tell him, "Stand." If he doesn't know the word, it's time he learned it; *stand* is a useful word for horses to know. Praise him and reward him for standing still. Climb the block, talk to the horse, get down, walk the horse around in a circle,

A smooth dismount should not shift the saddle.

bring him back to the block, tell him to stand, and repeat. With a clever horse, four or five repetitions should give him the idea. Move your arms and hands while you're on the block, wave, do arm circles. You're much taller than you've ever been — you're looming over the horse — and he needs to get used to this sensation.

Then bring in an assistant to stand by the horse's head while you mount from the block. The assistant's job is to keep the horse where you put him, so that you can take your time mounting and prove to the horse that the process isn't uncomfortable. But be sure that your assistant understands the job; it's not to hold the horse in place and keep him from moving, but rather to give him an additional reason for standing still, and to praise and reward him for standing still. Whenever you say, "Good horse, thank you" (or some other phrase of your choice), your assistant should give the horse a treat.

This is a lesson that all riding horses need to learn: The rider mounting is not a signal to move, and neither is the rider's leg touching the horse on the way over. There is only one signal to move off, and that's a squeeze from the rider's legs.

After a while, the assistant can then stand back so you can reach forward and give the horse the treat. The horse should still be standing quietly. Then you can sit up straight and organize your reins and ask the horse to move forward. Praise him for this, too. You're really trying to teach him two lessons that are closely connected: One is that *stand* means, "Don't move until you're asked," and the other is that the horse should move forward when you ask him to. One will emphasize the importance of staying put, no matter what is going on; the other will emphasize the importance of waiting until he's asked before he moves off.

This is a lesson that all riding horses need to learn: The rider mounting is not a signal to move, and neither is the rider's leg touching the horse on the way over. There is only one signal to move off, and that's a clear squeeze from the rider's legs (or a word and tap of the whip — whatever your signal may be). Actions that are not signals to move include the rider picking up his stirrups or adjusting his reins, scratching his nose, buttoning his shirt, or leaning forward to give the horse a treat.

We usually train horses to be mounted from the left, but they can also be trained to be mounted from the right. (If you were a Pony Club member, you would have to demonstrate that you could mount and dismount from both sides of the horse.) I'm guessing that you're probably not wearing a sword, so there's no compelling reason that you would have to mount only from the left. Either way, the mounting block is a good idea. You can use the block to teach your horse to line up with his right side next to the block, so that you can mount from the right. If your right leg is solid enough for you to stand on it comfortably while you take your left leg over the saddle, this might be a good alternative for you.

If you make your own mounting block or have it made for you, you can make it as tall as you like. Three feet or three feet, three inches is usually a good height, but if you want the perfect mounting block, measure the distance from the ground to your stirrup tread and use that as the height. With the mounting block at stirrup height, you can just step over the horse's back and let yourself down into the saddle. No pulling on the saddle and no back strain for your horse, and no extra lifting and heaving of that right leg for you. Stacking one or two straw bales next to the mounting block, on the other side of the horse, will make a good visual barrier to help the horse understand that he should stand still in the space by the block.

So you've got the horse, now get a mounting block! It's not special equipment for sissies; it's an essential item for any horseman who wants his horse to be comfortable.

CHAPTER 8

On the Trail

MOST RIDERS ENJOY riding on the trails, combining nature, fresh air, scenery, and quiet time with their horses. Most horses enjoy this, too, but for some horses, the trails are stimulating to the point of being frightening. Riders typically become very anxious and concerned when their horses exhibit "bad behavior" on trails. What many riders don't realize is that trail-riding skills have to be learned by horses as well as riders, and that with time, patience, and sometimes help from a friend or two, a horse's trail behavior can be changed. Feeling out of control isn't fun for riders; feeling frightened and "in charge" isn't fun for horses. Mutual trust between horse and rider can be developed through careful riding and handling, and will improve any trail ride.

Horse Kicks While Being Ridden

Q   A girlfriend recently bought a well-broke, seven-year-old mare that had been shown as a yearling at halter but has since been used for moving cattle and trail riding. The mare is well behaved the majority of the time, the exception being when another horse comes up behind her on the trail. She proceeds to buck and strike out until the other horse moves away. What may be going through her mind and what can be done to stop this dangerous habit? My horse and I have learned to just keep our distance, but my friend is troubled that she may injure someone else that unexpectedly comes riding up upon her mare from behind.

A   The first thing I would do is tie a red ribbon on that mare's tail! It's the accepted sign for a horse that has a propensity for kicking, and it can be an effective warning or signal to other riders. And if someone doesn't know what it means and asks about it, that person will be warned not to get too near. When I've taught group lessons in clinics with a horse with this particular tendency, I would take a 3" x 4" or 4" x 4" sticky label, write "kicker" or "kicks" on it with a thick marker, and stick the label to the horse's backside so that anyone riding behind that horse would be able to read it from a safe distance.

As to what's on the mare's mind, I would say that's pretty clear: She's worried about being attacked or crowded, and she's saying, "Back off — *now!*" She may have had a bad experience with a biter or an aggressive stallion or stallion-like gelding, or she may have had the rider behind her hit her with a rope to make her go forward. You can't know what started this behavior, but it doesn't really matter because you'll use the same procedure to try to change it.

The mare needs to be desensitized to horses coming up behind her, and, ultimately, the only way to do this is to have horses come up behind her.

You'll have to determine whether this is something the mare does only on trail rides. For example, what does she do when she's in a group of horses in the pasture and it's feeding time? Does she kick at the horse behind her? When she's tied or cross-tied, can other horses be led past her or tied behind her?

If she kicks only on the trail, then her owner will need to ride her on the trail with a few friends for a training session. They'll have to discuss the issue in advance. Be sure to choose quiet horses and good riders so that nobody will actually get kicked. Have the mare go first and have each rider in turn come from the back and pass her. Find out exactly what seems to provoke the kicking and whether she does it when another horse is anywhere behind her, when a horse is one horse length behind her, when a horse passes her, or when he comes up alongside her. In other words, figure out whether she is saying, "Get away, you're too close!" or, "Don't you even think about passing me!" There's a big difference.

If being passed is the problem, there are simple exercises your friend can do to change the behavior. Your friend will have to use her sensitivity and her knowledge of horses to determine whether her mare is afraid of having another horse behind her, or whether she is simply annoyed at having another horse behind her. If a horse has crashed into the mare and hurt her on a previous occasion, it will take some real work to bring her to the point at which she will stop worrying — just as if you've ever been rear-ended while driving, it took a lot of time for you to stop worrying about cars following your car too closely. The kicking, though, must be discouraged.

Your friend will have to be very calm and deliberate in her own actions. Set up a group riding situation, and make it easy for the mare to do the right thing. Your friend should first try to give the mare something to do when another horse is coming up behind her — bend, leg-yield, or anything that combines forward and lateral movement, which will make it more difficult for the mare to kick. The rider will need to keep her legs on the mare and send her forward; this

A kick can happen very quickly,
and severe injury can result whether the
kick connects with a horse or a rider.

will make kicking more difficult, as the mare will be using her hind legs to step underneath herself. There is almost always a pause before a horse kicks out, because she has to prop herself on her front legs for an instant. Keeping the forward motion and not permitting that pause will help a great deal. Keeping the mare on the move and listening to the rider also allows the rider to continually praise the mare for doing what the rider asks. This is important, because it reinforces the desired behavior and helps the mare build trust in her rider. A confident, secure horse that trusts its rider will typically be much less defensive than a nervous, insecure horse.

If the mare is annoyed rather than frightened, and if the above exercise, practiced several times in a week, didn't do the trick, the mare can still be taught that her rider finds calm behavior acceptable and kicking unacceptable. Do not do the following exercise if she is actually frightened, however, because it will just frighten her more.

The mare's rider will have to carry a loud popper with her and be ready to shout (don't shout "No," as it sounds too much like "Whoa" — make a very loud and unpleasant game-show-buzzer sound instead) and give the mare one very hard, loud swat on the behind with the popper if she kicks. The rider should be ready for the mare to plunge forward — keeping the reins loose and holding the saddle horn or the mane so that a sudden jump forward won't cause the rider to yank on the reins or become unseated. Be sure there isn't anyone directly in front of that mare. You don't want to create the same behavior in another horse by crashing into its hindquarters.

The second the mare becomes calm and moves forward normally, she should be praised. Every time she allows a horse to walk behind her or pass her, she should be praised. But every attempt to kick should result in a loud smack on her behind (nowhere else) with the popper, until she learns that kicking is not a rewarding activity. On the other hand, if she doesn't kick, nothing unpleasant happens to her, and her rider says "Good girl." Clever horses generally conclude that kicking isn't worthwhile, and if they forget on some later occasion and you feel them begin to pause or bunch up to kick, you can move them forward and make the buzzer noise, which is usually enough of a reminder. And even when the reminder is needed, don't forget to praise the horse for doing what you've asked her to do. Be absolutely clear about which behaviors you absolutely forbid, which ones you are willing to accept or ignore, and which ones you welcome and reward.

Human-Proofing a Trail Horse

Q I regularly ride my horse on trails near our farm. About two months ago, I took out a different horse — my young horse that I am training. He is four and has some experience on trails, but not a lot of experience with groups of people, especially children. My two friends and I had dismounted in a flat, grassy area to let the horses graze, and a group of adults and children came up to us and were very excited to see the horses. Several of the children went right up to the horses and started petting them. I told them to get away from the horses and explained that horses can be frightened by sudden movements and unfamiliar humans, and finally got them to leave us alone.

My horse wasn't nervous because I got the people to leave in time, but my question is how can I keep people from being so rude and inconsiderate? These were children accompanied by their parents, and yet their parents had obviously not bothered to teach them any manners. They ran right up to the horses and began to touch them! I know that I can't control the way other people raise their children, but mannerless children like these are a danger to themselves and others and could cause a horse to spook and injure them. Is there anything I can do other then tell such people, "Get back," and warn them that I won't be responsible if their bad manners frighten my horse and he hurts them?

A It's true that many children are poorly raised. It's also true that horses spook, and that sudden movements, strange humans, and the like can cause them to spook. But having said that, I must say that you are not in a position to change either of the above. You have no influence on child-rearing unless the children are your own; you have no influence on horse instincts and nature. Even yelling, "Get back!" may not serve you, as the yell may spook your horse — just what you want to avoid! And if you should encounter a child with a hearing impairment or one that doesn't speak English, even a really loud yell might have no effect.

Where you do have some influence, and even some control, is with your horse's training, behavior, and expectations. If your horse is going to be a trail horse, try to get him accustomed to children who want to pet him. Borrow some neighbor children and practice spontaneous horse-petting scenarios. You probably prepare your horse for other potentially frightening aspects of trail riding by introducing him to people on bicycles, bicycle bells, motorbikes, hikers with staffs and backpacks, and all of the other predictable "spook factors," so why not just add children? It won't guarantee that he will never spook, but if he can be made to feel at ease in the presence of swarming children, he will be much less likely to spook when he meets some on the trail.

At the least, this should buy you a few extra seconds in which to explain to the children and their parents that they need to stand back and come in one at a time to pet the horse by invitation only. But tell them with a smile, please! We do need to share the trails, and it's natural for children and even adults to

Make the effort to help your horse become accustomed to the sight and sound of children and dogs.

want to pet horses. I agree that it isn't always appropriate, and I agree that they should wait to be asked, but we both know that this isn't always going to be the case, and we can't count on other people being well brought up or wise in the ways of horses.

As for the liability issue, this is something that you would need to discuss with your insurance agent. These matters vary a good deal. It's best to assume that since you and your horse are on a public trail, it is your obligation to ensure that no harm comes to anyone because of your horse, even if he was severely provoked by an eruption of small excited children.

A horse, like a car, is large and heavy and has quite a lot of potential for causing injury. The children and their parents may not have any understanding of that concept, but you do, and you won't want to live with the knowledge that preventable harm came to a child on the trail because your horse was there that day. You need to ride defensively in the same way that you drive defensively — always with an eye to what could and might happen and with an idea of how you would deal with any situation. Of course, you can't predict every possibility, but you can offer your horse, yourself, and the children and adults that you may meet a modicum of protection by preparing your horse at home.

Dealing with children, bicycles, crowds, noise, kites, balloons, backpacks, and umbrellas should be part of every riding horse's education. It's especially important now that there are so many children and parents who have never even seen a horse close up and whose impression of horses and their riders may be changed forever by your reaction. Take the opportunity to educate them a little, and tell them how you have had to educate your horse. They'll be interested, they'll appreciate the information, and they'll be glad to have the chance to pet the horse — with your permission. And they'll remember what you taught them when they next encounter a horse and rider on the trails.

Avoiding Puddles

Q I'm wondering whether my horse has trouble seeing, is just ignoring me, or is playing a game of some kind. I've had him for six months and he's been a pretty good boy, but we haven't really had many chances to spend time outside. Now that it's finally good weather, we're riding the trails. He's a good horse for trails, except for one thing: At the end of our driveway and on the little piece of road I have to go down to get to the trails, there are often little puddles in the low spots. My horse totally refuses to step into those puddles, no matter how much trouble it is to step around them or how much I hassle him. On the trail he goes through water just fine. It's just the puddles on the driveway and the road that are a problem. Someone told me that he is frightened of his own reflection in the puddles, but that doesn't make sense to me. How would he even know it was his reflection? So what is the problem with him? Or is it something I'm doing wrong? It rains a lot around here, so we get those puddles at least once a week.

A Don't worry, you're not doing anything wrong, although you may want to reconsider the reasons behind your training strategy. "Hassling" your horse isn't likely to be an effective way to convince him to do something, but it can be a very effective way of causing a horse to "tune you out" and stop listening to you. What you really want is for your horse to offer an enthusiastic response to your quiet, polite request, and for that, you'll need his respectful attention and his trust. Try to think like a horse — ask yourself why he's doing what he's doing instead of what you've asked him to do. In this situation, your horse isn't actually doing anything wrong. You want him to go straight through whatever's in front of him, but he's protecting both of you by avoiding the puddles on the road. Horses really dislike stepping in places where they aren't sure what they'll be stepping into or on. The trouble with puddles on driveways and roads is that you can't ever be sure what's under that flat, reflective surface. It's not your horse's reflection that worries him (unless it's very clear, in which case he still wouldn't recognize himself, but might spook at the sight of something that seems to be alive and

Unless you are quite sure about what lies beneath a puddle, don't insist that your horse go through it.

moving). It's much more likely that he wants to avoid puddles because he doesn't know whether the puddle is half an inch deep or four inches deep or three feet deep. As a prey animal with flight as his primary protection, he's not eager to put himself at risk by stepping into the unknown.

I'd steer him around the puddles, if I were you. You can practice leg-yielding (asking the horse to move sideways and forward simultaneously), which is a useful exercise anyway. Since he goes through the little brooks and creeks that are always in the forest preserve, he's obviously not averse to walking through water — as long as he feels reasonably secure about what's under it. Part of good horsemanship involves taking care of your horse, and that includes not asking the horse to walk on or through dangerous footing.

If you were an event rider, you would put on your rubber boots and walk through every water obstacle at least once, noting the depth, the footing under the water, and anything else important before you ever took your horse around the course. Eventers don't ask their horses to jump, canter, trot, or even walk into "mystery water." There are good reasons for this. If the water is shallow, riders who don't mind getting splashed may choose to gallop or canter through; if the water is deep, experienced eventers will bring the horses in at a much slower pace. If the footing is slippery or rocky or full of frogs, you'll want to know before you ask your horse to step there. If the footing is uneven and has deep holes, it's not a suitable jump for an event course. You can encounter exactly this condition in the driveway or on the road.

In my area, there are roads that seem to "grow" potholes overnight. Not only do riders avoid taking their horses through innocent-looking puddles on the road, but drivers of cars and trucks are very careful to go around those puddles instead of through them, because a flat spot in the road on Monday can be a two-inch depression on Thursday and a six-inch pothole by the following Sunday. There's no way of knowing how deep the underlying pothole may be. It's not worth risking a horse's leg — or a car's axle — to find out.

You can go around those puddles. As long as you intend to go around them and indicate this clearly to your horse by directing and steering him around them, there won't be any question of disobedience. You'll be doing the sensible thing, and your horse will be doing exactly what you've asked him to do.

Crossing Water

Q My horse never had any trail experience until I bought him. He seems to enjoy being on the trail, but I can't get him across creeks or streams. He has extensive show-ring experience, including trail classes, and will cross small amounts of still water, but is afraid of running water when we're out on the real trail together.

A First, relax, and know that you're not alone with your problem. Many horses, especially ex-show horses, are unsure of themselves when confronted with water obstacles. Your horse doesn't mind a small pool or puddle of still water because he's been trained to deal with those, but, like many other horses, he's unsure of himself when asked to deal with running water.

This is very natural. Horses are prey animals and are afraid of anything unfamiliar — and of things that are familiar but move and therefore seem to be alive. Horses also like to see where they are stepping, and running water can make it difficult to see the footing under the water.

Teach your horse that he can trust you when you ask him to walk though a creek, stream, or pond. Keep in mind that you are training for the future, not just for today. Anyone can force a horse through a stream or onto a trailer once.

Your goal isn't just to get your horse to cross a stream once, it's to teach him that crossing a stream is something he can do calmly, confidently, quietly, and without fear.

You didn't specify your situation, so I'll give you some ideas for teaching a horse to cross running water, whether you have easy access to streams and other riders and horses, access to streams but have to ride alone, or no access to streams and have to ride alone.

Home alone, no streams

If, like so many other riders, you ride alone much of the time and don't have easy access to streams, you can use a hose to help your horse become familiar with running water. Find a place where you won't make a terrible mess, and set the hose on the ground. Turn it on so there's a steady trickle of water, and then bring out your horse in halter and lead rope. Bring his favorite grooming tools also. Hold him loosely on the lead rope and groom him. Don't ask him to do anything about the water, just allow him to be aware of it. If he wants to walk around a little, allow him to do it, and allow him to inspect the hose and water. Don't insist that he stand in one place, and ignore the water yourself. When he's bored with the water, you can begin to lead him in a big circle that crosses the water coming from the hose. When he's calm being led in one direction, go in the other direction, until he's bored with the whole idea in both directions. Then finish your grooming, put him away, and then turn off and move the hose. Or if your horse is absolutely calm, you can turn up the hose so that there's an actual stream of water coming out rather than just a trickle, and do it all again.

Doing this will tell you a lot about what you need to work on.

Find a wide, shallow, slow stream for your horse's initial training in walking through water. A narrow, fast-moving stream will tempt the horse to jump.

Does your horse lead easily, give in to a small amount of pressure on the halter, relax, and follow as soon as you release? If your answer is no, work on these issues first. If your answer is yes, do the basic work with the hose as above, starting with a trickle and moving on to a stronger stream of water. Then do the same walking exercise under saddle.

Since your horse did well in trail classes, he probably already walks and trots calmly over a plastic tarp. You can use a similar tarp in your water training. Set the hose on the tarp, let it trickle, and walk your horse across the tarp, first on the lead rope, then under saddle. If he's calm, increase the flow of water and do it again. Take it slowly, let him look and sniff, and praise him. If he needs a moment to think about things, wait and let him have as much time as he needs.

If your horse becomes anxious or tense at any point, be ready to back off. The idea here is not to force him to do what you want him to do; it's to make him comfortable doing what you want him to do. If he becomes worried, cut the speed (slow walk, or walk and stand and walk again, instead of a more energetic walk), or cut the water pressure (go back to a trickle instead of a stream). Keep him happy, and always keep him thinking, "I can do that!"

Some horses have had bad experiences with hoses — people spraying them in the face, water getting into their ears, or the sort of tense, angry atmosphere that too often exists in training or show situations.

If your horse is afraid of the hose, then you have another problem to deal with, and you may as well deal with it before you move on to the stream. Some horses have had bad experiences with hoses — people spraying them in the face, water getting into their ears, or the sort of tense, angry atmosphere that too often exists in training or show situations. Many horses are only bathed at, or just before, competitions, when their handlers are in a hurry and may be disposed to be rough. If he's afraid, he may be carrying some emotional baggage. Be aware of that, and be extra slow and extra calm.

Getting a horse used to a hose requires holding the horse loosely so that he can move around and using the hose to get water on the horse from the feet up. If the horse is nervous or afraid, never take the water higher than the middle of his cannon bones. Use your good sense: Don't attempt this on a cold day or with icy water, or when your horse is just coming out of his stall. Wait for a hot, sticky, sweaty day; do not put on fly spray; exercise the horse thoroughly; and take him out for some grass. Then pick up the hose. Even a traumatized horse with good reason to fear the hose will quickly learn how wonderful cool, running water feels on his feet and lower legs — and how the flies disappear at the water's touch.

On the trail with friends

First, choose the right stream! A suitable stream is wide but not too deep, with running water that doesn't move too fast and a safe, visible bed of sand or pebbles so that the horse can walk across on reliable footing. A deep stream, one with fast-running water, or one with bad footing can frighten your horse and convince him that streams should be avoided. A suitable stream should also have a gradual drop into and climb out of the water, not a sudden, dramatic drop-off that could frighten your horse or threaten his balance.

A narrow stream may look easy to cross, but it's an invitation for the horse to jump across rather than to walk through. Choosing the right stream will make this lesson infinitely easier. If you have any doubt about the footing, walk in rubber boots or waders beside your horse. A tipping slab of rock or an unexpected hole may cause you to get dunked, but better you than your horse.

If you have a suitable stream on your property or can trailer to a place with suitable streams, ask a couple of friends with water-savvy trail horses to come with you. But be sure that you stay in charge of your horse's education. One difficulty in asking for help from others is that there is usually someone who thinks she or he knows better, and believes that a whip or a pair of spurs and "getting firm" is the answer. It's not.

Sometimes walking through a stream can be achieved easily and calmly just by letting the other horses walk through first and allowing your horse to follow. If the first two horses go through at two-horse-length intervals and each is allowed to stop, sniff the water, and drink, the third horse will usually follow the others. If you're out with one friend and his horse is willing to walk into the water and stand in it quietly, your horse will want to join the other horse and will be much more interested in getting into the water. Your horse can also be "ponied" (led by another horse) across the stream. If the "pony horse" is calm, your horse will want to stay close, and will most likely calmly cross the stream.

On the trail alone

If you're riding alone, know that there's a suitable stream nearby, and are willing to invest some time, you can teach your horse to walk through the water.

Take a book with you. Not a book about making your horse walk through water — a long book that you will enjoy reading while sitting on your horse's back. The kind of fat paperback novel you'd take with you on an airplane is ideal. You need to keep alert and the book shouldn't require all of your attention, but it can be a great way to alleviate the boredom if the waiting process happens to take several hours.

Horses are individuals. Their reactions, experiences, and histories are unique. For one horse, this process might take half an hour or an hour; for another, it might take four or five hours. That's why you brought the book. I hope you chose a good one.

When you get near the stream you plan to cross, listen to your horse. If he is anxious and worried, just stop and stand facing the stream. When he's standing quietly, take out your book and start reading. The idea that you want to convey to your horse is not that you can make him cross the stream, but that you are totally calm, interested in going forward and across the stream, but not in any hurry. Your horse may be nervous and not want to go across. That's fine; you won't force him, but — this is key — you won't allow him to turn away from it or move in any other direction. He has to stand facing the stream. He's going to stand there until the sight, sound, and smell of the stream have become familiar and boring, and until your horse figures out that the movement and sound have nothing to do with him, and that he's in no danger.

At some point, your horse will decide that he would like to move, and although you won't allow him to turn to the right or the left or back up, don't push him to move forward — just let him know that the door forward is open if he'd like to move through it. Gentle encouragement is fine. Praise and pat him whenever he takes even a tiny step forward, even if he then takes a step backward, but don't push. The idea of going forward across the stream is yours. If you're patient, eventually it will become your horse's idea, too. Don't worry; even if you make progress one tiny step at a time, or two steps forward and one step back, you'll reach that stream before you finish your book.

If, when you reach the stream, the horse wants to look at it closely or touch it with his muzzle, that's fine — he's just figuring out what it is. If he wants to drink, even better. He may not want to walk into it immediately and that's fine. He can stand there. Don't push. Just wait and read your book. Keep him facing the stream. Horses are naturally meant to be on the move, and they are naturally curious. Your horse is going to want to move, and since you're permitting movement only toward the stream, he'll decide to investigate it more closely. Eventually, he'll put a foot in — maybe even both front feet. Praise him, pat him, and again, don't push, and don't punish him if he jerks his feet back out of the water and takes a step back. It's a new sensation, and he doesn't know how deep the water is. When he's done this two or three times, he'll realize that the ground is still there, there's safe footing under that moving water, and stepping into and out of the water didn't hurt him. Your praise and pats will tell him that he's doing well. Your lack of pushing and punishing will tell him that you're just going to let him figure it out, and your relaxation tells him that you're calm, not in a hurry, happy with him, and not at all worried about the water. At this point, he'll probably go a little farther in, and then a little farther. Stay relaxed, praise, and don't push. He'll walk into the stream.

Praise and pat him whenever he takes even a tiny step forward, even if he then takes a step backward, but don't push. The idea of going forward across the stream is yours. If you're patient, eventually it will become your horse's idea, too.

At this point, if he makes himself anxious and rushes through the water to the other side, let him. Fighting with him won't make him enjoy the water more or want to stay in it longer. If he's not in a hurry, gently ask him to stop in the stream and stand for a moment. This is the point at which many horses decide that the stream is a good place. When you're on the other side, go for a walk or even a trot or canter. Have fun. Turn around and come back at a walk, and let your horse walk through the stream calmly in the other direction. Don't make a big deal of it; it's just water you're going to cross, in the same safe location, on your way back to home and supper. If he balks, handle the situation just as you did before. The process is the same, but it won't take as long this time.

Over the next days and weeks, repeat this exercise once or twice daily until your horse says "Ho-hum" when he approaches the stream.

It can be easier and faster to make a horse do something than to wait for your idea to become his idea, but in horse training, going more slowly often means getting where you want to go — and getting there more quickly. Educate

---

10 STREAM-CROSSING DOS AND DON'TS

1. DON'T ask your horse to walk across a stream with a strong current.

2. DON'T ask your horse to cross where the footing is slippery, rocky, or full of holes. If you aren't sure, go by yourself the day before, wear your waders, and check out the footing.

3. DON'T punish your horse by circling him if you ask him to cross the stream and he refuses. This is hard on his legs, bad for both of your attitudes, and doesn't help him learn anything about crossing streams.

4. DO plan to cross where the entry is gradual and easy — no steep slopes or heavy undergrowth.

5. DO look for a wide stream; avoid the small, narrow ones that may tempt your horse to jump across.

6. DO choose a stream, not a puddle, for this lesson. Horses are clever enough to know that going around a puddle makes much more sense than going through it and will try to do just that.

7. DO be patient and calm. If you're tempted to kick, squeeze, or push your horse before he's ready, make yourself sit and wait. The object isn't to force him across the stream this one time; it's to help him learn that the stream is harmless and that crossing it is enjoyable, so that he'll be happy to cross it the next time.

8. DO keep your horse from rolling! If he stops midstream and wants to drink, fine. But if he begins to paw, ask him to move on. Enthusiastic pawing is cute, but it's generally followed by the horse lying down for a lovely roll in the water.

9. DO remember to leave your tie-down at home. If your horse is wearing it, unfasten it before you get near the stream. Accidents can happen. If your horse slips and falls, if he steps into a deep hole, or if the stream is much higher than usual, he'll need to put his head up high to breathe. If he can't get his head out of the water, he'll have roughly one minute of life left, and that may not be long enough for you to unfasten or cut the tie-down. Every year, a few horses drown because their riders left the tie-downs fastened.

10. DO know when not to cross a stream, even if your horse knows about streams and crosses them calmly. If the water seems higher than usual and the current seems faster than usual, be sensible. Also realize that the footing may be different under these conditions.

your horse about streams. You want him calm and thinking, because if you plan to do a lot of trail riding with him, especially competitive trail riding, the water he'll be asked to cross won't always be moving slowly, and crossing it won't always involve descending a gentle slope and walking across a firm, visible creek bottom. Always think ahead. Start slowly with the ideal stream, and teach your horse to enjoy crossing it. When you later teach him to cross water that is moving more quickly or that has a more rocky, slippery bottom, he'll be calm, confident, and thinking right along with you as you both look for the safest path to get to the other side.

Frightened Trail Horse

Q I have an eight-year-old Missouri Fox Trotter. I have had some problems with him, but now he is coming along nicely. Yesterday, a friend and I were out on the trail getting ready to do a 25-mile ride at a state park. There were two other riders behind us, we were in a wooded area, and my horse couldn't see the other horses but could hear them. They were traveling at an extended trot. Well, my horse bolted when he heard them. It was very scary, but I did get him to stop and turn to face the other horses.

This scared me badly because it happened so fast. He is a big, strong horse and can really move when he wants to. He is not normally spooky, but he seems to have a problem with things coming up behind him. I could tell that he was really scared. After we had both calmed down, we continued with our ride and had a really great one. We passed other horses, saw wild pigs and scary tents and a very long-eared mule, and even though he looked, he didn't spook. So he isn't really what I consider a spooky horse.

A It sounds as though you should plan to do some work at home before your next long, organized ride on the trails. Your horse doesn't sound spooky, just concerned. I'll make a couple of suggestions that might help him become less worried about things coming up behind him.

One of the most useful exercises for any riding horse is the one I call "leapfrog." This involves two, three, or more riders playing a passing game. Get a few friends to help you, and do this at walk and trot in an arena and then at walk, trot, and canter in a large field before you begin to practice on the trail.

Walk in single file, separated by two horse lengths. When everyone is walking calmly and maintaining a safe following distance, the last rider should pick up a trot, pass all the other riders, take the lead, and come back to a walk. When everyone is walking again, the new last rider should pick up a trot, pass all the others, take the lead, and walk. Continue doing this until each rider-and-horse combination has had many opportunities to trot up to and past all the others. Then have everyone pick up a steady trot, still maintaining a safe following distance. The last rider will canter past the others, take the lead, and resume trotting. Continue doing this until everyone has had the chance to take the lead several times.

Change the order of horses periodically so that your horse isn't always following and being followed by the same horse. Create variations on the game by having everyone walk and then letting the last rider canter past the others and by having the last two riders trot or canter past the others. The idea is to get your horse, as well as all the other horses, completely familiar with the idea of being passed by others without becoming agitated. Every horse in the group should be improved by this exercise, as they will all learn to go first, last, and in the middle, and to pass others and be passed by others without making a fuss.

If machinery passing your horse is also a problem, then in the field or out on a familiar, quiet trail, enlist the help of friends who have mountain bikes or ATVs. Playing the same "leapfrog" game will help your horse learn to accept being passed by scary motorized monsters. If he's very frightened, you can combine what you've already done (stopping and turning to face the "monster") with a more aggressive lesson on "chasing" the monster. Understand horse logic! The same horse that spooks at another horse trotting past is using this logic: "Something is behind me, therefore it is chasing me, therefore it is dangerous and scary." Playing "leapfrog" or the more aggressive "chasing" of another horse (or a bike or an ATV) makes good use of the same logic, but from a different perspective. It teaches the horse to think: "I am behind this and it is running away from me, therefore it is afraid of me, therefore I am not afraid of it."

If you get caught on the trail with a worried horse in need of a quick refresher course, don't forget that you can approach someone with a suitable horse or vehicle and ask for help. There are a lot of very nice people out there, and it shouldn't be too hard to find one or two who will take a few minutes to let your horse sniff their vehicles or even drive slowly along the trail so that you and your horse can "chase" them.

*With training, horses can learn to remain calm when they hear
other horses coming up behind them.*

In addition to the "leapfrog" exercise, which involves others, there's something you can do without help from anyone. Teach your horse a signal that means, "Everything is fine — relax." You can't teach your horse a "Don't" signal. "Don't panic," "Don't worry," and "Don't be frightened" are simply not teachable. "Relax" is something that *can* be taught.

Again, you must use horse logic. In this case, the logic involves the horse's posture. A tense, frightened horse will hold his head high and his attention (eyes and ears) focused on the object of his fear. A relaxed horse will be much more low-headed and will have at least some of his attention focused on the rider. You can teach your horse to assume the posture of a relaxed horse; in doing so, the horse will make himself much more relaxed.

Choose a signal that will be easy for you to give without getting out of position — in other words, don't teach him to respond to a tap of your fingers on his hip or his chest. I find that a good place for giving this sort of signal is halfway up the horse's neck, just under the mane. You can teach your horse to respond to being tapped here (I usually tap three times), or to some other signal like a long stroke down the side of the neck, beginning as high as possible (again, without you getting out of position) and ending on the shoulder. Either way, the idea is to teach your horse a specific cue that means, "Relax; drop your head and neck."

Once you've taught the horse this cue, practice it hundreds of times, until the response is instant and automatic. Then you'll have yet another useful tool in your trail-riding toolkit: a cue that tells the horse, "Everything is fine, get into your relaxed position now."

Horses that learn to respond this way to cues will typically respond to it even when there are exciting things going on around them. Once they've put themselves into the calm, relaxed position, it's easier for them to actually relax. It's as though they're running a little mental audiotape that keeps repeating, "I'm relaxed, I'm fine, my rider says I'm fine, I guess maybe I could be fine after all," and this simply drowns out their initial, "Oh, no, what was that, I think I'm afraid!" tape.

Having a cue isn't magic. It won't take every horse from totally terrified to utterly bored in two seconds, but it's a very useful tool. It helps both horse and rider relax and breathe, which then makes the scary situation seem less scary. Any tool that can give you enough time to sit up, breathe, and relax while your horse drops his head (even a little) and relaxes is a good tool to have with you at all times.

CHAPTER 9

Shying and Spooking

HORSES THAT SHY OR SPOOK are reacting to something, real or imaginary, that they perceive to be a threat. A brief "startle" at a sudden movement or sound in the environment is nothing more than the normal reaction of a healthy horse — the horse "spooks" for an instant, often without moving its feet at all, and then his attention returns to his rider. A prolonged or exaggerated overreaction, such as the sort of shy that takes a horse and rider halfway around a large arena, is also normal — for an insecure horse that lacks trust in his rider. When a horse spooks, punishing him and comforting him are equally useless — the true solution must involve the rider building the horse's confidence and holding the horse's attention.

Horse Shying at Home

Q My horse has been inattentive and spooking lately. It has gotten to the point where most of my rides are focusing on damage control.

I moved him to a new barn this last spring. He now has a good-sized paddock he can run around in, and his stall is always open to it so that he can self-exercise whenever he needs to. His feed supplement was changed as a result of the move (the barn didn't offer the same thing). We started with a name-brand senior feed (it was too high in molasses), changed to cob (which still had too much sugar for the lively boy), and then changed to rolled oats (which is what he was on at a previous barn, where he was more mellow). You could really tell that he was whacked out with all the sugar — he just had so much nervous energy. He has calmed down some, but he still spooks quite a bit in the arena at this place.

When I first brought him there I rode him in the arena, and he was fine the first few days until the sugar kicked in. When we jump him in the arena he is fine, I suspect because he has something very interesting to do. But when we

*If your horse habitually pays close attention to you, his attention
will come back to you quickly, even after a spook.*

work on our dressage he is flighty. He will tense up when he rounds a particular corner. He has a favorite side, although some of his more spectacular spooks and rearing have occurred on the other side. I think we have gotten past the rearing, and it was a function of the rider not letting the horse go forward into a spook.

Last week I took this horse to a dressage schooling show, and he never spooked — not even when people would ride down out of the woods. We had a much better ride at the show than at home. I have ridden him out in the field at his stable, and he is more relaxed there than in the arena.

I don't know if the horse really fears something or has lost interest in dressage/basic flat work. He moved so well at the show that I know he is capable, and his back was up and relaxed. I don't know if he is truly afraid or just unwilling.

I have been watching his ears, too, when I ride, and I wonder if he has just decided to blow me off. I have tried talking to him, clucking, squeezing with the inside leg and tweaking the rein in order to get one ear to cock back at me, but it doesn't happen very often, and more importantly, it doesn't stay there. I have tried nagging at him, but I don't think this will help either.

Can you offer any insight or suggestions? Do I need to do some groundwork to get his attention focused on me before I get in the saddle? How do I keep his attention once I get it? How do I make it important enough to him to give me his attention? I suppose it is easier for him to give me his attention and not spook (whirling is a lot of work) but he doesn't seem to think that way.

A If your horse prefers to work outdoors — and most horses do — why not work him outdoors as much as possible? Dressage isn't just for dressage arenas. Horses can get bored or at least very tired of repetitive unpleasant experiences, and if your horse has become tired of arena work (for whatever reason), you might try working him outside instead.

I often hear about horses that seem bored indoors yet perk up visibly when they go out. That's normal. Horses tend to be much more alert when they're exposed to sights, sounds, breezes, and smells that are all lacking in an indoor location. Even the shift in footing can help them become more focused.

Your focus matters, too. Going outdoors also tends to make the rider more focused on the horse; riders can become very complacent in an indoor arena and begin to do their work by rote instead of paying close attention to their horses. Outdoors, you're always looking up and listening, and you're always aware that something interesting could happen. Indoors, it's very likely that you may be looking down and thinking of things other than your horse.

If your horse has had an actual bad experience — perhaps one that didn't involve you — in the indoor arena, he most likely won't feel safe and secure there, and a nervous horse is not going to relax and lift his back easily or consistently. The quality of your work will probably be better if you take the horse elsewhere to school him, at least for a while. If there's a flat field you can use, or even a slightly sloped one, you can do everything that you would do in the arena and gain the extra benefit of learning how to maintain consistent, steady gaits whether you are working up or down the slope.

If there's a trail or path nearby, use that. Your horse will already be thinking about moving forward as you go down the path, and you can improve your lateral work tremendously by doing it from side to side on that trail or path. Leg-yield, shoulder-in, half-pass, travers, renvers, and all manner of transitions are perfect for work on trails.

Once you're in the saddle, you're invisible, and your horse can't tell what you want by watching you. This is where the language of the aids becomes all-important.

It's a good idea to watch your horse's ears, but if he isn't paying attention to you, it's not because he's made a conscious decision to "blow you off." Horses don't think that way. They are very, very reactive, however, and will become tense and upset if the rider is constantly pestering them. If your horse's ears are swiveling around to catch sounds, that's normal. If one ear keeps swiveling back toward you, that's normal, too. But don't try to adjust your seat, reins, or voice just to make the horse bring an ear back. It won't work, and the effort will interfere with your riding.

Groundwork is fun and can be an excellent way of teaching riders more about horse body language, but there won't be an automatic carryover to under-saddle work. Body language isn't so useful when the horse can no longer see you — once you're in the saddle, you're invisible, and your horse won't be able to tell what you want by watching your posture and your gestures. This is where the language of the aids becomes all-important — your communication with your horse will now be a matter of balance, pressure-and-release, weight shifts, and a soft voice. Instead, I would suggest working outdoors and then going into the arena to cool down, have a few treats, and have fun. If your horse learns to associate the arena with pleasant, relaxed communication, he will become much less spooky about it, and much more attentive to you when he is being ridden indoors.

Spooking, Rider Fear, and Horse Learning

Q How fast does a horse learn bad habits? I am no expert when it comes to riding, and yet I love it. Three years ago my boyfriend and I bought a 25-year-old horse. She is a wonderful, healthy, and well-behaved horse, and she taught me a lot about horses and riding these past three years. But I am still sometimes really scared, although I know there is no good reason for it.

When I do not feel secure before I start riding, I don't ride. I just groom, walk, longe her, or play with her in the paddock. I am never afraid when I'm on the ground, even if she is a little too exited. But sometimes I feel good, saddle up, and start riding, and then the trouble starts.

My horse is very forward-going, willing to work, and is rather sensitive. When something strange happens, she spooks and gets very tense. For the next five minutes, anything else that happens, even things that normally don't bother her, gives her good reason for either spooking or running away. This is when I get scared!

When this happens, I want to get off my horse, but I always stay on and keep trying until she is a little more relaxed. That takes quite some time, because I'm scared and she feels it and gets more scared. I don't want to stop because I am worried that she might learn to think, "When I am running and spooking, my rider gets off and I can go back to my stable." So when I quit today, I am afraid that tomorrow she will just put her head up and start running because she knows I will quit again.

Do you think that will happen? When does a horse connect running and spooking with a rider getting scared and stopping? Will she learn to be annoying just to avoid working?

A Horses learn in the same way, regardless of us labeling what they learn as good or bad. It's easy to create a habit in a horse; whether or not we like the habit is another matter.

Trust yourself. When you're scared, there's a reason for it, and there's no point in telling yourself not to be afraid when you're sitting on a spooking horse. It's perfectly sensible of you to be scared when you're on top of a thousand pounds of horse that is bouncing and fussing and taking no notice of you. You like your horse very much, so I expect that what frightens you is partly the possibility of getting hurt and partly the reality of being high in the air and not in control and wondering how and when you will get back in control.

Since your mare comes back to herself and listens to you again when you get past those initial five minutes of silliness (which, if you time it, may prove to be more like one minute — it just seems longer when you hold your breath), and since during those five minutes she doesn't actually rear, buck, or attempt to scrape you off on the wall, I would say that you're participating in a classic feedback loop. Your mare startles at a sudden noise or motion, you startle because she is startled, she becomes more anxious, you become more anxious, and then you suddenly say to yourself: "Oh, no, I must make myself calm and stay on this horse. I can't get off, as that will teach her that becoming anxious and dancing around is a profitable behavior."

Alternatively, you may initiate the process yourself by noticing that another horse is leaving the barn or by hearing a noise that you think will cause your

This mare is paying close attention to something and no attention to her rider.

mare to spook. This makes you become tense and apprehensive, so you hold your breath and become rigid, at which point your mare, rather cooperatively, spooks, and the two of you proceed as above.

Your mare may or may not be in the habit of spooking with you, but either

It's better not to think in terms of getting rid of a habit. Instead, think in terms of establishing a new habit.

way, you will need to take a slightly different approach to the problem. It's probably better not to think in terms of getting rid of a habit, because you never do get rid of a habit in the sense of erasing all previous behaviors and erasing the memory of the habit. Instead, think in terms of establishing a new, stronger habit by teaching the horse a different behavior and repeating the lesson until the new behavior becomes a habit. The success you will have in retraining any horse largely depends on how well you understand this.

For example, a young racehorse at the race track learns from repeated experience that on race days, he will be saddled and mounted while he is moving. This is not a bad habit, it is a habit that is perfectly acceptable and, in fact, absolutely normal from the trainer's and jockey's point of view. When the horse's racing career is over, it begins a new life with a rider who wants to do, say, dressage or eventing. The new rider wants the horse to stand still for saddling and mounting. At this point, if the horse moves off while the rider is trying to mount, the rider can choose to punish the horse for "being bad," which the horse will understand only as a sudden personal attack from the rider, or the rider can choose to begin teaching the horse the desired behavior by asking the horse to stand, rewarding each still moment, and asking the horse to stand again when he starts to move off.

From the horse's point of view, neither moving off nor standing still is better, in the sense of being "more moral" or "more ethical" or "superior" — the horse doesn't understand such terms. The horse does understand consequences, though, and when he learns that a particular behavior has pleasant consequences, he will learn to repeat that behavior. The rider who understands this will have little difficulty retraining the horse.

It's important for you to understand why horses do the things they do. A horse that learns that the rider will get off whenever she bucks, rears, or refuses to move is usually a horse that did those things for another reason (usually fear, confusion, or a combination of the two) and then learned that these were behaviors that humans *want*. That's an important distinction: It's not a matter of a horse thinking "I'll be very bad and the human will get mad and go away"; it's a matter of a horse remembering, "The last time I did this, I got something very nice for doing it!"

Getting off and taking off the tack is actually a very useful training tool, and it's brilliant as a reinforcer if your horse has just done something that you really wanted her to do or shown you that she's getting the idea of something you really wanted her to do. However, getting off and removing the tack is not a convenient way to reinforce a behavior if you happen to be a few miles from home or even if you're at home but just beginning your ride.

I don't think that your mare is in any danger of learning to spook to get out of work, for two reasons. First, you aren't dismounting and putting her away when she spooks; you are dealing with her in the best possible way, by trying to calm her and by staying on board until she is calm again. Second, she enjoys her work and has no reason to want to avoid it. All of this speaks very well for your horsemanship.

So why does she spook? She will spook if she is not paying proper attention to you, and thus is easily distracted. She will spook if there is some benefit for her, even if you can't quite figure out what that benefit might be. She will spook if she thinks you want her to spook because she is rewarded for spooking. And she will spook if you spook first, even if you are just spooking because you think that she is going to spook.

If the horse or the rider isn't paying attention

If your mare is truly paying attention to you, she won't have much focus left for anything else. If she is totally focused on you, she won't spook; she may look at or flick an ear at something, but she won't spook. If she is almost totally focused on you, and if she is in the habit of keeping her focus on you, she may spook briefly at a sudden movement or sound, but it will be just for a heartbeat, and then her focus will be on you again.

There's a trick to this, though: Her focus will be on you to the same degree that your focus is on her. If you are thinking about every movement of yours and hers, every breath, and every footfall, and if you are maintaining a constant, close dialogue with her, any spook is likely to be a mild reaction that may not even cause her to take a single fast step. If you are daydreaming, not paying close attention to your riding or to your horse, or are thinking about other things or perhaps looking around for something that might possibly cause your horse to spook, then she'll spook, because your mind isn't on her and hers isn't on you. So practice keeping your attention on her and asking for her attention in return. You'll find that it's much easier to hold her attention when your own attention is on her in the moment.

If there's a benefit to the horse

Sometimes, when a horse is bored or becoming uncomfortable, a spook provides all sorts of entertainment. It gets back the rider's attention, and it affords the horse a chance to change direction, pace, speed, or frame. If a horse routinely spooks after ten minutes at a trot, for instance, and always takes the reins away from the rider when he spooks, it's almost invariably because the horse has given up on more subtle (and unsuccessful) ways to tell the rider about his discomfort and has found that the only way to get enough rein to accomplish a badly needed neck stretch is to bounce suddenly and then lean against the bit. The solution here is to listen to the horse in the first place, notice when she is beginning to become uncomfortable, and offer her a change of pace, speed, or frame, or the chance to stretch. This way, the horse will never need to demand these opportunities by taking the rein away from you.

If you have asked for the spook

If you have, in the past, ever rewarded a previous spook by dropping the reins and patting or caressing the horse, by dropping the reins and stopping the horse, or by doing anything else comforting that the horse may have construed as a reward, you may have inadvertently taught the horse that this is a behavior you appreciate and enjoy. If you teach your mare that spooking means, "Time out, relax; I'll pat your neck and talk softly to you," then why on earth wouldn't she spook?

If you started it

If you are always aware that your horse might spook and are afraid of what will happen if she does spook, then you are likely to be constantly looking out for anything that might cause your horse to spook. If you have even a nanosecond of worry, anxiety, or fear when you notice something like that, *your* spook probably precedes hers. She's a herd animal, and when you're riding her, you're all the herd she has. If you spook, she will spook. It takes a very mature, secure animal to carry a spooking rider and act out the horse equivalent of "There, there, you're fine, nothing's wrong." Most horses don't do this. The ones that do are usually in great demand as school horses, worth their weight in gold, and generally priced accordingly.

In any case, there are ways around all of these causes, but it does help to figure out which ones may be causing the spooking. When you've figured that out, you'll be better able to eliminate it. In the meantime, I'll give you a wonderful exercise that can be tweaked and used for a huge number of purposes. In this case, it's a grand anti-spooking exercise. But before I describe it, I'm going to give you homework to do both on and off the horse.

Let's assume you are riding around the arena. All is well, but then someone takes another horse out of the barn and you feel your mare become tense. When this happens, instead of you becoming tense and holding your breath, sit tall, take a very deep breath, and let it out slowly.

Your homework is to breathe. The lovely part of deep breathing is that as long as you are doing it, you cannot become tense. Practice when you're off the horse. Learn the basic technique from a video if you need to, such as a yoga or tai chi instructional video; each will help you with breathing along with slow, coordinated, gentle movements. Do the breathing exercises at the table, at your desk, in your car, when you watch television. Practice breathing deeply and slowly whenever you are upset, angry, or startled. Make it your habit to react to surprises with deep breathing. It's good for you, and the benefits to your riding will be truly amazing.

When you're on the horse, practice the same exercises, and notice how the breathing that makes you calm and steady will invariably make your horse calm and steady as well. Do it at a standstill, at a walk, at a trot, at a canter. Find a rhythm that corresponds to your horse's stride, and breathe deeply and slowly at all three gaits.

Here's your specific exercise, so that you will have a plan and know precisely what you are going to do as soon as your mare becomes tense and nervous. Your strategy should be to keep her busy, allow yourself to sit up straight and breathe deeply, and offer her neither a reward nor a punishment. You're not going to praise or condemn her tension and nervousness, you're not even going to let on that you notice them; you're simply going to ask her to show you something else instead.

I'm sure that you can sense the moment before your mare becomes tense and bouncy. Let's assume that you are riding around the arena, tracking left. All is well, but then someone takes another horse out of the barn and you feel your mare become tense. When this happens, instead of you becoming tense and holding your breath, sit tall, take a very deep breath, and let it out very slowly. Then take another, and another. While you are sitting up and breathing, ask your mare to bend smoothly to the left for a few steps, as though you were intending to ask her to circle left, then straighten her and ride her absolutely straight for one step. Then ask her to bend smoothly to the right for a few steps, then straighten again, then bend left, straighten, bend right, and so on.

Pay attention to your breathing and to your horse. If she bends nicely and is listening to you, tell her, "Good girl," and immediately ask her to straighten and then to pick up the next bend. Praise her and lengthen the reins a little when she tries; if she doesn't listen, lengthen your reins a little and ask again. If your reins keep getting longer, good. If you're doing this correctly, she will follow the bit, looking for that comforting contact, and you will feel her neck becoming longer and longer.

This is a very good exercise for both of you. It will help you improve the coordination and subtlety of both your aids and your breathing. It will help her gently stretch and loosen her neck and back, relax emotionally, and remind her to pay constant attention to you. It will also make you pay attention to her — not to what you think she may be thinking or to what you fear she may begin to do, but to what she is doing right now. You'll be giving her constant input about what you want her to do and constant feedback about what she is doing, and because you will also be sitting up and breathing, you won't be telling her, "Run! Run! Tigers are chasing us!" That's exactly what your body tells her when you hold your breath and become tense.

If you ever get to the point where you're really scared to death and can't possibly sit up straight or control your breathing, dismount, because you won't be able to accomplish anything useful. But don't put your horse away. As soon as your feet hit the ground, begin immediately to do work in hand, asking for steps sideways, steps back, turn on the forehand, turn on the haunches — anything and everything you can think of. Make it clear that whether you're in the saddle or out of the saddle, a spook or a spook followed by a dismount doesn't mean "stop working."

Here are three more ideas you may want to keep in mind.

The last lesson of the day matters most. Always end on a good note, always end when something is going well, and if you want your mare to pay maximum attention to any one lesson, make it the last thing you do before you dismount and remove the tack. Whatever happens then is going to have the most significant impact of all, so take advantage of that fact and make it count. Whatever is most difficult for you and your horse — for example, a square halt, backing, turn on the forehand, turn on the haunches, or standing quietly on a loose rein — is what you should do just before you dismount.

Clicker training may help. If you want to try incorporating a bit of clicker training into your work, there's nothing quite like it for keeping humans focused on their horses. You can become more observant and perfect your timing on the ground, then carry both qualities over to your ridden work. After a time you can phase out the clicker and phase in a verbal signal or a pat, and you'll be doing very old-fashioned dressage, in the classical style, which involves total awareness of the horse and her actions and reactions. Clicker training is just one of the many roads by which you can approach clear communication with your horse.

From the horse's point of view, habits aren't good or bad. They are all just behaviors, and depending on how you react to them, the horse will perceive them as either profitable or not profitable.

Keep your mare's age in mind — not because she's too old to learn new habits, but because she is 28 years old, and age does make a difference to physical comfort. I have a mare of that age at home, and I can assure you that at 28, any horse is bound to be a little more stiff and uncomfortable than she was even three years ago. She'll also need a longer warm-up.

Some older horses appear to be more nervous and excitable than they were when they were younger, and it's not really a matter of excitement but rather discomfort. In her younger days, I'm sure your mare could toss her head up and bounce once or twice without feeling twinges of pain in her legs and back. Now that she's approaching 30, she is bound to have some arthritic changes in various joints, and the natural spook reaction of holding the head up, making the back tight, and bouncing is likely to cause her some pain, which will probably make her react with annoyance and yet another bounce.

Warm her up in a half-seat, and after you've walked — always do this after a long warm-up — let her decide whether to trot or canter. Older horses sometimes can't stretch their backs, hips, and stifles effectively — and thus can't do any useful work at trot — until they've had a chance to canter. If your mare is one of them, it may help her both physically and mentally if you follow up your opening walk by allowing her to canter a few times around the arena on a long or even a loose rein, with you in a half-seat, before you ask for any real work at trot.

Horses can learn habits very fast, but from the horse's point of view none of them are good or bad. They are all just behaviors, and depending on how you react to them, the horse will perceive them as either profitable or not profitable. You'll find that your training and/or retraining always proceeds better if you think in terms of encouraging the behaviors you want. Keep your training positive, and keep breathing!

Eyesight and Spooking

Q I just got my very first horse at the age of 40, and love him dearly. Sinbad is six years old, possibly a Quarter Horse–Arab mix. I don't know his history; he was purchased at auction. He is boarded at a farm where there are seven horses. Most of our riding is around the property and up and down the driveway. We do a little ring work as well. He is turned out all day with five other geldings and a mare, and he's king of the hill, as far as they are concerned.

From the day I bought him, I've had a problem with him shying. He trots along and then suddenly slams on the brakes and leaps ten feet to the left. It happens at different places and at different times. The only consistent thing that spooks him is fluttering plastic bags, which he doesn't see often.

When I feel him tensing up I tell him "No!" and try to keep looking where I want him to go and drive him straight ahead with my legs. Sometimes it works and sometimes it doesn't. I haven't come off yet, but there's a first time for everything.

The other day I had a friend ride him and I watched him carefully, and suddenly it all came together. He carries his head slightly to the right all the time, especially when cantering. He always shies to the left, away from something on his right. Could it all be because he has a problem with the sight in his right eye? Are sight problems common in horses? I don't plan on showing so I'm not concerned about the head-tipping, just his safety and mine. Do they make blinders for bridles? Would something like this help, or just make things worse?

A   You may have already figured out Sinbad's problem — if not, you've certainly found a good starting point for a physical exam. When your veterinarian comes out to do spring shots, ask him to do what he can to check the horse's eyes. It's not always easy to diagnose eye problems without special equipment and lights, though, so warn him in advance that you'll want him to look at your horse's eye. You might also want to talk to him long before he comes out, in case he wants to come a little earlier than June. Eye problems are best dealt with immediately, although I agree with you that this problem is probably a long-standing one and it's just the diagnosis that will be new. Don't count on your own ability to tell whether Sinbad can see. Someone will probably tell you to

An eye exam can help determine if frequent spooking has a physical cause.

brush your hand past his eye several times and see whether he blinks, but this is not conclusive, because horses will often blink from feeling the air current caused by your hand. You definitely need a vet's help here.

There are other possible explanations for your horse's shying and head-tipping, including neurological damage from accident or illness. Your vet will be able to offer a diagnosis and prognosis, so I'll limit myself to a discussion of various ways to cope if the diagnosis indicates, as you suspect, vision problems.

Many horses have vision problems of one type or another, and many horses have only one eye and manage to get along very well indeed. Some forms of competition even allow one-eyed horses to participate.

Many horses have vision problems of one type or another, and many horses have only one eye and manage to get along very well indeed.

Blinders won't help Sinbad if he's losing his sight; what will help is you doing everything you can to make his life easier. If you know that he can't see things coming up behind him from the right and you know he can't see things on his right side, be careful to present him to anything new or potentially scary by showing it to him on his other side and letting him sniff it.

Most horses will spook at fluttering plastic bags — that's nothing strange. I suggest that when you feel that he is about to spook — when he becomes tense — you try this: Instead of becoming tense yourself and telling him "No!" (which only convinces him that there is something scary there and that you are afraid of it, too), take a deep breath and let it out slowly while you bend Sinbad and ride him forward on a curve or in a circle. Practice will teach you whether it will work better to the right or to the left, but it will almost certainly work better than trying to make him go straight ahead. It's harder for horses to become tense and stiff if they are bent and moving on a curve.

If you are aware that he doesn't see well, especially on the right, you can ride him and handle him in ways that make it easier for him to cope. Always let him know where he is in relation to the rail on the right side; always warn him if someone or something is coming from that direction. He'll learn to understand you — horses are amazingly adaptable. I once knew a blind dressage horse whose owner could ride him anywhere. She had taught him voice commands ("right," "left," and so forth) and could even ride him over curbs just by telling him when to step up and down. He was a lovely horse, and he isn't unique — there are others who cope every bit as well. The secret seems to be having a sensible, understanding rider.

Spooky Corner

Q I have a mare around seven years old. I've been riding her for about two-and-a-half years. We both started out green, and it's been slow going, but she's great.

My question has to do with how to handle her fears. Although she's much, much better than she was at our start, she is still pretty spooky. For example, just yesterday I had her in a group lesson with about five other horses, in an indoor arena she'd never been in before. (All of these horses are barn mates, and her best pal was in the lesson, too.) At the far end of the arena was a noisy exhaust fan and some parked trailers, and the strong outdoor winds were making lots of rattling noises in the arena.

Although many of the other horses were a little nervous at first, they all settled down to work. On the other hand, my mare was still spooked by that far end of the arena after an hour and a half of going round and round. Every time we took that bend, she'd stiffen up and divert all her attention from me to the scary corner.

I'm not sure exactly how I should handle her when she's like this. I guess my present tactics are pretty ineffective if she never really relaxes. Yesterday, I tried to keep her attention on me by talking to her and wriggling the reins as we neared the scary corner. If I'm not in a lesson, I usually try to give her some unexpected command or something to do at the time I feel her stiffening up. Then I always pat her, reassure her, and congratulate her if she makes it past the scary bits without swerving.

Is all this talking and cajoling the wrong approach? I'm beginning to think that maybe I'm actually rewarding her for being silly — maybe she thinks that if she acts scared and tense she'll get extra attention and sweet talk. When we started out together, she was a true basket case about all sorts of spooky things, and she really needed to hear lots of soothing talk and encouragement. But maybe I need to expect more from her now.

A It's true that unfamiliar places can be scary, and that wind and noises are scary to a horse. But those things shouldn't matter as much as the fact that your horse has a job to do and needs to focus on doing it.

Your instincts are excellent — you do need to expect more from her now. She's not a basket case any longer; she's a grown-up horse that deserves to be treated with respect and allowed the dignity of a job to do.

Your best approach is not to comfort or cajole — this will merely convince your mare of one or two ideas, neither of them useful: that the corner really is scary, and that you, too, are scared of it, or that you want her to spook at that corner, since you praise her for doing it.

Talking to her and wriggling the reins won't do anything except convince her that you are nervous. Instead, put this mare to work! Decide what you are going to do long before you go past that corner, then do it. This means getting and keeping her attention, not on you but on her job, which is whatever you tell her it is.

In other words, instead of saying, "Oh, brave mare, please go past that scary corner," or "Poor scared mare, that corner really wasn't all that

The world is full of scary things competing for your horse's attention.

scary," you need to be saying to her — with your body and your breathing — "Go forward, bend, balance, keep your rhythm, go forward a little more, steady up, bend, balance." If you do this, you'll be able to let her know that the corner is no big deal.

In order for your mare to keep her focus where it belongs — on what she is doing — you need to keep your focus where it belongs: on what she is doing. Don't make room in your mind for what she might do. Instead, be very clear, to yourself and to your horse, about what you want and what you expect her to do.

Make clear demands and hold your mare to them. You cannot say to your mare, "Don't spook here!" That makes no sense to a horse. You also cannot say,

"Oh, honey, let me try to distract you from the scary corner by wriggling my inside rein." It's a natural human instinct, but it just won't work as a training method. Neither will sudden unexpected commands; she'll just learn that she needs to worry about that corner, because whenever she gets there she'll be ambushed with a surprise demand. This might distract her briefly, but it doesn't do what you want, which is to help her become calm, relaxed, and focused on her job.

What will make sense to her is knowing exactly what her job entails. If you're going around the arena tracking left, her job is to move evenly and rhythmically, with a very slight bend to the left, and her head and neck in "position left" so that you can just see her inside eyelashes and nostril. Her job is to keep going until you ask her to do something else. Your job is to keep her in this position, keep her coming forward, and keep one step ahead of her. As you come through the corner, think about your next ten steps.

It's very important for you to be aware of your own body and your aids. If you lean to the inside as you approach the scary corner, for instance, or if you collapse over your inside hip, your body is telling her to go to the inside of the arena, away from that corner. If you pull her head to the outside to make her go into the corner, she will bend her entire body away from the corner and be moving toward the left while bent to the right, which isn't very useful. If you pull her head to the inside, she will fall over her inside shoulder, lose her rhythm and forward movement, and move away from the corner. If you hold your breath as you get to the corner, your physical tension will make her tense and convince her that there is something really bad in that corner. So you have a very active role in this, but it's more to do with you than with your horse: Sit straight, post rhythmically, look out and ahead, and breathe deeply and steadily. If you do those things and your mare is already in position (very slightly bent to the inside), you will be making it easy and comfortable for her to do what you want, and you will get through the corners without a hiccup.

It'll be easiest for you to do this at a trot, since her head position and your hands will be very steady, and you can regulate her rhythm by regulating your own posting. Be ready to add a little leg if she starts to slow down, but that is probably all you will need to do. If there's any hesitation or unevenness, just keep breathing and push on. Don't reprimand her if she hesitates; send her forward. Don't comfort her afterward — she doesn't need it. And don't try to go into the corner by pulling her nose to the outside. Just keep her in position and send her forward into that corner, as if you were going straight into the wall.

Don't change your own position, her bend, your rhythm, or your breathing (keep it slow, deep, and steady, in rhythm with her gait) and keep looking up and out, between her ears. When she is about to reach the next wall, look down that wall and ride her through the turn without changing anything. Ride her through the turn and up the next wall in a steady rhythm, and then ride a circle halfway up the next wall. When you come back to the rail, still in position left, still keeping the same rhythm, come down the rail to your next wall and do the same thing. The circles on each side will prepare her for the bend through each corner. You aren't going to ask for a sudden bend; all you want is for her to go where you send her and not change her position.

If you stay busy with *your* job — telling her with your weight, breathing, and posting rhythm that you want her to go forward smoothly while maintaining her position and bend — she will get busy with *her* job and be able to take pride in her own ability.

Do you remember when you were little and scared about doing something (first time at a sleep-over, at the skating rink, at camp) your parents told you to stand up straight and act confident, because acting confident would make you feel confident? It worked, right? Standing up tall with your head up and your shoulders back and walking confidently and breathing deeply will make you feel more confident; you can act your way into a

By creating in your mare the posture of a forward, listening, confident horse, you are making it difficult and highly unlikely for her to spook or for you to tense in anticipation of the spook.

feeling. And it works just as well with horses, although they don't act deliberately. If you can put your horse into the position that a confident, bold, forward-moving, focused horse would assume and keep her there, then your horse will be much more confident, bold, forward-moving, and focused.

By putting yourself in the posture of a strong, confident rider and by creating in your mare the posture of a forward, listening, confident horse, you are making it difficult and highly unlikely for her to spook or for you to tense in anticipation of the spook. Instead of getting worried and trying to distract her — and thereby making yourself incoherent to her, which will only make her anxious and more likely to spook — you are making it possible for her to become as businesslike and confident as you insist that she seem.

The day will come when you are riding through that corner or a similar corner and something scary will happen — a car will backfire, a bird's nest will fall from the arena ceiling, or a barn cat will pounce on something suddenly. But your mare will either ignore it all or she will startle for a second and then go right back to work.

Suddenly Scared Horse

Q I have my own horse, and just recently he seems to be spooking at everything, like a long patch of waving grass, plastic bags, or a piece of paper half-buried and not moving on the ground. The most recent incident was when he saw something (I don't know what) and he reared, slipped, and fell. He was not hurt but was very shaken. He also refuses to jump anything colorful. I don't know what to do. He is a great horse, and up until now he has been a fearless horse. I am beginning to be a bit scared to get on him, as I often fall off when he shies. Please help me; I don't want this to get any worse.

A It's my long-standing practice to look for a physical problem first whenever a horse's behavior changes dramatically. In your horse's case, I would strongly suspect that his eyesight is no longer what it once was. You didn't mention his age or his breed; some horses are more susceptible than others to certain diseases of the eye. But regardless, it definitely sounds to me as though your horse's vision has changed.

Call your veterinarian, explain what is going on, and ask him to take a look at your horse. Then, if he can't find anything obviously wrong — a lesion, an infection, or a scar, for instance — ask for a referral to a good veterinary hospital with a resident ophthalmologist. Eyes are a very specialized subject, and they are also very delicate organs, especially in equines. The equine eye is particularly susceptible to injury and infection, and there is no such thing as a "generic" treatment. Don't use any ointment containing atropine or belladonna unless you are in a position to keep the horse out of direct sunlight (in his stall, for instance). Ointments containing steroids can be destructive if there is a cut or lesion in the eye itself. Your vet may suggest that you wash out the eye with saline solution while waiting for him to arrive, but as a general rule, it's best to avoid using *any* eye ointment without your vet's recommendation. Using the wrong medications can make things worse instead of better, and you can't afford to take a chance with your

Two types of problems should always be considered red-alert situations for a horse: colic, and any sort of eye problem.

horse's vision, so just make the horse as comfortable as possible and wait for the vet to arrive.

There are two types of physical problems that should always be considered red-alert situations for a horse: One is colic, and the other is any sort of eye problem. Don't wait a day or two or three to have an eye injury checked by the vet, and don't hesitate to trailer the horse to a specialist. It's much better to hear, "Oh, this isn't a big problem: Here's something that should clear it up in a few days," than to hear, "Oh, dear, if you'd brought him in a few days ago, we might have been able to save the eye."

In your case, I wouldn't ride the horse until you have a better idea of what is going on with him. Do you have a safe place to turn him out and let him exercise himself? Just for safety's sake, carefully inspect the turnout paddock or field and ask yourself, If I blindfolded a horse and turned it out here, could he trip over or get caught in anything? Don't count on the horse's ability to see and avoid anything that shouldn't be in the field. Anything, from a broken bit of fencing to a piece of old farm machinery, could be dangerous. These things would be potentially dangerous to any horse, but especially to a horse that can't see them or can't see them well.

In the meantime, while you are waiting for the vet, do some detective work. Find out whether there has been any other change recently — perhaps a dietary one? Horses that suddenly begin spooking at everything are sometimes not vision-impaired (although you should still have that checked) but overfed or being fed an improperly balanced ration. To a horse that is on a normal diet, a piece of paper on the trail may be worth no more than a glance or a single step sideways, but to a horse that is suddenly being stuffed with high-energy feed, a glimpse of that same single piece of paper could prompt an equine version of the macarena.

If you aren't the person who feeds your horse, visit the barn at feeding time and look closely at what he's being fed. It's possible that his diet has changed drastically. I've had that experience myself, long ago when I was boarding a mare at a very nice barn. The person who usually fed the horses was replaced by another person, and the new person didn't pay much attention to the instructions on the various feed cards. In one week, my mare went from sweet and cooperative to a nervous, aggressive creature who spent altogether too much time on her hind legs. It took me almost two weeks to figure out that her feed was at fault, because she didn't get fat. When I discovered, quite by accident, that she was being fed ten pounds of alfalfa and five pounds of sweet feed instead of her usual ration of grass hay and a handful of whole oats, I was horrified and saw to it that she was put back on her proper ration. One week later, calm was restored, and she was once again friendly and sweet and had remembered how to move about on four legs instead of two.

By the way, you are right to worry about falling off — it's something that sensible riders try to avoid. Riding is a risky sport, but there's no reason to take unnecessary chances. Whatever is going on with your horse, the result is that he is, at present, dangerous to ride. If you don't ride your horse while you are waiting to find out what's wrong, you're not being a coward; you're being intelligent.

CHAPTER 10

Herd-Bound,
Barn-Sour

HORSE OWNERS ENJOY seeing their horses relaxed and happy in their pastures, paddocks, and stalls, but they are often much less happy when they want to go for a ride and their horses appear uninterested or even unwilling. It's very frustrating for riders when their horses seem to be obsessed with their pasture buddies or with the barn itself.

New Herd Member Is Herd-Bound

Q My new five-year-old Thoroughbred is getting along fantastically well with her new herd members. In fact, I got her on a Wednesday, and we had them together in the same pasture for an hour or so on Thursday and alone together by the weekend. Chamois, a 29-year-old palomino quarter horse, is the boss; Queen, a 32-year-old Tennessee walking horse is second; and Baby, my mare, is third and just happy to have buddies.

A horse's buddies represent the safety and security of the herd.

This is where my problem arises, however. The horses are so close that Baby and Queen were sharing hay piles, nose to nose, within the first week! When I try to take Baby away to work with her, Chamois and Queen whinny up a storm, and, of course, Baby gets all stressed out and calls back to them. I am very touched that she's been so quickly accepted and that they can't do without her, but I have a hard time keeping her attention.

I rode her about five times over a month-long period before I got her, and she was usually a dream to ride. She was fine when taken away from her herd mates into the indoor ring at her former barn, but no one was whinnying to her.

The first time I took her outside to ride at the previous stable, I did a senseless thing. She hadn't been ridden outside since the previous summer/fall, she was in heat, and there were stallions around in the next paddock. As soon as we walked outside, she tensed up. At this point, I should have either gotten off and longed her or taken her back in, but I thought, I've handled stubborn/nervous horses before — no problem. Well, the stallion around the corner whinnied, and she gave a pathetic whinny back and then bucked. On the third buck, she put her head way down between her legs, and I flipped right over her head. I wasn't hurt, but lost my nerve! I took her back in the arena, got back on, and we were fine. But when I heard her whinny like that again yesterday, I had a little flashback!

There is nowhere to ride indoors at the new stable, but Baby was ridden outside all the time at the other place and had never bucked anyone off. The afternoon that she bucked me, a very experienced teenager with "Velcro legs" got on her and Baby tried to buck her. This girl stayed on, though, and had no more problems with her inside or outside in the following three weeks before I bought her. She jumped her (which I won't do until she's a little older) and worked on flying lead changes, and Baby did fine.

I know the best advice is to take it slow and just work on building a good relationship with her. We've got lots of years together still. I just wanted to know what advice you have on getting the horses used to being separated, since your advice on introducing them worked so well! Baby is extremely happy at her new home and is very calm. She's even letting me touch and rub her face now, something I wasn't able to do before (the former owners were a little rough with her).

A I'm glad that Baby is fitting in so well with her new herd. Separating horses is always a problem, as you are finding out. This is where you have to realize that you are putting a few weeks, months, or perhaps years of training up against millions of years of evolution. Horses know that their safety is in their herd, and they don't want to be separated from the herd.

This anxiety isn't permanent. The "talking" may be, but that isn't anything to worry about. Horses often call to each other when you take one away to work in the arena, but the one that's being worked quickly loses interest in talking back if you keep her attention on you, give her things to do and think about, and keep a conversation going between the two of you.

There's a difference between a nervous horse and a mare in heat talking to a stallion! A horse can't really pay attention to two things at once. This works in your favor when you're training, because a horse that's really paying attention to you is less likely to spook at strange things, and when she does spook, you get her attention back very quickly. But this can work against you when something happens that is guaranteed to command your horse's attention, because your horse won't have any attention left over for you. That's what happened with Baby and the stallion. For all practical purposes, she forgot that you existed. Here again, we're talking about millions of years of evolution, plus hormones. Trying to ride a young mare that's in heat when there's a stallion calling her is almost impossible. In fact, trying to get her attention is almost impossible — her hormones are talking to her a lot louder than you are. You're right that you would have done better to get off. But that's all behind you now, and you'll know what to do if the situation arises again.

My advice is that you go very easy on the riding. Baby needs a lot of basic work and basic training anyway, and there's no point in asking her to do things that she may not be in physical condition to do (flying changes and jumping, for instance). Baby is only five years old. She needs to know you and trust you, and she needs to build a relationship with you. Likewise, you need to build a relationship with her and confidence in her. That takes time — not just quality time, but quantity time! Take her for walks on a lead rope and hand-graze her. It doesn't matter if the grass she's eating is exactly the same grass that's in her pasture; the important thing is that she'll learn to associate your presence with calm, pleasant experiences. Groom her a lot, work with her from the ground, and talk to her all the time.

Right now, she's anxious about leaving the others because she found out that sometimes when she leaves the other horses in her herd, she never comes back and never sees them again. You have to teach her to accept you as a consistent presence in her life. The first time you take her out alone to graze, you may have to stay in sight of the other horses; if you take her where she can't see the others, Baby may spend all her time whinnying and turning in circles. Don't worry; she'll learn. If you take her out often, and every time you take her out she has a nice time with you before you put her back, she'll be less worried when you take her out the next time.

Don't worry about the calling back and forth — Baby is young, and it sounds as though the older mares have "adopted" her. The first time you separate a mare and her foal, perhaps when the foal is around two months old and you start to work the mare lightly, they both yell. The next time you take the mare away, they both yell. The time after that, they both yell — but not as much or as loudly. After a week or two, you notice that you've groomed the mare, tacked her up, and ridden her for half an hour, and then the baby yells, and the mare answers — or doesn't!

Those "sound effects" are temporary. The mares will yell, Baby will yell back, but eventually they'll get bored or Baby will be too busy having her head groomed with a nice scratchy brush and she won't answer as quickly, or at all. When they all figure out that the one that goes away eventually comes back, the yelling will subside. Keep in mind that the other mares may be calling for another reason, too: Baby is being taken out for food, grooming, or attention, and they aren't. I have one horse that will scream with total indignation whenever I take out her neighbor — not because she wants her neighbor back, but because *she* wants to be the one getting the attention. When it's her turn to leave the others, she never says a word.

Buddy-Sour

Q My horse doesn't pay enough attention to me when I ride him. His attention is on the other horses, even if I ride him away from them. He calls to the other horses, and if they answer him he doesn't pay any attention to me at all. Last week, I rode him alone in a big field, and he was good for about fifteen minutes. Then someone else rode with us for a little while and left. My horse started calling and calling the other horse. Then he went from a slow trot to a very fast bumpy trot and he wouldn't listen when I told him to slow down. I yell at him and kick him when he does this, but it doesn't seem to help. Why does he do this, and what can I do to make him stop?

A You're probably familiar with the expression "There's safety in numbers." For horses, this is absolutely true. In nature, safety for a horse means staying with the herd, so it's natural for a horse to worry and call when he is separated from the other horses. A horse in a natural herd is secure; a horse alone,

Walking the last mile home is more than just a sensible tradition — it's a good safety habit.

separated from the herd, is in constant danger and may well end up as someone's dinner.

Your horse is calling out of fear and insecurity. He knows that he's not with his "herd," and he hasn't yet accepted you as a source of security and reassurance. He can learn to do this, as all good riding horses do, but it won't happen until you are able to offer him security and reassurance.

You need to get your horse's attention and gain his trust. He doesn't need to think that you're another horse. But he needs to feel that you are a trusted companion, or at least a benevolent presence, and he needs to understand that you are in charge so that he doesn't have to be.

Right now, when he is with you he thinks that he's all alone. You need to teach him that he's not alone when he's with you. It will be a gradual process, so start now, asking him to do simple things — a lot of simple things. Praise him when he responds, praise him when he responds promptly, and praise him when he's quiet. Plan your rides so that you are constantly asking him to do something and praising him for doing it or for trying.

Yelling at him and kicking him when he's worried about being the only horse left in the world will only convince him that he really is alone and in danger — from the predator on his back! So keep him busy, ask him to do little tasks, and praise and reward him. The way to keep his attention focused on you is to keep your own attention focused on him. Over time, he will learn to trust you, and he'll relax more. He'll eventually learn that you're in charge, that he can rely on you to keep him safe, and that nothing horrible happens to him when he leaves the other horses or when the other horses leave him.

Barn-Sour

Q I spent the summer with my dad and had to lease my horse to a friend for three months. My friend would always let him run back to the barn. Now my horse is barn-sour and insists on running back to the barn whenever we go out. If we go on the trails by ourselves or even with other horses, he still wants to run back to the barn as soon as we get close to home. I have tried lots of things, such as doubling him and yanking the reins, but he's not any better. Why does he keep doing this? My friend says that I can fix this problem by working my horse so hard that when we come back to the barn, he will hate it and not want to be there at all. I guess this makes sense, but I would like my horse to think that work is okay, so I don't like this idea so much.

A For your horse, that barn is a great place — it's his safe place. For wild horses, security means the herd, and they don't want to be separated from it. For many domestic horses, kept separated from other horses most of the time, barns and stalls have taken the place of the herd. Those horses don't know what it is to feel safe in a herd, but they do feel safe in their familiar barn and stall. So although it seems to you that your horse is foolishly attached to a silly building, from your horse's point of view, he's trying to get back to his safe place — his substitute herd.

Instead of fighting with your horse on the way back to the barn, try using a little psychology instead. Your horse wants to go back to the barn as quickly as possible, and you want your horse to walk and pay attention to you. You can both have what you want, if you use your good sense and patience to teach your horse a lesson.

Since your horse's desire is to return to his safe place, you shouldn't punish him for trying to get there faster than you would like him to. Frightening him will only make him more determined to reach sanctuary as quickly as he can. Instead, try this: Do most of your work when you are headed away from the barn. Do your trotting and your cantering, work on your transitions and leads, or whatever you are trying to improve, on your way out. On your way back, ask your horse to walk. As long as he walks quietly, talk to him, give him small jobs to do, like stepping sideways or lengthening or shortening his stride, and praise him for every effort, no matter how tiny.

For many domestic horses, barns and stalls have taken the place of the herd.

If he begins to speed up, don't fight with him, just turn him around and begin riding away from the barn again. Do some more work, and when you're certain that you've got his full attention and cooperation, turn around and begin walking toward home again. If he begins to speed up, do just what you did the last time. The lesson you're going to teach your horse is that speed is fine — but only when you ask him for it, and only in the direction that you choose, which just happens to be away from the barn.

During the summer months, when your friend was riding your horse, your horse learned that when he's going home, toward the barn, it's perfectly fine to be fast and out of control. You can't erase this lesson, or go back in time and keep the horse from learning it, but you can teach your horse a completely different lesson: that going away from the barn means work, but coming back toward the barn means a nice relaxing walk. He'll also learn that whenever he goes faster than the nice relaxing walk, he gets to turn around and do some work in the other direction. Keep it pleasant at all times. This work is not a punishment — it just involves more effort than a nice quiet walk toward the barn, and it's going in the "wrong" direction. Let your horse figure this out for himself.

Your instinct is good, and your friend's advice was bad. "Doubling" the horse and yanking the reins are actions that use the bit for punishment — something no rider should ever do. Making the barn unpleasant for the horse isn't the solution to this problem, either. If your horse is hurrying home because he's tired and would like to lie down in his stall or field, then it can be effective to do some more work when you get home instead of immediately dismounting and putting the horse away. Whether you solve your problem by working your horse on the trail going away from the barn or after you've come back to the barn, or both, the work itself should always be pleasant.

CHAPTER 11

Napping and Bolting

WHAT'S WORSE: the horse that plants his feet and refuses to move, or the one that runs away with you? Most riders would prefer not to have to deal with either problem, but it's a rare rider who hasn't been faced with one or the other. When a horse is presented with something that it perceives to be frightening or worrying, he may be able to relax and accept the new situation or the new demand, or he may not. If he's unable to cope, he will probably try to avoid the source of his fear, either at a dead standstill (napping) or at top speed in any direction (bolting). Riders who know how to help their horses relax can often avoid such problems altogether, but when faced with either situation, it helps to have a plan and follow it calmly.

Horse Is Glued to the Ground

Q I've taken on a "problem horse" for the summer as a favor for a friend. The horse's problem is that he just decides that he's going to stop somewhere on the trail and then that's it; he won't move. My friend said she was going to sell him, but she really likes him, so I said I would take him home for the summer and try to cure his problem. Now that I've experienced this for myself, I realize that I have no clue why he is doing it or what I can do to fix it, but I still want to try.

A "Napping," or stopping and refusing to go forward, is an extremely annoying behavior. Some horses react to unpleasant or worrisome situations by stopping and refusing to move in any direction. Nervous or timid horses, reluctant to leave the herd or the barn, will sometimes reach a point at which they refuse to continue: They become "glued" to the ground.

Some horses nap because they simply don't know what they are supposed to do next and feel more secure about stopping and standing still than they do about moving forward. If the horse naps in familiar surroundings — the home arena or on a familiar trail — then he may be doing so because he is uncomfortable. Check your tack. Some horses with ill-fitting saddles, for instance, will cooperate with the rider until the discomfort becomes unbearable, and will then nap. Under the circumstances, it's certainly preferable to other possible extreme reactions, such as rearing, bucking, or running back to the barn.

It takes a strong and confident rider to encourage a nervous horse to go forward despite his concerns.

If your horse naps only when faced with the unknown — a new trail, an unfamiliar arena or show ground — then he is far more likely to be napping out of fear. If he naps only when faced with specific objects, this, too, is probably out of fear. Pay attention to the surroundings and circumstances when your horse naps. There may be a pattern, and you may be able to figure out what is worrying him. Some horses are terrified of passing cattle pens or dog kennels, others are afraid to cross water, and some are made nervous when ridden from an open field into the crowded darkness of a stand of trees.

It takes a very strong and very foolish rider to force a frightened horse to go forward by making him more afraid of the rider than anything else. It takes a strong and confident rider to put a nervous horse's mind at ease and encourage him to go forward *in spite* of his concerns. In most cases, it makes more sense to take a low-key approach, working with the nature of the horse. Just remain calm and wait until the horse relaxes and puts his own mind at ease.

The easiest and most successful method of putting an end to napping is also the most time-consuming, at least in the beginning. To put this method into practice, you simply sit. Give the horse a long enough rein to stretch his neck, but not long enough to graze, and just sit there until the horse makes up his mind to move forward. The key word here is *forward*.

Don't kick or yell or pester your horse, but don't permit him to move to the left or the right, back up, or turn completely around and head in

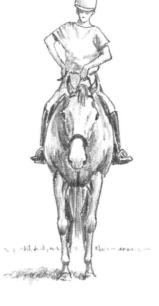

One of the simplest and safest ways to reform a 'napper' is to wait it out.

the direction of home. The message you want your horse to get from you is that he is welcome to stand still and is welcome to move forward, but those are his only options. Don't insist on movement of any kind, but don't accept movement in any direction other than straight ahead. When the horse offers any forward movement, praise him generously.

As usual, training is progressive and improvements are incremental. If your horse naps at the entrance to the trail, it may take an hour before he feels sufficiently safe (or bored — the two are closely connected) to move forward. But the next time it may take only half an hour, and the time after that, perhaps no more than five or ten minutes. If you have a good book with you, you can lengthen your reins, sit quietly, and wait patiently without becoming bored, and the results will be much better than they would if you fought with the horse. Just don't immerse yourself in the book to the point where you're no longer aware of your horse and the environment. Some riders will use this time to carry on long conversations with friends, using a cell phone, but I prefer the traditional book.

Horse Runs Away

Q   I have a lovely 12-year-old called Kaptein. Most of the time he is well behaved, but occasionally he will take me or another rider and he will run and run.

No amount of turning him in a circle, pulling back, or trying to stop him will make any difference. He seems to run until he wants to stop. The more you try to stop him, the more he fights for mastery and continues to run.

A   This is not a question I can answer for you; I can make a few suggestions, but you're going to need some hands-on help from local experts who can look at the actual horse and watch him being tacked up and ridden.

First, have this horse thoroughly checked out by a good veterinarian. If there's a tooth problem or a saddle-fit problem, that could be causing the horse enough pain to make him take off running. There may even be another problem, but it's best to find out if the veterinarian can detect it.

If the vet can't find a specific cause but the behavior keeps happening with no consistency or pattern (same rider? same saddle? same venue? same length of ride?), then you may want to ask your vet to refer the horse to a veterinary hospital for more tests.

Usually a "pulley rein" can help bring a bolting horse into a large circle and slow it down.

There have been cases of horses with brain tumors that caused them to just start running for no apparent reason and to keep running until they hit something. This isn't an annoying habit; it's a dangerous problem. By all means stay off the horse until you know what's causing the trouble. If it's a tack, training, or riding problem, it's probably something that can be solved. If it's a medical problem, that's another story. Don't take chances.

Bolting over Jumps

Q I've been riding for ten years and feel very comfortable on a variety of horses. Last year I purchased a five-year-old mare that was supposed to be an experienced eventer with the owner's 14-year-old son. I tried her out in a small outdoor arena at walk, trot, and canter, and jumped several jumps, a cross-rail, a vertical, and an oxer, all about 2 feet high, and she was quiet and obedient. Hindsight is 20-20. I now realize that I should have tried her out in an open area, on the trail, and over some cross-country-type jumps and some bigger jumps, but I am not very comfortable jumping anything over 2 feet high and so didn't ask them to raise the jumps.

When I brought her home, she was fine for a few months. For various reasons I didn't ride her for six months and when I started again, she began bolting with me. The land next to my boarding barn is a forest preserve where we can ride for miles on all kinds of trails. On a couple of the trails, people from my barn and a few other local barns have built ten low jumps out of logs and rocks. I have jumped those before on other horses and everything went well. This mare likes jumping so much that she starts to speed up when she sees a jump, then as soon as you get into jumping position she bolts forward and jumps very fast and lands and bolts again.

I was afraid I wouldn't be able to turn her by the end of the arena so I rode her on that trail to jump her. She jumped the first one from a nice trot, then as soon as I got into jumping position she bolted all the way down the trail over all the jumps, much faster than I wanted to go. After the last jump there is an uphill slope into a field. Once we were in the field she slowed down to a trot, and I got into jumping position just for a moment and she bolted again. All I could do was lean forward and hang on. I didn't know how to stop her. I tried pulling one rein and then the other, and that worked, she slowed and then I could sit up straight, and then she decided that she was fine to trot and walk! We walked home and she was very good but now I don't trust her because I am afraid that she will bolt whenever I ask her to jump. She has extensive eventing experience, so I can't understand why even small jumps would make her bolt. I don't like to be afraid of my horse.

A There are several things that come to mind here. One is the horse herself, the second is the rider, and the third is saddle fit. First, the horse: Since you didn't try this mare over natural jumps in a field or on a trail, you had no way of knowing how she would deal with such obstacles. I know that you were told that she had "extensive eventing experience", but when you bought her, she was five years old, so it's not likely that her experience was truly extensive. An eventer with several years of good training and useful experience will not have to race flat-out, because it will be balanced and have the ability to lengthen and shorten its stride according to the rider's wishes; a relatively inexperienced horse, or one that lacked good training and a sensible rider, might have no such balance and no such abilities. It's quite possible that even if your mare had done a few hunter trials or one-day events with a young teenager in the saddle, all her "experience" might consist of running fast and jumping whatever she's pointed toward. This doesn't mean that she is a confirmed bolter, or even a bolter at all. A horse will typically take a course of jumps in the way it's accustomed to taking them, unless the rider has other plans — or unless there's an element of pain or fear involved.

Second, the rider: You've said that you hadn't ridden in six months — it's probably safe to assume that you were less fit and probably less comfortable on a horse after so much time off. You've also said that you aren't comfortable jumping anything over two feet high. Your reaction to fear, nervousness, and insecurity on horseback is very typically human: You curl up on the horse's neck! This reaction is absolutely natural, but the message it sends to the horse is: "Run, run, go as fast as you can!" Unfortunately, when this happens, your legs are not in a position to help your mare engage her hind legs, and your body is not in a position to help her bring her balance back. Her initial leap brings you forward into a sort of "jockey" position, and from that moment on, her speed makes you curl up, and your curling up asks her to run faster. The only way out of that situation is for the mare to be backed off by a physical obstacle, or for the rider to sit up straight and ask for more engagement.

Riders who are nervous and unfit can also find it very difficult — especially on an unfamiliar horse — to distinguish between a horse that is bolting and a horse that is simply going faster than the rider wants to go. I don't believe that your mare was truly bolting, and this is why: She came back to trot in the field, after the last jump; also, when she began running again, you were able to bring her back to trot by using alternating rein pressure. That tells me that the mare knew that you were in the saddle, and was listening and responding to you. When a horse is *truly* bolting, it isn't listening to you at all, and in fact probably doesn't even realize that you are there. To establish control over a bolting horse, you first have to establish communication with it — and you always had communication with your mare. I think that your mare was simply going too fast for your comfort, and that she was doing it for several reasons. *Habit* is one reason — I suspect that this is how she is accustomed to going over cross-country jumps. She probably began rushing out of anxiety, as most horses do, and then continued to rush because her rider was quite happy to race around taking low jumps in stride. Now she believes that this is the way she *should* jump. *Obedience* is another reason — she probably thought that by charging her jumps and running fast, she was doing exactly what you were asking her to do. When you leaned forward on her neck, this was a clear signal to go faster. Practice your jumping position in the arena, on the flat, so that you can be sure that you are *folding* your body rather than curling up or standing up and leaning forward.

Your reaction to fear, nervousness, and insecurity on horseback is very typically human: You curl up on the horse's neck! This reaction is absolutely natural, but the message it sends to the horse is: "Run, run, go as fast as you possibly can!"

Finally, I'm a little suspicious about the fit of your saddle. After six or seven months without being ridden, your mare's musculature will have changed significantly, and even if her saddle fit her perfectly when you bought her, it may not fit her now. Also, she is still rising six, which means that she is still growing — the last area of the horse's skeleton to develop is the area just in front of and under the saddle. Saddle position matters, too — even a well-fitting saddle will fit badly and cause the horse pain if it is positioned too far forward on the horse's back. An unfit rider — understandable after more than half a year without riding! — will not be as balanced or as coordinated as a fit rider, which means that there will be more movement of the saddle on the horse's back, and probably more pressure in certain areas of the saddle.

The fact that your mare seems to react so strongly to you getting into a "jumping position" tells me that she may be experiencing pain, especially if you are leaning forward rather than folding your body. When you lean forward on her back without folding your body, it brings more of your weight to bear on the front of the saddle. If your mare has lost muscle or gained some height in the withers, both of which are very likely given her time off and her age, your saddle may be putting painful pressure on her whenever you assume that position.

Don't think of her as an experienced eventer; think of her as a green horse that you are training from the ground up. In every sense that matters, it's true.

Be aware of all the possibilities. Horse behavior doesn't come "out of nowhere": It's always a reaction to something. Our job as riders is to find out what that something is, and then to change it so that the horse can learn a different reaction. If the saddle, or the combination of the saddle and its position and your position, causes pain to your mare, no amount of training will persuade her that the pain doesn't exist. To change the reaction, you'll have to begin by changing the reason for the reaction.

When you're certain that there are no equipment issues or residual soreness to deal with, you can begin your real work — teaching your mare to relax and listen when she's jumping on the trail. When you are certain that your mare is comfortable in her tack, and that both of you are fit enough to work effectively as a team, begin work on the flat. When you can easily "rate" her — asking her to speed up and slow down, asking her to lengthen her stride and shorten it — in the arena, go out and practice the same things on the trail, but still without doing any jumping.

When it becomes easy on the trail, go back to the arena and incorporate some small jumps into your routine. Set them at related distances so that you will be able to ask the mare, for example, to take six long strides between jumps — or seven short strides. Talk to her, praise her, and several times during each session, ask her to jump a single small jump from trot and then from canter, stopping on a line after the jump. Praise her as she slows down in response to your request, and praise her for stopping and standing in response to your request. Once that becomes easy, make it a habit — and once it's a habit, you'll be able to take her out on the trail and start the same jumping routine all over again from the very beginning.

Don't think of her as an experienced eventer — think of her as a green horse that you are training from the ground up. In every sense that matters, it's true. You're teaching her a new way of approaching jumps, a new way of moving on after jumping, and an entirely new attitude about the whole process of running and jumping. It will take time and effort, but the results will make it all worthwhile.

The Chronic Bolter

Q My new horse (Thoroughbred, three-year-old ex-racehorse) seems to be a chronic bolter. I am heartbroken because he is so beautiful and such a good mover. He is everything I have ever wanted, except for this problem. There are certain things that just seem to scare him to death, and he just whirls around and runs blindly. One of the other riders who boards here has a lot of experience training horses. She says I am doing everything wrong, and I will only make his bolting worse. Here is what happens: We will be in the arena or sometimes in the field, and he will see something that scares him. I never know what it will be. Last time it was a bendy tree moving in the wind, the time before that it was a mailbox, and the time before that it was an upside-down manure bucket that somebody had put in the arena to use as a mounting block. None of these things are scary and he should have seen them all before. He was fine when the tractor came past in the next field, pulling a big harrow.

I try to get him as close as I can to whatever it is, then just sit there quietly so that he can calm down. I thought it was working but the other rider says I have to make him put his nose on it or he will keep bolting away. Well, I tried that, and he got totally scared and whirled and ran away and it took me a long time to get him under control. It doesn't matter how much pressure I put on the reins, he just goes faster and faster. He calmed down after about ten times around the arena, and he does the same thing in the field.

I am afraid to take him on the trail because of this, and I don't know what to do. I really like this horse and want to keep him. I don't want to put a twisted wire bit in his mouth as someone suggested for a brake. How can I stop him? I've heard of something called a "pulley rein;" should I use that?

A Actually, your own instincts are wiser than the advice you've been getting. It's true that a horse that will go up to something and put its nose on it probably won't panic, whirl, and bolt — but the horse has to approach the item itself, and put its nose on it out of interest and curiosity, not because someone has forced it into contact with the terrifying object. If you want him to approach something scary, get as close to it as you can without him going into panic mode. Then sit tall, loosen your reins, and let him stand there. If you make it clear that the choices are "stand still" or "investigate the object," his natural curiosity will eventually take him closer and closer to the object, and he will probably put his nose on it eventually — at which point he may jump back. If he does, start over, but don't punish him. Your goal is for him to figure out that the object is (a) not harmful, and (b) boring — and he can only learn these things if he's allowed to figure them out for himself. Forcing him is not only pointless, it's counterproductive.

Your horse is a three-year-old Thoroughbred off the track — possibly very recently off the track. In a way, this is good, because in many ways he's a blank slate, and you have a chance to teach him all the things you want him to learn. In a way, this is also inconvenient, because there is so much he needs to learn, including a lot of the things you probably expect him to know. He doesn't bolt when he sees the tractor and harrow because those are familiar to him — he's seen similar equipment all his life, at the training barn and at the track. He's seen manure buckets, of course, but never upside down in the middle of an arena. He has probably never seen a mailbox in his life, and depending on where he was trained, stabled, and raced, he may never have seen a tree moving in the wind. He's in a completely new environment, and it's up to you to teach him that he is safe there. Don't take anything for granted. He's seen heavy machinery, trucks, trailers, and manure spreaders, but he may panic at sights that other horses at the barn will barely notice, such as a "road closed" sign, a child on a bicycle, or even someone setting up three barrels in the outdoor arena.

Steady rein pressure won't have the effect of slowing him down, for several reasons. One is that a bolting horse is literally out of its mind: Fear is its motivator, and speed is the only way it knows to deal with fear. A horse's natural defense is speed, and for a frightened horse to run away makes perfect, logical horse sense. Another reason is that this horse has been trained to race, and steady, strong rein pressure is exactly what he expects to feel when he runs. He won't understand it as a signal to slow down or stop, especially if the rider is doing what comes naturally to frightened humans, and curling up on his neck in fetal (and, coincidentally, "jockey") position. The combination of tighter reins and a lighter seat encourages the horse to run. When he runs off, see if you can bring yourself to change your position in exactly the opposite way: Sit up as tall as you can, deepen your seat, and lessen the pressure on the reins. From that position, you will be able to use a pulley rein if necessary.

He has probably never seen a mailbox in his life, and depending on where he was trained, stabled, and raced, he may never have seen a tree moving in the wind. He's in a completely new environment, and it's up to you to teach him that he is safe there.

There is no point in adding pain to the situation by putting a twisted-wire bit in this horse's mouth — and incidentally, no twisted-wire bit should ever be put in any horse's mouth at any time. Increasing the pain he feels won't decrease his speed or his fear or his instinct to run away. If anything, causing him pain will simply make matters worse. Your goal is not just to get your horse under your control again, it's to offer him the calm reassurance that will make him less likely to run off in the first place, and more likely to listen to you when he does run off. Pain won't accomplish this — no horse finds pain calming or reassuring.

If your horse is running off but is aware that you are there, you can ask for a response almost immediately. If your horse is truly bolting, you'll have to make him aware that you are there before you can hope for a response. In either case, the tried-and-true methods still work well. Directing the horse onto a large circle will help you gain some control, and even if he is still going much faster than you would like, at least you won't have to worry about *where* he is taking you. You may need to use a pulley rein just to get the horse onto that large circle, but once you're there, don't try to force him to a stop. Instead, try to sit up and

Anything that helps your horse become calm and attentive is the right thing; anything that makes him more anxious is the wrong thing.

ride, just keeping the horse on the same circle until it eventually realizes that nothing is chasing it. At the point where the horse remembers you exist, you'll be able to begin to take control in a reassuring way, by asking it to do things and praising and patting it for each tiny effort. By "do things" I don't mean stop, necessarily — begin by asking for a slight change of direction, or by using your weight and leg aids to increase or decrease the size of the circle. Each small change is good. As he begins to pay more attention to you, ask for more frequent and more complicated changes — changes of direction, changes in stride length, changes in gait. Be sure to praise him for each effort, no matter how tiny. At some point, you will find that you are once again in charge of your horse.

During the next year or so while you're giving your horse his basic training, keep him focused on you. Any horse can become frightened, and any horse can bolt, but training has an enormous effect on the frequency with which a horse will become frightened, the amount of fright it experiences, and the way it expresses that fright. A horse that knows you, trusts you, and is in the *habit* of paying attention to you and responding promptly to your aids will be much less likely to bolt or run off. If he does either, he will relax and "come back to you" much more quickly. The best way to keep his focus on you and his attitude positive is to ask him for things he knows how to do, and praise him for doing them. Practice transitions — hundreds of thousands of transitions, between gaits and within gaits. Practice turns at all gaits, and again, always praise the horse for every effort.

Your aim will be to do so many transitions and turns, and to improve your horse's skills and your own so dramatically, that you will both develop new habits. Your new habit will be, "When in doubt, ask for a transition or a turn, then praise the horse," which is an excellent way to avoid problems by preventing them. Your horse, meanwhile, will get in the habit of responding to your signals instantly, automatically, almost reflexively, without thinking. This is essential, because it will pay off when he *isn't* thinking. If he panics and bolts, he won't be thinking — but you'll be able to call on his habits and get his body moving in the direction that you want, and his brain will eventually come along.

And, incidentally, improving your transitions will make your horse much stronger and more supple, and will make you a better rider. It's a win-win-win situation.

If you have to use a pulley rein at some point — to get the horse onto that large circle, for example — here is what you'll do:

Sit up as straight as you can, and stretch your legs down around the horse's body. Breathe. Decide where you want the circle to be — which way you want the horse to turn — and prepare to begin asking for the turn. Let's say that you're entering the big field and you want to make a big circle to the left. Put your right hand down by his withers, hand closed tightly on the rein, fist pushing into his neck. This will help steady and support your upper body. Now lift your left hand up (toward the crest of your horse's neck) and begin using your left rein in a series of strong "take and release" movements. "Take" the rein up towards the crest, then "release" your left hand down and forward, then "take" again. Continue until your horse shifts into the turn and onto the circle. After that, use it only as needed to keep him on the safe circle. Now put your focus on sitting tall, relaxing the rein pressure as much as possible, and talking to the horse. Don't overuse a pulley rein — it's very powerful. As soon as you sense that he is listening to you or even becoming aware of you, loosen the reins a little and begin asking for transitions, etc. Make the situation normal and familiar so that your horse — and you — can relax.

Horses startle and run when they are surprised, when they are afraid, and when something hurts them. Ignore those "helpful" people who offer new and different ways to surprise, frighten, and hurt your horse — those tactics can cause a horse to panic and run, but they won't help the horse feel secure enough so that he doesn't panic or doesn't feel the need to run. If you want a rule to follow, try this one: Anything that helps your horse become or remain calm and attentive is the *right* thing; anything that makes him become more anxious or fearful is the *wrong* thing.

CHAPTER 12

Bucking and Rearing

BUCKING AND REARING are every rider's worst fears. These two behaviors are always mentioned when someone is describing a horse out of control. Anxious parents often ask for assurances that the horses their children ride "will never buck or rear," but horsemen know that both behaviors are natural and that, with enough provocation, any horse can exhibit either behavior. As with other unwanted behaviors, the secret to dealing with bucking and rearing is to discourage the behavior itself while simultaneously searching for and eliminating its cause. Because bucking and rearing can be so dangerous, it's especially important for riders to be aware of particular situations and conditions that may lead to these behaviors.

Once a Bucker, Always a Bucker?

Q My horse has become such a concern of mine that I am grappling with the decision of whether to sell him. Ninety-eight percent of the time he's a very sweet, people-oriented horse, but the other two percent of the time he can be dangerous.

My horse, Tristan, is a nine-year-old Trakehner-Thoroughbred cross, and stands 16.3 hh, with a large build. He was sold to me a year and a half ago as a green eight-year-old who had been turned out for most of his life. Right there, alarms should have gone off in my head, but I didn't pay much heed because I loved so many other things about him. He was just learning to jump low rails and didn't have much knowledge of flat work. Beginning only a few weeks after I purchased him, he had one lameness issue after another, all of which I have systematically cared for with the help of my farrier, veterinarian/acupuncturist/chiropractor, trainers, and a lot of patience. My horse is very heavy in the front end and abdomen, with a longish back. His hindquarters are a normal size. I'm told that with his conformation working against him, I have to get his hindquarters and back into shape very carefully so that he doesn't eagerly do more than he is physically able to and hurt himself in the process.

Tristan is on a diet of a quarter scoop of a mixture of pellets and sweet feed twice a day and five flakes of hay per day. This diet has helped him trim down some, and I believe he is in good flesh.

I consider myself to be an advanced intermediate rider, stand only 5'3", and have been riding hunt seat on and off for about 30 years. In the year and a half that I've owned Tristan, he has bucked me off three times, in the ring and out on the trail, at the trot and at the canter — mostly after spooking and bolting, but once while following another horse at a canter through tall grass on the trail. I've attributed the behavior as having physical roots because after each incident he developed some kind of soreness or lameness in the back, hip, or foot. Now I believe that he is physically sound, more physically fit than he has probably ever been in his life, and on a regular exercise routine of riding out on hills and trails four times a week and doing ring work once a week. He has learned a lot of flat work, engages behind, is learning to balance better, and is responsive and obedient. He has come a long way but is not an Olympic contender, and I don't need him to be. He is intended to be a pleasure horse to ride out, jump 2- to 3-foot fences once in a while, and possibly do some local showing.

Most of the time, Tristan is docile, very willing and eager to please, and not prone to flakiness. In fact, he often has to lead others on the trail because of his good temperament. But recently, he spooked in a field where we were working on hills. We were cantering balanced and relaxed. He accidentally brushed against some branches (which normally doesn't bother him at a walk), bolted, and as I attempted to regain control before we reached the woods, he fought me by shaking his head and bucking. This time I managed to stay on, pulled him up, and gave him a light whack with the crop since he's very afraid of it. Now I think that I shouldn't have done that, but have gotten different opinions about what would have been an appropriate action.

Can buckers be retrained, or will they always carry that in their bag of tricks when the going gets anxious? I'm afraid Tristan has learned that in dire situations, it is a viable alternative. The last time Tristan bucked me off I landed in the ER with a concussion. I don't want to repeat that experience, but I've been through so much with this horse and I love him, and I want to give him the opportunity to be good. If I can stay on, what should I do to correct or calm him? Or do you think that, as some of my friends suggest, I should sell him? Since the behavior is so intermittent, once every two or three months, it's tough to send him somewhere to be retrained. What would you do in my situation?

A   Your situation is very interesting. You've had a lot of riding experience, your horse sounds very sweet, and it seems that you've enlisted the help of just about every professional who could help. It's quite possible that the most I'll be able to do for you is give you my thoughts and perhaps help you clarify your own thinking.

Let's begin by taking an objective look at the horse and the situation. Pretend that you're reading about someone else's problem.

This horse has had soundness issues since his owner purchased him and quite likely from long before she purchased him. She purchased him as a green eight-year-old who had spent most of his life turned out. His size and conformation alone would make it difficult to get and keep him truly sound and fit. It's entirely possible that he may have been started young and then turned out and left out because of some injury that is now coming back to haunt him. It's very likely that some physical problems are causing him pain, and they are doubtless exacerbated by his size and build.

On the plus side, the horse is sweet and people-oriented, and an enjoyable

*For a reprimand to be
effective, the rider will have to
offer it while the horse is bucking,
not after he has stopped bucking.*

ride 98 percent of the time. And he's honest; it's significant that after each bucking episode, a physical problem was clearly involved. That makes it highly likely
that the lameness was already coming on before the bucking episode, and when
it got to the painful stage, the horse wasn't able to tolerate the pain and a rider,
and so he bucked. If this horse had been bucking with his rider on a daily or
even weekly basis, I would classify it as a chronic physical or behavior problem.

How often does the horse buck? The rider has come off him only three times
in 18 months, but is that because he has bucked only on those three occasions,
or because those happened to be the only three occasions on which the rider has
come off as a result of his bucking?

What should the rider do? You're right that hitting him after pulling him up
was the wrong response. A quick, loud smack with a whip can be a useful teaching tool, but only if the timing of the smack occurs while the behavior is in
progress — otherwise, the horse will create no useful association in his mind. A
loud yell *during* the behavior is of far more use than a smack after the behavior.
The problem is that he will associate praise or punishment with whatever he is
doing at the moment the praise or punishment is offered. That's why patting a
horse after he's completed his jumping round (for example) doesn't convey,
"Well jumped," it conveys, "What a good boy you are for trotting" (or walking,
or standing still, or whatever the horse is doing at the time he is being patted).

When a horse bucks, rears, or bites and is punished *while* the behavior is in progress, he will associate the punishment with that behavior. When a horse bucks, rears, or bites and is punished after the behavior, the punishment conveys, "No, you should not stand still" (or put all four feet on the ground, or close your mouth). It's all a matter of timing, and in this case, your timing didn't say, "Bucking is bad and I don't want you to do it," it said "Bucking is fine, but do not come back to hand and pull up."

Horses are very sensitive to loud noises, and your horse, being mostly Thoroughbred, is likely to be more sensitive than most.

This is why punishment too late is worse than no punishment at all. And since it can be difficult to coordinate a whip smack when you're riding a horse that is actually bucking at the time, try yelling instead. Horses are very sensitive to loud noises, and your horse, being mostly Thoroughbred, is likely to be more sensitive than most. A sensitive, people-oriented horse that likes to please will usually be affected by a really loud "No!" or "Stop!" or game-show buzzer sound. It certainly leaves no doubt in the horse's mind that whatever he is doing when he hears that noise is something he should cease doing immediately.

If you can smack the horse during the objectionable behavior, you can often eliminate that behavior from his repertoire. If you can't smack the horse and stay in the saddle, don't bother smacking, just yell and send the horse forward. "Open a door" for the horse with your reins and direct him through it with your legs, so that he has somewhere to go. As soon as the bucking stops, pat, praise, and reward. The horse will not think he's being rewarded for bucking. This is a difficult lesson to learn, not for the horse, but for the rider. Sitting on a horse that bucks or rears is frightening, and fright creates an adrenaline surge in the rider. The rider's instinct is to grab the reins and try to wrestle the horse to a standstill, but the best solution is to ask the horse to go forward in the direction the rider chooses, and under the rider's control.

The rider's instinct is also to get the horse under control and then punish it, which is actually counterproductive. For example, when a horse bucks or rears, the rider's impulse is to cling to the reins, and when the horse's feet touch down again, the rider's impulse is not to praise the horse but to hit him — and this is something that the rider simply must not do.

Bucking and rearing are both problems that require active, energetic, forward movement as part of the solution. These problems are typically the result of horses being given clashing aids — hearing both "Go" and "Whoa" at once — and are made worse by timid or fearful riders who think in terms of making the horse stand still. When confronted with a potential or actual buck or rear, don't pull back on the reins. If you need to administer a short, sharp verbal or physical correction, do so, but what's most important is that you decide on the direction and the gait you want and encourage your horse to move forward with energy.

Rearing Mare

Q I am exhausting all my options before I have to make the worst decision of my life. Recently, my normally willing but strong willed, very intelligent nine-year-old Arabian–Quarter Horse mare has taken up rearing. I have had a trainer working with her since last September on simple Western pleasure movements — headsetting, lead changes, working off the hind end, and so on. All this work has been done inside an arena. She had really come along great.

About a month ago, I decided it was time for her to get back out on the trails. I had one rearing incident on the trail a while back, and I knew she needed more work there than in the arena. So for five days I had my trainer take her out to see how she'd do. The trainer would longe her first in the arena, then take her out. Not until the fifth day did the nightmare begin. My mare started going up before she even got down the driveway — a walk she has taken a million times. But my trainer made her go and continued for about three and a half hours. I can't believe the endurance this horse has. She was dripping wet when they returned.

Rearing is dangerous for both the rider and the horse and should not be taken lightly.

A few weeks prior to the trail training, a yearling had been put in my mare's paddock. We think that the yearling has bonded with my mare and that she thinks she's her mother. Prior to the new yearling's arrival, I had ridden my mare all over the farm with no more than a little easy-to-deal-with spook now and then. I tried taking her out of that paddock, but she got through the fence and paced back and forth in front of her regular paddock so we put her back in. Could it be possible that my mare wants to be a mother, or is she really just buddy-sour and spoiled and getting away with it? How can you tell, and how do you fix this?

A First, rearing is very dangerous and not something that you should be trying to deal with yourself. Second, rearing is usually the action of a horse that is very uncomfortable or frustrated. Third, although you've come up with some possible reasons for your mare's rearing, I think you've overlooked several more likely possibilities. The most likely cause for rearing is physical pain, and that would be the first area to investigate. As for your suggestions, here are my reactions:

Does your mare want to be (or think that she is) a mother? Almost certainly not. Horses don't function that way. A barren mare in a field with other mares and foals may, under certain circumstances, "steal" a newborn foal. And a mare in heat may be reluctant to leave the sexy stallion in the next field. But both of these scenarios are other situations altogether.

Attachment to a buddy is certainly possible, and if your mare has a close friend in the same or a neighboring paddock, she may very well want to stay with or return to her friend. But this is probably secondary to the fact that your mare has spent the last several months working at this barn, in an arena, and sees the barn as her herd and her security. Asking a horse to leave her safety zone and go down the trail alone after many months of arena work, especially if the horse is in pain, is a good formula for creating a horse that will rear, buck, or bolt.

"Getting away with something" isn't an idea I apply to horses. I haven't yet met one for which it's appropriate. Horses do what comes naturally to them and what they have been taught to do by humans, and horses also do things in reaction to the painful, frightening, pleasant, or reassuring things that humans do to them. Horse reactions are *horse* reactions, not human ones; they don't think like humans, which often confuses the humans to whom they are reacting.

A child who feeds a horse jelly beans or little carrot pieces from a cupped hand runs the risk of having a finger bitten, not because the horse is vicious and demanding more treats, but because the child doesn't know how to feed a horse a treat. A horse that steps on the foot of the human who is leading him is not acting out of spite or revenge or trying to get out of being ridden; he is just stepping where he steps (he can't see his own feet), and it's the human's fault for putting her feet under the horse's.

A horse that rears is almost always a horse that is in pain or badly frightened. It's possible to train a horse to rear, but even that usually begins with a rear that happens out of pain or fear. Here's how to induce a horse to rear: Ride the horse, perhaps a sore-backed or sore-footed horse, with a saddle that doesn't fit. Use bits and auxiliary reins that make it impossible for the horse to move her head and neck or put them into comfortable positions. Kick the horse forward while holding her mouth painfully. After a time, unless the horse is a true saint, she will rear. She's responding to the rider saying, in effect: "I can hurt you a lot and make you go forward and hurt even more, but, surprise, I won't let you go forward. I just want to hurt you!" The horse, already in pain and deprived of her ability to go forward, will go up. Sometimes she will go up and over . . . and sometimes the rider will be killed.

Horse reactions are horse reactions, not human ones; they don't think like humans, which often confuses the humans to whom they are reacting.

To confirm the training, put the horse in the same position over and over again, and you'll make the rearing into a habit. If nothing changes about what the rider is doing, nothing is likely to change about the horse's reaction.

Sore backs, sore mouths, and unhappiness or discomfort from other causes are the usual suspects when a horse begins to rear. For example, your mare may have a hormonal condition that would make her more susceptible to rearing. She could also have a sore back from a painful follicle, or she could have painful cysts on her ovaries. These are matters for your vet to determine, and if you suspect that there is any chance of a physical problem, I hope that you will have the vet come out immediately.

In the meantime, though, I would look at more ordinary causes of pain. Saddle fit is always worth investigating, particularly in the case of a horse that has been undergoing intensive training. Her back has undoubtedly changed shape since the training began, and even if the saddle fit her at the beginning of training, it may not fit her now. Mouth pain from a severe bit, from a heavy-handed rider, or from the constant use of draw reins can send a horse straight up into the air. Mouth pain is made infinitely worse if the horse's teeth are in need of floating. Have your vet or equine dentist look at your mare's mouth and do any necessary smoothing of rough edges and sharp points. Her wolf teeth (if any) may need to be removed.

Sore feet can cause rearing. Many horses with navicular disease and laminitis reach a point at which they simply refuse to go forward, especially on hard, uneven, extremely painful surfaces. Such horses will sometimes stand still and sometimes walk on their hind legs in an effort to avoid putting weight on their sore front feet. It's something that your vet and farrier can help you investigate.

Training can cause rearing, because training can cause pain. *Headsetting* is really not an acceptable term or concept for a horseman, because the only thing it does is hurt, frighten, and damage the horse. Training a horse to carry its head in a fixed, unnatural position causes mental discomfort and physical damage to horses. The forceful, painful methods and equipment used to achieve a "head-set" are unacceptable, and the goal itself ought to be unthinkable. Horses that are worked hard while their heads are held in a fixed position are going to be sore in several places. Horses with headsets are invariably sore in their mouths, necks, and backs and often have sore hind legs as well. It's not a good practice, it's not fair, and it's not going to create a comfortable or happy animal. On the contrary, it will create an unhappy, uncomfortable animal in the short term, and an unhappy, uncomfortable, and unsound animal in the long term.

If your vet, equine dentist, and farrier find nothing overtly wrong with the mare physically and ultrasound reveals no cysts or large follicles that could be causing a problem, look very hard at the tack fit and at the selection of tack. Horses wearing saddles with very long skirts can buck or rear because of the painful contact between the back of the saddle (or the edge of the pad) with their hips. If this is the case, you might change to a saddle with shorter, rounded skirts, like a barrel saddle, and see how your horse reacts.

Horses wearing unsuitable or cruel bits can rear — or buck or bolt — when the pain in their mouths becomes overwhelming. Try using the gentlest bit possible or no bit at all; a week or two in a Bitless Bridle, English jumping hackamore, or soft, padded side pull never hurt any horse. You might think that this would lessen the rider's control, but you'd be mistaken. Riders (and tack) should not control horses through pain.

For the same reason, I would advise changing your mare's training and trying to restore her normal movement and range of motion. This may take quite a lot of time, and you may need the services of more experts; massage and chiropractic help are often necessary to put a horse back into a normal shape after she's been subjected to headsetting techniques. The muscle damage alone can require months of daily massage.

As for the long fight between your horse and your trainer, a horse that is exhausted from a three-and-a-half hour fight is not a calm horse, it's just a very tired, and very unhappy, horse. The way to get a horse away from the barn and out onto the trail is not to make the experience as unpleasant as possible for as long as possible. If the horse stops on the way and refuses to go forward, instead of beating her and fighting with her, try sitting on her and keeping her pointed in the direction that you want her to go.

Instead of forcing her, try waiting. It may take hours, but your goal must be to make the horse decide to go forward. You can do this simply by being very patient and making it clear to the horse that she isn't going to be allowed to go sideways, backward, or in any other direction than the one you want to go.

Instead of forcing her, try waiting. It may take hours — if you do this in summer, wear sunblock — but your goal must be to make the horse decide to go forward. You can do this simply by being very patient and making it clear to the horse that she isn't going to be allowed to go sideways, backward, or in any direction other than the one you want to go.

Some horses take twenty minutes to figure out that their only useful choice is to go forward. Some horses take two hours or longer — but it's two hours of standing, not two hours of fighting. A horse that's standing still, with a choice and a place to go, isn't going to panic or go up and over. But a horse that's being pushed and pulled and kicked and yanked won't have the peace and quiet to figure out her options, and after a point will panic and buck, bolt, or rear.

Think about it in terms of your ultimate training goals. Do you want to force the horse down the trail right now, today, no matter what you have to do, and then have it take twice as long to get the horse down the trail next time? Or do you want to invest the time it takes to let the horse come to the correct conclusion, and have it take half the time next time? It's up to you.

I think that the yearling's brief presence in the next paddock was a coincidence, not a cause of your mare's rearing. It's far more likely that the problem has to do with the shift from arena work to trail work, with all that this implies about longer sessions, harder footing, and leaving the security of the farm.

Your mare is trying to tell you something. In my experience, "I'm in pain," and, "I'm frightened," are the most frequent reasons for rearing. Listen to her and bring in some experts who may be able to listen more closely and hear more accurately. Have your vet look at your mare in case there is a specific physical problem. I also suggest, in the strongest possible terms, that you bring in someone who is good at evaluating tack suitability and fit.

If I can leave you with one thought about horses and training, I'd like it to be this: Horses that seem to be saying, "No" are almost always really saying, "It hurts!" or, "I'm afraid!" or, "I don't understand what you want." Base your training on that, instead of on the idea that your horse has some complex psychological plan based on human thought and motivation. If this response has seemed stern, it was intended as such. Your horse is hurting, and you or your trainer will get badly hurt if you don't start dealing with the cause of the problem.

Buying a Rearing Horse for a Beginner

Q My sister is looking at an eight-year-old horse to use as a trail horse for her husband. The horse is an Appaloosa gelding that has been used in the park service on trail rides in the mountains. My sister events at novice level and has some dressage experience. She wanted to work with the horse this weekend and noticed that when the horse was by himself he did not want to leave the barn. She tried five or six times to move the horse away from the barn, and on the last try the horse evaded by rearing. My sister did not know if this was a habit or a freak occurrence. The horse does not like any kind of contact with the bit. I recommended that my sister have the horse's teeth checked, but she does not want to put a lot into this horse unless he proves to be safe for beginners. Is there a way to know if a horse habitually rears? Is there anything she could safely try to see if this horse uses rearing as its evasive technique?

A   This is really several questions in one. First, would this horse be a good trail horse? Second, why is he rearing? Third, can he be convinced not to rear? Fourth, is he likely to suit a beginner rider?

If this horse has been a satisfactory trail horse with the park service, that's a good sign. Your sister should talk with the horse's regular rider/handler and find out whether the horse is regarded as a good trail horse or just a barely acceptable one — after all, he *is* for sale, and it would be good to know why. She should enlist the rider/handler's help to try this horse, and if he is unwilling to ride, that will be a bad sign. In addition, you need to determine whether the horse is a good trail horse for a beginning rider, as not all horses are well suited to beginners.

If the horse is very barn-sour, as he would tend to be if he hasn't been ridden for some time, he is likely to do just about anything that will keep him from leaving his "safe" place. This includes balking, backing, rearing, and bolting back to the barn when the rider gets him away from it. It's obnoxious, but not unusual, especially if the horse hasn't been ridden for a while or is used to going out in the company of others. If the horse just lifts up slightly on his hind legs as opposed to going straight up in the air, I wouldn't think that this is necessarily a habit.

First, check the horse over — teeth, tongue, back, legs, and feet — just in case there is some physical reason for his behavior. Then check his equipment; a painful bit or a badly fitting saddle or one with a broken tree can cause a horse to rear or even fall over. If the horse seems fine and the tack isn't causing any

Moving the horse forward and down can interrupt an impending rear.

problems, your sister should ask to see him ridden at the barn and away from the barn. Ideally, she could ride another horse on the trail and watch this horse under another rider, preferably his usual rider. The horse should also be ridden with his usual saddle, bridle, and bit.

By the way, whenever you are looking at a horse to buy, it's always useful to see him under his regular rider. If the rider is reasonably competent and the horse goes badly, you may save yourself a potentially dangerous trial ride.

If your sister likes the way the horse goes with his regular rider, she should then try him herself (wearing an approved safety helmet, with the harness fastened) and take him on the same trail, again in his regular tack. That will give her a good idea of how he reacts. If he is calm and quiet, she can deliberately spend some time riding like a beginner and find out how the horse reacts to an unbalanced rider, conflicting signals, and so forth. If she still likes the horse, she should put her husband on him (in a confined area, wearing a safety helmet, and preferably with his instructor present). If everyone likes the horse at that point and your sister's husband is comfortable with the tack, it is time to call the vet and have the horse checked out.

One warning: The combination of rearing and not accepting contact from the bit is very worrying, and would make this horse unsuitable for a beginner rider — or for any rider who wants to be safe. No matter how beautiful or talented the horse, I would think twice before riding, much less buying, him. But keep in mind that a horse ridden on painful contact, especially sudden or prolonged painful contact, will often rear in protest, so rider behavior is something to consider as well. Riders who are used to riding on contact often get into trouble when they get on horses that have been

There are a lot of nice, uncomplicated horses in the world, and your sister has only one husband.

ridden Western and taught to go behind the bit, on a loose rein. These horses don't understand what the riders want if they try to get direct hand-to-bit contact through the reins. The rider thinks he is asking for contact; the horse thinks he is being punished for moving forward and that the rider wants him to run backward or rear. That's another good reason to watch the horse as he's ridden by his regular rider. It gives you a chance to see how the horse moves and reacts, and how he is accustomed to being ridden.

If the horse is basically quiet and well trained but has had a bad or inconsiderate rider recently and needs some retraining, this can probably be achieved. But is it worth the time, effort, and expense? And will the horse be suitable for a beginner, even after retraining? If the horse is injured, sick, or has been ridden badly for so long that he dislikes the whole idea of being ridden, I would look for another horse, one better suited for a beginner. In addition to having the vet look at the horse, it would be a good idea to bring her instructor or her husband's instructor, or both, out to see the horse work and give their opinions — after all, if she buys the

If this rider were leaning back and raising her hands, she would risk pulling the horse over backward. The way out of a rear is forward.

horse, those people are going to be working with him. There are a lot of nice, uncomplicated horses in the world, and your sister has only one husband. Safe is always better than sorry. If she decides to buy this horse, it should be on the basis of as much solid professional advice as she can get.

Novice Rider Needs Help with Rearing Horse

Q I bought my gorgeous, sound, athletic Thoroughbred last October. He is an excellent horse in many ways and full of potential. Unfortunately, the people who sold him to me "forgot" to mention that he rears when frightened or angry. Of all the nasty habits, this has to be the worst a horse can have. I probably wouldn't have bought him if I'd known, and there was no indication of this trouble until two weeks after I'd brought him home. He has pulled this on three different riders now, today being the worst.

It started with a gravel truck unloading just outside of our lesson ring. He freaked out, spooked, reared fairly high, humped up his back, and bolted. The gravel truck that caused the spook stayed there, and it took me too long to calm him down, so by that time it was too late to punish him. My trainer said this was a mistake, and I agreed.

My trainer is suggesting that after he has reached the peak of rearing and is at a lower angle, grab the mane and one rein and pull him around so that he cannot repeat the rear and at the same time give timely discipline. This I agree on. Turning his head around is an old trick to arrest forward movement and gain control. Unfortunately, it was the last thing on my mind today, and I feel like a failure.

I would love it if this were a situation that I could set him up for and have a professional on his back. But these are unpredictable events. What other techniques are there, and what would you have done in the same situation? Also, selling is out of the question.

A This is a serious problem, and if you have a good go at it and can't solve it, my suggestion, regrettably, would be to get rid of the horse. Rearing is perhaps the single most dangerous habit a horse can develop, and it isn't worth risking your life. I commend your determination to work through this, but if that proves impossible, please consider your own safety. Having said that, though, there are some tricks that you can try. First, before anything else, have the horse's teeth checked, just in case there's something causing mouth pain. Check his bit for fit and suitability. Similarly, check the saddle fit; it's possible for a horse to be comfortable in ordinary riding, then hump his back in fear and hurt himself, and then rear because of the pain. It's always best to begin by investigating and eliminating all possible physical causes of a behavior problem.

Your trainer's suggestion was absolutely correct. When a horse goes up, you can only bring him back down onto all four feet by immediately sending him forward and into a turn. This has three effects. First, it shifts the weight of the horse's forehand to one side, and he will naturally try to put his front feet down to balance his weight. Second, it puts his attention on you, because you aren't just yelling at him, you are telling him to do something. Third, it's a distraction. Often, a horse taken sharply sideways and forward will put his front feet back down and forget that he was thinking about rearing. You *do* need to think "forward," though. Whether you're preventing or stopping a rear, you must ask and allow your horse to move forward. Far from being part of the problem, forward movement is an essential part of the solution.

Prevention is the best cure. Anticipate situations that will frighten your horse and be instantly aware of the sounds and sights that will make him anxious, and then keep him very busy. This works by keeping him occupied, listening to you, and thinking about what you are asking him to do. He can only think of one thing at a time — which is precisely why he forgets about you when he spooks. Additionally, what you are asking him to do can be helpful in avoiding a rear. A horse can't rear if he's moving forward.

When a horse rears under saddle, there is always that brief moment before the rear when he must stop and shift his balance backward onto his hind legs. If this happens, send him forward and into a turn, just as your trainer suggested. Lean forward, loosen your outside rein, and take your inside rein quite low, bringing his nose in the direction of (but not all the way to) your knee. At the same time, use your legs strongly to send the horse forward. The result should be a circle in the direction of your low inside hand. Again, put your weight and his onto his forehand and take his head and neck to the side while sending him forward. He can't rear until he has both hind legs together underneath him, and he can't get them there if he is moving forward into a turn or a circle.

You've probably heard the saying "When in danger or in doubt, run in circles, scream and shout." I'm going to suggest a variation of this for you and your horse, because going forward and turning in a circle is a time-honored way to

A rearing horse can lose his balance and fall over backward.
This type of fall is every rider's nightmare.

discourage rearing, and because a scream, shout, or loud buzzer noise can be a significant distraction for your horse.

When in danger or in doubt, try shoulder-in! It's an ideal movement for the purpose, since you can bend him toward or away from the source of his fear and yet keep him energetically moving forward. Any good bending or lateral work will make rearing physically difficult; with his body bent and his inside hind leg stepping under his midline, he's balanced correctly to do a lot of different things, but rearing isn't one of them.

If your horse spooks and rears before you can prevent it, immediately lean forward, loosening the reins and stretching your arms around his neck, and get ready to kick your feet out of the stirrups if an emergency dismount becomes necessary. Weighting his forehand like this may send him down and forward or it may not, but at least it will make it more difficult for him to rear straight up, and very difficult for him to go over backward.

You must be sensitive to what the horse is doing and thinking and keep your focus on him and on the information he is giving you. It's much easier to avoid a rear than it is to deal with one that's in progress.

Whatever you do, do not sit back, lift your hands, or pull on both reins; this just makes it easy for the horse to rear, and, in fact, encourages him to rear. He will also be more likely to go over backward. If you feel him going up high enough that he is likely to go over backward, take your feet out of the stirrups immediately, lean forward with both arms around his neck, and slide off to one side. If your horse does go over backward, you do not want your body to be pinned between him and the ground.

The keys to all of this are knowledge, planning, and focus. You must know what is involved in a rear and in what position the horse must place himself to be able to rear. You must have a plan so that you can act without hesitation at the very moment that the idea of rearing comes into the horse's mind. And you must be sensitive to what the horse is doing and thinking and keep your focus on the horse and on the information he is giving you, so that you will sense that tiny hesitation and send him forward into a turn before the rear actually happens. It's much easier to avoid a rear than it is to deal with one that's in progress.

Rearing Horse, Novice Rider

Q I have a nine-year-old Thoroughbred gelding that hadn't been ridden for a while before I got him. I'm schooling him, but I have a problem: If he doesn't want to do something, he rears. He's already fallen on me once and I don't want a repetition of that. I have tried some basic leg-yield exercises and I would like to teach him a rein-back. But how do I go about doing this? I give him the correct aids, but no such luck. I don't want to argue with him in case he goes up.

A Please do not ride this horse until you can get a good instructor or trainer to come out and help you with him. Rearing is one of the most dangerous things a horse can do. If he's already fallen over backward on you, you're lucky to be in one piece! Find someone who is qualified and trains kindly and correctly, and make an appointment for that person to come do an evaluation. It will cost you a little money in the short term, but it may save your life in the long term.

Before you work with the horse, even with help, have the veterinarian look at him. Not even the best trainer in the world will be able to help you if your horse is rearing because he's in pain. Tell the veterinarian what has been happening, and ask him to check the horse thoroughly, particularly his mouth (teeth, tongue, bars, and cheeks), his back, and his feet. Show the veterinarian your tack, tack up the horse, and ask him to evaluate the fit and suitability of your saddle and bit. If there's a piece of equipment that's hurting the horse, you won't be able to put the horse's behavior right until you've taken away the pain and whatever caused it. A harsh or an ill-fitting bit can cause a great deal of pain, as can a saddle with a broken tree, a saddle that doesn't fit the horse's back, a cheap or badly made saddle that doesn't fit any horse's back, or a perfectly nice saddle that fits well but is placed incorrectly on the horse's back (too far forward is very common). And sore feet can make any horse reluctant to move forward.

While the vet is there, tell him about the horse's living conditions, diet, and exercise program. Even a quiet, naturally docile horse can become agitated and out of control if he is overfed and kept in a stall. If this is the case with your horse, you might have a much easier time if he were fed according to his workload and allowed to live in a field.

If the vet finds a physical cause — or suggests a drastic change in management — don't do anything else until you've made the changes. If the vet can find nothing wrong anywhere, call the trainer, explain what you've just done, and confirm that appointment!

When you have someone to help you, and you are both wearing your helmets (that meet current ASTM/SEI or BSI standards), you can begin checking other possibilities.

The rein-back is the *last* thing that you or anyone else should be trying to teach this horse right now. His problem is a lack of forward movement — when you ask him to move, you want him to go forward, not up, and certainly not over backward. Leave the rein-back off your list of things to do with this horse. Don't even think about it until the rearing problem is fixed.

In fact, if you keep this horse, I would stop riding and go back to basics. Groundwork, longeing, and long-lining are indicated here. Take your time, make everything clear to the horse, and train him from the ground up, as though he were a green three-year-old just up from the farm. You're going to have to begin again and establish — nicely — who is in charge of whom! It sounds as though the horse is in charge right now, and he's probably not very happy about that. Horses prefer to follow; they would like *you* to be the leader.

Repeating aids that he doesn't understand will simply make him frustrated — just as you would be frustrated if someone were shouting at you in a language you didn't know.

You have no way of knowing what your horse's past experiences have been or what his expectations are — he may think that you want him to rear. You've said that you don't want to argue with him, but he may think that when he rears and you stop telling him what to do, it's because rearing is the behavior you wanted.

It's also quite possible that he doesn't know as much as you think he does. When you give him the correct aids and he doesn't respond, consider the possibility that he doesn't know what they mean. Horses aren't born knowing the aids; they have to be taught what the aids mean and what responses the rider wants from each aid and combination of aids. Repeating aids that he doesn't understand will simply make him frustrated — just as you would be frustrated if someone were shouting at you in a language you didn't know. If the shouting continued and you couldn't get away, you would probably do one of two things: ignore it entirely or react violently, hitting or pushing the person who was shouting. So you can understand what the horse may be feeling.

You can't know or change his history, so what you will have to do is create a new history, beginning *now*. You can do this if you are willing to invest the time and effort, and if you truly feel that it is worth the risk. Think hard before you decide to keep a horse that needs retraining, that has a dangerous habit, and that frightens you. Riding should be enjoyable, and you would be better off with a horse that is well-trained and fun to ride. You can't learn or improve while you are tense, and you won't be able to relax on a horse you don't trust. There is no shame in being sensible and giving up a horse with this sort of problem. And there's something else to consider: Even with a "normal" horse, training is an art, and my impression is that you are not yet experienced enough to be training a horse, let alone one with a dangerous problem. You will gain that experience in time, but you need to learn on more suitable animals.

I understand that you don't want to waste this horse's potential, but what worries me is his potential to hurt you. Horses generally develop characteristic resistances (usually for good cause, but that's no comfort to you when you're in the hospital!) and revert to those resistances when they are frightened, hurt, or in new situations. I would worry that this horse, even in the hands of a very experienced, kind, and competent professional, would revert to this behavior at a show or on the road.

Many trainers are unwilling to take on a horse that rears and goes over backward, because they know exactly how serious this problem is and how dangerous it is for the rider.

There are many nice horses in the world, and many horses with good potential. It would be great for you to live long enough to enjoy a series of nice horses, and someday have the pleasure of training a nice young horse of your own.

CHAPTER 13

In the Stall

HORSES THAT MISBEHAVE in stalls can be very frightening to their owners and handlers. In most cases, the misbehavior is the result of poor training or lack of training and can be remedied by a patient handler who is willing to fill the gaps in the horse's education. It isn't always easy to deal with the so-called "vices of confinement," but horses' behavior can be changed, provided that their owners are patient and that they understand that the key word is not "vices," but "confinement." It's important for horses to learn how to behave in stalls, but it's equally important for their owners to understand that a natural, comfortable, healthy environment for a horse involves open spaces and freedom of movement.

Crowding

Q My horse likes me so much that he tries to be right next to me, and sometimes he just about jumps on top of me. He's not a mean horse, but sometimes he steps on my feet or bumps my head really hard just because he's trying to get so close to me. He does this when I go in his stall and when I groom him and lead him. It makes me happy that he likes me so much, but it hurts when he steps on me.

A There can be several reasons for horses wanting to get too close to you. A nervous horse that sees you as a source of comfort and security may try to get as close to you as possible or even hide behind you. A horse that has learned to see you as a treat dispenser may crowd you in an effort to get more treats. If the horse has never been taught to respect the personal space of humans, he may crowd you because he can; by making *you* move away, he asserts his dominance over you. Or, as in your case, a horse can just be very happy to see you and not have any idea that you don't want him right on top of you. Some horses haven't had the benefit of being well brought up in a herd; some were taken away from their dams and put into stalls at a time when they should have been learning manners from their mothers and other mares in the herd. Some — usually the worst behaved of all — were orphans that were hand-raised by well-meaning humans who felt sorry for the foal and didn't teach it any manners.

The problem is that no matter what the horse's reason for crowding you, being crowded is dangerous. You've already noticed the effect on your toes and your head.

If you were a horse, you would nip, kick, and shove to show a gauche youngster exactly when he had trespassed into your personal space. Since you're not a horse, you need some other method — and a piece of equipment — to help you make the same point. A short whip with a thick, solid butt is an ideal tool for this job. Carry it with you at all times, because you'll be using it whenever you lead this horse. You don't have to use a whip, of course; as long as the implement is reasonably rigid and the end is solid but not sharp; you could use anything, including your grandfather's old cane or a piece of smooth, splinter-free wood. (If you've forgotten your whip and you're bringing your horse in from pasture, you can use your elbow as a substitute. Hold it out so that if the horse crowds you, the contact will be his shoulder to your elbow, not his foot on your toe.)

By keeping the whip horizontal, with the butt end toward the horse, you can teach the horse to maintain a respectful distance. Hold the whip so that the horse won't come into contact with it unless he crowds you, and then lead your horse around the farm, turning in both directions, letting the horse run into the end of the whip whenever he begins to crowd you.

As the horse learns to respect your space, you'll be able to teach him to respond to a light tap with the end of the whip, accompanied, if you like, with the spoken word, "Over." This will improve your comfort and safety, help your horse learn to be

This handler is in a good position to keep control of the horse and stay safe.

led much more efficiently, and lay a foundation for work that you will do later when you teach your horse to move his hindquarters away from pressure.

If you teach your horse turn on the forehand, turn on the haunches, and sidepass from the ground, you'll have a better mannered horse, and later you'll find it much easier to teach him those same skills under saddle.

Cornered by Horse

Q I was caught in a bad situation the other day. My young colt, Nic, trapped me in a corner of the paddock. Normally, this would not be a concern to me, but I could tell by the way Nic was approaching me that he had other things on his mind; he was waving his head and started to rear. I truly believe he had no intention to harm me, and I think he just wanted to play. He is not even two years old yet. This is the second time it happened. I had to hit his shoulder with my crop a few times to get him to stop. I prefer not to hit him, but if I didn't I could have been seriously hurt. I need suggestions.

A Nic probably doesn't have evil intentions, but his intentions don't matter; it's his behavior that you have to change. You have several things going on at once: Nic is full of energy and needs exercise; he is a young horse who needs the company of other horses (horses are social animals and they need to play with one another); and he is approaching you as he would approach a peer, not as he would approach the alpha horse in his herd. He needs to learn that rearing and pawing at you are simply not acceptable.

The first problem is easily solved if you can find a way to provide Nic with more exercise. He's a bit young for longeing, but you could certainly take him for walks in hand. You'll be very fit, and he'll be less bored.

The second problem is trickier. The horse is a gregarious animal by nature and requires companionship. If you can't find another horse or large pony to share the field with Nic, consider bringing in a small pony or a goat.

The third problem is one that you will have to solve by reminding Nic that you are the leader of this particular two-member herd. He must be taught to respect your space, but you can't afford to put yourself in danger while he is learning that he can't play colt games with you.

Carry a whip whenever you go into the enclosure, and use it if he crowds you (push the handle end against his chest or shoulder). Tell him "No" very clearly or make a noise like the wrong-answer buzzer on game shows. It works very well. Then if he backs off and settles down, just go about your business as usual.

If the noise isn't enough, make the noise and bump him hard in the chest with the handle end of the whip. You don't want to lift it high and hit him with it, because a hit on his rear will provoke a kick and a hit on the chest or neck will make him think that you are doing your best to rear and play the game he wanted to play in the first place! If you do have to smack him in the chest with the whip, bring it across at him, not down on him.

Nic is approaching you as he would a peer, not as he would approach the alpha horse in his herd.

When you work around Nic, stand tall and move in a determined way — make your body language slow and clear, and let him know that you expect him to move out of your way. Playing with you, rearing, leaning on you, and crowding into your personal space are all behaviors that, if allowed, will cause Nic to think that he outranks you. This is an attitude he must change as soon as possible; you don't

In horse language, crowding and shoving means, "This space is mine."

want to be dealing with a larger, heavier, more mature Nic who still thinks that you are subordinate to him.

Don't worry that reprimanding Nic will make him stop liking you. In fact, he'll be a happier horse if he knows where the limits are and what he is and is not allowed to do. It's a small herd, but that doesn't make him your equal. You can be dominant without being aggressive, and that's what you have to do if you want Nic to be a good horse and a happy follower. This isn't just about you and Nic, either. You want him to learn how to behave around humans so that he doesn't frighten them and make them feel that they should punish him. Your vet and farrier will appreciate your efforts.

Sweet Horse Getting Mean

Q I am fourteen years old and have been riding in lessons and at summer camp for three years. For the last two years at camp, I rode a horse called Starlight. He was my ideal horse. At the end of camp last summer, my parents bought him for me and had him shipped to our farm. I was so excited. Now I don't know if it was a good idea. I still love Starlight, but I just can't control him.

He rears a lot when he is turned loose to play (he gets an hour of turnout to play in a paddock every morning). Then when I ride him, he jumps around when we go on the trail and he tries to run home. Now I am only riding him in the fenced ring instead of on the trail, because I am nervous that he will rear when I am riding him. Sometimes he gets very light in front and sort of bounces, and I am pretty sure his front feet are off the ground, but he doesn't stand up straight like he does when he rears in his paddock. I am starting to get scared of him, and I don't want to be scared of my best friend.

I thought that he would be happy living with me, but maybe not. He was great for the first month, but then he started to get cranky. I don't understand why. He gets his stall cleaned two times a day here, and the alfalfa hay and sweet feed are much better than the camp feed; they only fed oats and their hay was old grass. He has gained weight since September and looks shiny and beautiful. He is fifteen years old.

I can't ride him for a month or two because we got too much snow and there is ice in the arena, so he just goes out every day for his turnout time, even though it is very cold. I am very worried that in the spring he will be too hard for me to handle if he acts like he did last month. What can I do? It's not like he is cranky because of too much work. At camp he was in lessons and on the trail for about five hours most days. I only ride him for one hour. I have already checked his saddle, and it fits fine. His bridle is the one he had at camp and it fits too, as does the bit. Do you think he misses camp and his friends? My parents say this is silly, but they never saw how sweet he was at camp. They think this is his normal personality, but I know it isn't how he usually is.

A I think you can change Starlight back to his sweet self without too much trouble. You're trying to do everything to make him comfortable and happy, but that's just the problem: You're doing too much! Your story is a very familiar one. Your horse isn't turning into a monster; in fact, his personality probably hasn't changed at all, but he's having difficulty dealing with the changes in his life.

If someone wanted a guaranteed-to-work formula to make a nice, quiet horse into a maniac, the easiest method would be to increase the horse's feed intake and protein level dramatically while dramatically decreasing the horse's usual amount of exercise. Does this sound familiar?

Starlight, at age fifteen, was doing very well on a steady regimen of low-protein, high-roughage hay and a handful of oats. He was getting lots of steady exercise — not hard work, but exercise — for four or five hours a day, probably including two hours of walk-trot lessons with a bit of cantering and two or three hours of walking on the trail. Now that he's a privately owned horse instead of a summer-camp horse, everything has changed. He's getting much more feed and at least twice the amount of protein he was used to, and his exercise is limited to a single hour of turnout in a paddock and one hour of riding once a day. If he's making you nervous, you probably aren't even riding him for a full hour. The combination of more and higher-protein feed and a drastic reduction in his physical activity level is creating the problems you're experiencing.

Begin by changing two things: Starlight's diet and his exercise routine. Find some grass hay. If you can't, find some mixed hay with a high proportion of grass. Stop buying sweet feed and use whole oats instead — and use them sparingly. A cup or two of oats with his alfalfa may even help, because the oats are actually lower in protein than the alfalfa. If Starlight has lots of grass hay, he'll get his nutrition and stay busy longer each day. It takes much longer for a horse to eat ten pounds of grass hay than ten pounds of alfalfa.

If you don't already weigh your hay, start doing this. A flake of grass hay is not the same as a flake of alfalfa, so if you're feeding alfalfa by volume, you're compounding the problem. A "big fat" flake of grass hay may weigh five pounds and look much larger than a thinner flake of alfalfa, but if you weigh them, you may be surprised to find out how heavy that flake of alfalfa is. Your horse needs the roughage and the chewing time, not the high-octane fuel.

Change Starlight's exercise program, too. There's no reason he should be in his stall all day and night if you have a turnout paddock for him. Let him use the paddock! If it's attached to the stall or a run-in shed, so that he can find shelter in really bad weather, let him have full-time access to the paddock. If the paddock is a separate turnout area without shelter, turn him out there for at least

High protein feeds are like high octane fuel and can 'supercharge'
a horse and make him difficult to handle.

four or five hours at a time, on as many days as you possibly can. Since this is your family farm, you may want to talk to your parents about arranging full-time turnout with a shelter for Starlight. If he can exercise freely all the time, he'll stay healthier and you'll both be happier.

I don't think that Starlight is pining for the summer camp. He probably enjoys living on your farm, and I'm sure he enjoys all the focused attention. But if you can manage him in conditions a little bit more like the conditions at camp — lower-protein feed and a lot more exercise — you'll find that your horse will become sweet again.

Don't worry when you see him rearing and bucking and bouncing around in his paddock. It's just a sign of excess energy, and you'll see less of it as his feeding and exercise programs begin to match his actual needs. Horses that are overfed and under-exercised do tend to explode into frantic activity when they are turned out; horses that are fed appropriately and permitted many hours of turnout every day may dash around for the first few moments when they are turned out, but will quickly settle down and graze, roll, or wander around and doze in the sun.

By trying to make Starlight's life perfect for him and by trying to make everything better at your farm than it was at camp, you've supercharged your horse! Now let him relax and just enjoy his new home, without the excess feed and more exercise. You'll both be happier, and by spring, you should once again have the horse you fell in love with.

Winter Stall Behavior

Q Bubba is a nine-year-old Quarter Horse gelding. I have had him for one year. He is awesome with me or with other adults, but quirky with other horses. He prefers to be by himself — he doesn't want other horses paddocked with or next to him, stalled next to him, standing next to him, and so forth. There is no horse that he likes or prefers, yet he is a gentleman with adults and children.

Last winter he was at another farm. The place was very small, with horses crammed into the barn and paddocks and open stalls through which other horses could stick their heads in his stall. To make a long story short, he almost took the place down by kicking out doors, walls, beams — you name it.

In February, I moved him to a place where he has his own paddock alone, has a very large stall with metal bars around the front so no one can bother him, and high wood walls on either side so he really can't directly see anyone next to him. His caretakers are conscientious, observant, and know their stuff. From February through the summer, the stalls on both sides of him were empty. An additional boarder arrived midsummer and was put into the stall on Bubba's left side. No problem.

But toward the end of the summer, this new horse taught all the others — Bub included — how to chew/crib fences. It was a passing phase for everyone else — except Bub. He really likes it, so now he wears the Weaver Miracle Collar during the day.

December must be the magical month, because Bubba increased his cribbing to include his stall walls, *and* he has begun to kick in his stall. This place is constructed well, but he certainly is making dents. Another boarder is now in the stall on the other side of him, and Bubba is kicking the walls on both sides.

There are observable changes during winter, not because of the season, but because of the confinement that horses often experience during that time.

I cannot find the source of angst that led him to begin cribbing and kicking, and I am feeling stupid. Bubba gets an appropriate amount of food, and he is meaty but not fat. I ride four times a week. Rides alternate from arena work, conditioning by a local lake, and trail riding where we sometimes do our flat work and other times just plod along. I sometimes ride alone and other times ride with someone else. Bubba likes being ridden. I groom him almost every night, and he seems to like that, too. He is not crabby under saddle, but he is increasingly crabby with something in his environment.

This is a small farm. When they are full, there are only five horses. The people who run it are low-key and safety-conscious. Bubba cannot be stressed from a crazy environment, such as a large show barn. I've been taking his temperature every night and before and after riding. It is completely normal. I have sent a urine sample in to the lab just to rule out a urinary tract infection.

My husband and I have been discussing offering to pay for arena lighting so that I can ride five to six nights a week. It does seem that when I ride, he is less

Some horses react to confinement by kicking the walls of their stalls.

agitated later on. I have also ordered some flower essences. I'm willing to try anything — especially something that is all natural.

The barn owners suggested that Bubba may have winter behavioral issues, as his kicking occurs more during this time of year. They are very patient with him and with me, but I do not want him to injure himself. I also don't want him doing damage to someone's property. Am I missing something? What can be going on?

A I can't tell you exactly what is happening, but I can make some suggestions. First, I'll assume that you've ruled out that urinary tract infection, and that his blood work is normal.

Winter behavior isn't different from summer behavior, because horses are horses regardless of the season. With breeding-age, intact animals, spring and summer are the seasons that are generally associated with behavior changes, but there is no increase in sex-hormone production in winter.

However, there are observable changes in many horses' behavior during winter, not because of the season, but because of the confinement that horses often experience in winter. This isn't a seasonal issue; it's a horse management issue, and the same behavioral changes could be produced at other seasons if caretakers restrict a horse's activities.

Confinement isn't natural to horses. The combination of confinement and overfeeding is even less natural, and yet this is what many horses experience in winter. Instead of turnout and free-choice hay, they are shut in stalls and fed higher levels of concentrates. In this situation, they have a great deal of energy and no way to dissipate it through play or work. The days are shorter, the nights are longer, humans aren't around as much, and there's less to do and less to see in the barn. But horses' sleeping patterns don't change — they are still awake for roughly twenty hours of every twenty-four.

You'd be surprised to see how infrequently a horse will choose to spend time in a shed in winter weather, given the choice between shed and pasture.

During these twenty hours, confined horses can exhibit a variety of annoying habits, such as kicking, cribbing, and weaving. These are called *stall vices,* which simply means that they are the result of confinement. This isn't unique to horses, by the way. Weaving can be observed at any zoo in which animals are kept in very small, non-stimulating areas. The constant pacing of zoo elephants and big cats is a reaction to confinement. And small children confined to cribs and given no attention will similarly develop vices of confinement — rhythmic head-banging, for instance.

The best solution for your horse would probably be full-time turnout with free-choice hay. If he is extremely territorial about his stall and this is causing problems for the barn owners, perhaps he's better off without a stall in the barn. If he really objects to the presence of other horses, a field and shed of his own would seem to be the ideal solution. If the weather is horrible, put a rug on him for the worst, wettest, windiest days. You'd be surprised to see how infrequently a horse will choose to spend time in a shed, given the choice between shed and pasture.

Flower essences probably won't do your horse any harm, but I think it's his physical being that is agitated, not his mental or spiritual self. In my experience, many flower essences are more helpful to the rider than to the horse, and I suspect that the alcohol content may have something to do with the relaxing effect on the rider. Horses are intelligent and sensitive beings, but they aren't unduly complicated ones, and putting them into situations that are good for their bodies and minds will usually sort out their spiritual sides as well.

See what you can do about your horse's management. Since you have cooperative caretakers, ask if they will help you with feed and exercise issues. A nine-year-old Quarter Horse that is being ridden very lightly is a horse that probably needs no grain at all, unless the hay is nutritionally deficient in some way. Hay, water, and salt should take care of his needs, and enough hay will also serve to keep him warm and occupied.

If full-time turnout in a larger paddock or field is not possible, perhaps you could arrange with the barn manager to have your horse turned out in the riding arena (with hay, of course) at night. Even this much freedom can make an immense difference.

Horse Aggressive about Food

Q I have a 10-year-old mare that I bought a few months ago. When we feed her, she becomes very aggressive toward our other mare. We feed them separately in their stalls to avoid any problems outside, but she can also become very protective of her feed — even toward me if I bother her while she is eating in her stall.

Yesterday, I was just watching her eat and talking to her, to see if I could show her I wasn't after her food. She threw a kick in my direction and hit the water bucket, destroying the bucket. I'm glad I was outside of the stall when she did this! I took her food away, and a few minutes later she was back to being her normal gentle self. But when I gave her back her food, she pinned her ears back against her head. This is the only time she gets this way; any other time she is a sweetheart, letting me do anything I want, but when there is food around we have to leave her alone.

A Some horses are aggressive about food because they feel that it's something they need to fight for or defend. Horses that have been brought up in large fields with good grazing and full-time access to forage are not typically as aggressive as this. I would guess that your mare has either had a previous owner who put out hay in an insufficient number of piles and let the horses battle for their feed, or was kept on a farm where grain was offered on a come-and-get-it-now-before-someone-else-eats-it basis.

Wild horses that have spent a good deal of time in Bureau of Land Management (BLM) pens are often aggressive about hay — which isn't the case with wild horses on the range or with properly raised domestic horses. This kind of food-protection aggression is clearly a behavior that the horses learned after being captured. The combination of overcrowding, limited space, and limited feed creates a hostile environment in which aggressive horses get food and timid ones don't. In such an environment, any horse can become aggressive toward other horses, and the aggression can carry over to humans later in life.

Taking her food away and giving it back is not useful. The horse cannot possibly understand that you object to her attitude about her food; she will just perceive you to be playing a cruel game with her.

You know that you have no intention of stealing your mare's food and that you wouldn't want to eat her food anyway. *She* doesn't know that, and she perceives only that there is another being hanging out in the vicinity of her dinner and that the other being must therefore be a threat, because if it didn't want her food, it wouldn't be hanging around. I know it seems very odd for a horse to pin back her ears and attempt to bite or kick you to "defend" her dinner when you've just *given* her the food, but that's precisely what happens. The food, to your horse, is her food, not something that you have kindly given her.

Taking her food away and giving it back is not useful and is more like teasing. The horse cannot possibly understand that you object to her attitude about her food; she will just perceive you to be at best playing a cruel game with her, or, at worst, trying to get her dinner.

It's not going to help to try to remind your mare that you are the "alpha horse" in this herd, because food-related aggression has nothing to do with herd hierarchy and everything to do with simple survival instinct. The best solution is simply to do what you're doing: feed in the stalls so that there are no horse fights over food and so that you can be sure of exactly how much hay and grain each horse is getting, and leave her alone to eat in peace. If the aggression is something that comes out only under certain circumstances and you can easily

A horse that is aggressive about food can extend that aggression to people.

avoid creating those circumstances, you don't have an enormous problem.

I would guess that her acts of aggression toward your other mare — which happen, you say, only when you and both mares are together — are just an extension of the food-defending aggression. The daily situation that puts you and both mares together is, after all, feeding time, so you can understand why the mare might react that way if her brain has shifted into dinner mode.

As you now know, the destruction of a water bucket doesn't take a very hard kick or even an aimed kick, but just a kick that happens to bring a hoof in contact with the bucket. The destruction of a human head or hand can take place just as easily. Stay out of this mare's way during meals. If necessary, put her feed in her manger before you bring her into the stable.

You may want to take a look at your feeding ration and routine. If your mare is working hard for several hours each day, she may actually need grain; if she isn't, she would probably be much better off on a diet of good hay. Some horses become vastly more aggressive if they are overfed. As the old ranch hands say, "Some horses just can't stand prosperity." An overfed, active horse that doesn't get enough exercise can easily become a troublemaker.

It's not uncommon for a horse to become aggressive over a limited-quantity treat, which is what grain is for most horses. It's much less common for a horse to become aggressive in the defense of one pile of hay among many piles of hay. If you find that your mare does not, in fact, need supplemental concentrates, you may be able to eliminate the aggressive behavior by keeping hay in front of her at all times. If this isn't possible, you can at least provide four or five piles of hay for your two horses. They may keep moving from pile to pile, but they are unlikely to battle over the hay as long as there is plenty for both. Eventually both horses will be adequately fed, with no danger to buckets (or human body parts).

If the aggression continues or worsens in spite of different feed and management practices, you may consider having your vet test the mare's blood. There are some hormonal problems that can make otherwise nice horses very aggressive. Sometimes a thyroid supplement is all that's needed to make an aggressive horse sweet again. Your vet can give you details and tell you whether your mare's thyroid levels are unusually low.

If you ever raise young horses of your own, you'll be able to teach them to stand back calmly and wait pleasantly while you serve their meals. Horses can be trained to step back and stand while you fill their feed tubs, but you'll need to begin their training early — something the previous owner of this mare obviously did not do. In the stall, move calmly and slowly at feeding time. Don't become aggressive yourself, but *do* take every opportunity to remind your mare that she must not enter your personal space — even when you are carrying feed to her.

CHAPTER 14

In the Stall: Boredom Breeds Vice

THE KEY WORD in the phrase "vices of confinement" is not "vices," but "confinement." The horseman's saying "Boredom breeds vice" is the equivalent of the teacher's observation that "The devil finds work for idle hands to do." Enforced boredom is bad for horses, just as it is bad for humans. Confinement to a stall is not conducive to health or happiness, but it is conducive to boredom and to the development of annoying and sometimes destructive behaviors. Bored children may twiddle their hair, bite their fingernails, or bang their heads against the wall. Bored horses may chew wood, paw their bedding into heaps (or dig holes if the stall flooring permits), kick the walls, or turn their attention to learning how to unfasten locks and latches. Imagine the frustration and destructive potential of an intelligent small child locked into a portable toilet for twenty-three hours a day, and you'll have an idea of what stall confinement means to a horse. We should not be surprised if confined horses exhibit the vices of confinement; instead, we should recognize that these unwanted behaviors are the *effects* of confinement, and act appropriately. Appropriate action does not mean punishing the horses — it means turning them out.

Pawing

Q My horse paws all the time in his stall. It's very irritating. He's also started to paw when he is on cross-ties and when he's in his stall and the other horses are being fed. I would like to get him to stop pawing, or at least to know why he does it.

A Pawing is a natural and very practical action for a horse in the wild. In winter, that's how wild horses get to the grass under the snow, and it's also how they break ice when they need to drink from a frozen stream. In summer and during a drought, wild horses will sometimes dig in dry streambeds to get water.

Domestic horses paw, too. Many horses will paw the snow in their pastures and turnouts, even if they've just been fed. If you watch a horse turned out in a drylot or a sandlot, you'll see him paw before he lies down to roll — in this case, he is digging to loosen the dirt and create a more comfortable area for rolling (and loose dirt will give him greater protection from insects).

Pawing can be a useful sign for an observant owner. Pawing is one of the signs that can indicate that a mare is about to foal. When a horse is beginning to colic, he will often paw the ground. If a horse never paws under normal circumstances, pawing should alert his owner to the possibility that something may be wrong.

Horses that paw in their stalls and on cross-ties are usually expressing their impatience and frustration, as well as the wish to move freely instead of being prevented from moving. Horses that paw in the trailer are usually expressing impatience, nervousness, or a combination of the two. Impatience makes a horse frustrated because he would like to move and can't; and nervousness makes a horse even more desperate to move.

If a horse paws in anticipation of being fed, his behavior is unintentionally rewarded.

The problem with horses pawing at feeding time is that the pawing behavior is reinforced with every feeding. The horse might begin pawing out of hunger and frustration, but even a horse that casually paws once or twice, out of sheer boredom, will quickly learn to associate the action of pawing with the consequence of getting fed. Because there is so much reinforcement for this kind of pawing, it's very difficult to eradicate the behavior. Sometimes it's not even appropriate to try, because pawing is one of a horse's more acceptable manifestations of frustration. Stall-kicking and rearing are much more dangerous to the horse and to anyone near the horse.

If the pawing is a relatively recent phenomenon, you may be able to figure out what is wrong and make some changes in your horse's environment. A confined horse is more likely to paw than a horse that's turned out in a field 24/7. A horse that is confined and overfed is more likely to paw than a horse that is merely confined. A horse that is confined without exercise is more likely to paw than a horse that is taken out for several hours of exercise each day. Pawing can be the equivalent of a child kicking the legs of his chair — a way of saying, "I'm bored. I want to go out and do something!"

Managing the horse that paws means providing appropriate feed, plenty of exercise, and as much turnout as possible. Use rubber mats under the bedding in the horse's stall so that the pawing won't produce dangerous holes in the stall floor. In fact, use rubber mats in all the areas where your horse is likely to be asked to stand for long periods — the cross-tie area, the wash rack, and the trailer, for example.

If the horse has been pawing for years, you may not be able to get him to stop. Punishing a horse for pawing takes a lot of attention and excellent timing and is probably not worth the effort. If your horse has plenty of exercise and isn't overfed, and yet continues to paw, the action may simply have become a well-established habit.

Horse Bangs Stall Door

Q I have a five-year-old Saddlebred-Thoroughbred mare, Dancer, who is just wonderful, but she has developed a bad habit and I don't know what to do. Early this spring she started banging on her stall door at feeding time. I thought she was using her foot, but my son watched her one day and said she was using her knee. Now she is doing it whenever she hears someone in the barn, not just at feeding time. I think she does it to get attention.

I was worried that she might hurt her knee or that she will start to paw the door with her foot and maybe break it. My dad has always had horses, and he

Stalled horses sometimes find noisy or destructive ways to alleviate their boredom.

said to put a tire on the inside of the door, but that hasn't stopped her, and now I am worried that she will catch her foot in it somehow. Also, he said to tie chains to her legs so that she will hit herself with the chains when she paws or kicks. I'm not sure that is a good idea. What do you think?

My riding teacher suggested that Dancer might be bored. She has a nice stall and can see the rest of the barn through the front, which has bars halfway up, so I don't know if this is true. Also, she goes outside every day for at least an hour. I would like to let her stay out longer, but that's as long as I can supervise her, and I don't want her to spend time alone in a field. I don't want to get another horse because I want Dancer to look to me for friendship and fun. My riding teacher said that there are some toys that will keep horses entertained and wants me to buy one for Dancer. What do you think about that? Will a toy really help?

A From your description, I'd say that your instructor is right: Your mare is bored. One hour of turnout time is not enough; that leaves 23 hours a day for her to stand in her stall. Horses are meant to be out and about, walking, playing, eating, and staying on the move. When they are confined, kept in a way that is contrary to their nature, they *do* get bored, and they develop various ways of dealing with the boredom. Stall vices, such as this type of pawing, are often the result.

My first, last, and most important suggestion is that you manage to get this mare more turnout time. If she can spend an hour in the field, why not four hours or eight hours or, better yet, all of her time when you aren't working with her? If you're worried about her being alone, you could get her a companion; that would probably be the best thing you could do for her. Since Dancer truly does need a companion, why not adopt one that's been rescued? It doesn't have to be another horse — a pony, donkey, burro, or goat would also be a good companion for your mare.

Horses are social animals, and it isn't fair to think that the one or two hours she spends with you each day will make up for spending the rest of the day alone. Letting your mare lead a more normal life, with freedom and companionship, will make her a healthier, happier horse, and that can only make your time with her better.

Don't worry: If she enjoys your company and the work you do with her, she will still look forward to your visits and your rides. But don't try to be everything to her — you can't do it, even if you turn her out 24/7 and spend all of your time walking around the field with her. Instead of trying to be her only companion, be a good, responsible owner and do what's right for her physical and mental health.

Don't use chains on her, and don't count on tires or stall toys to make a significant difference in her behavior. You're right to worry about her pawing and kicking her stall, but by trying to figure out how to make her live in a stall without being bored, you're answering the wrong question. The right question to ask is: How can I make Dancer's life more normal *for a horse,* so that she won't be bored?

Weaving

Q At the barn where I board my horse, there is one mare that never gets out of her stall. She is what they call a weaver; she walks along one side of her stall, swaying her head, and then turns and walks back. That's all she does all day, and maybe all night, too. I thought it might mean she needed more turnout, but the owners told me that they tried turning her out and she just did the same thing along a little corner of the fence. Is there any way to cure a confirmed weaver?

A Weaving and pacing are both expressions of boredom, frustration, and a desire to be somewhere else. Over time, they can become such strong habits that even if a horse is taken out of its stall and put into a field, it will continue to weave or pace, just as this mare does.

However, it's been my experience that enough time in the field will eventually result in a return to normal walking and grazing behavior, even for a long-time weaver or pacer. Horses will generally begin weaving along a piece of fence line approximately the same length as their stall wall, then gradually make use of a larger area, and finally begin to step away from their invisible line and start to graze at least part of the time.

Enough time doesn't mean a few hours or even a few days, though. Even if the owners could arrange to have this mare turned out permanently, it may be months before you would see a significant change in her behavior.

It's well worth making the effort, though. By weaving constantly in her stall, this mare is probably damaging her legs. The constant swaying and turning puts

Early leading lessons should establish the habit of cooperation.

extra stress on the tendons and ligaments of her forelegs. But even if she's elderly and retired and no one is worried about her physical condition, she would be better off — and happier — turned out with other horses to lead a more normal, healthy life.

Should I Purchase a Cribber?

Q I found the perfect horse for me. He's a little older, bombproof, and a great trail horse, to name a few of his attributes. However, when I turned him out, he walked over to the fence and started to crib. My question is, should I purchase a great horse that is also a cribber?

A If this is a great horse, and he certainly does sound like a great horse, and if your vet likes him, don't let the cribbing stop you. You can minimize the cribbing by good management. Be prepared to keep him outdoors as much as possible, and keep hay in front of him whenever he's indoors. Don't feed a lot of grain; in fact, don't feed any grain unless he needs it. Try to meet his nutritional needs with hay. Your vet can help you work out a good nutrition program.

Habitual wood chewers can do serious damage to buildings and fences, as well as to stalls.

We used to believe that cribbers swallowed air and could become predisposed to gas colic, but it seems that this is not true. The most recent studies indicate that there is no connection between cribbing and gas colic, so we're left with two problems: wear on the incisors and over-development of some of the neck muscles. You already know that you enjoy riding this horse and feel that he's perfect for you, so it's fair to assume that the neck muscles aren't a problem. As for the worn teeth, there may come a time when your horse may need to be given a complete pelleted feed along with his hay, just to be sure that he's getting all the nutrients he needs. But this won't require a lot of extra effort on your part.

Cribbing begins as a horse's response to stress, and because the horse learns to cope with stress by producing endorphins through cribbing, he generally adopts the behavior for life. However, it's not a behavior that endangers either the horse or his owner — it's just a sometimes inconvenient behavior that annoys some owners very much and doesn't bother other owners at all. I can think of any number of behaviors I'd take much more seriously as red-flag warnings; this one really comes down to personal preference. Don't buy him if cribbing makes you crazy, but if you don't mind, he sounds like a lovely horse.

If you keep him at home, you'll need to replace a fence board from time to time. If you board him elsewhere, be sure to let the boarding-stable owners know that he cribs. Some barn owners don't allow cribbers in their barns, either because of the annoyance of having to replace boards or because they fear that other horses will "catch" the behavior. The Weaver Miracle Collar has been successful in discouraging some horses from cribbing. Some farm managers have saved their wood fencing by installing a line of electric fence six inches to the inside of the top board. Vulnerable stall edges can be trimmed out with metal. But even if you manage to protect the horse's environment from the effects of its cribbing, it may not be possible to eliminate the cribbing itself.

Horses That Chew Wood

Q I have two horses that are not cribbing, but are chewing wood fencing and trees. Immediately after finishing their hay, they begin to chew. I suspect they are chewing out of boredom, since I do not have grass in the paddocks in the winter months. I can't give them more hay than they are getting, as they are not working much. I've tried various products, but the chewing continues. Is there anything that I can put on the fence and trees to stop them? I've lost three beautiful birch trees, and I'll be replacing fence boards all summer!

A There is almost certainly more to this than boredom. Horses are grazing animals; it's their nature to eat all day and most of the night, nibbling constantly at their natural food source: low-protein, high-fiber grass. We can keep them in large fields, large paddocks, small paddocks, or stalls, and we can feed them grain at regular intervals and give them treats and supplements, but we cannot change their basic nature or the fact that their digestive system is designed to function nonstop, around the clock, processing small amounts of low-protein, high-fiber food.

You don't mention how much hay your horses are given, but I'm going to guess that it isn't enough, especially since you say they begin chewing the fence as soon as they finish their hay. It would be best if the hay were always there, so that finishing it would not be an option. Horses should always have some source of fiber in front of them: grass when there is grass, hay when the grass is gone.

I know you are worried about overfeeding your horses, but please talk to your veterinarian about this. Horses that are not in work often do very nicely without grain, but they need hay, and not just for its caloric value. Feeding

Even mature trees need protection from wood-chewers. Once a tree is 'girdled' it will eventually die.

free-choice, stemmy hay won't necessarily result in hugely fat horses, as the process of digesting hay uses up calories and produces heat. This is why horses in cold climates are fed more hay in the winter: The process of digestion is what keeps them warm. If you can't offer free-choice hay, you should be able to give a large quantity of hay several times a day, so that the horses are never without hay for very long. Grass hay is best; lucerne (alfalfa) is too high in protein to be a practical option for ad-lib feeding. Your veterinarian will be able to advise you about the types of hay available in your area.

You should feed as much hay and as little grain as possible — grain can cause digestive discomfort and ulcers, which can lead to cribbing!

Also be sure that your horses have constant access to salt. If horses are salt-deprived, they will sometimes chew on any surface that presents itself. Putting a 50-pound mineralized salt block in their field shelter is a good idea: It may help solve the chewing problem if salt deprivation is a factor, and, in any case, they need the salt.

As for the property damage, there are ways to protect your trees and fences. You can protect your trees by enclosing them in small fences, or by wrapping the trunks with chicken wire — both are common practices on horse farms.

Still, your horses should find the fence less attractive when they are getting enough hay to satisfy their need to chew. If you find that they eat the fence even when they have hay available at all times, you can also cover that top board with chicken wire — this too is done on many horse farms. Another option would be to attach a single strand of electric wire just inside the top rail; this discourages chewing. It also discourages horses from leaning against the fence in an effort to reach the grass on the other side.

CHAPTER 15

Tying and Cross-Tying

Is your horse fit to be tied? Horse owners and horse buyers tend to take it for granted that all horses can be tied and will react by standing quietly until someone unties them. This isn't always the case. Some horses are accustomed to being tied in one specific way and are deeply suspicious of other methods; some are terrified of being tied at all.

Horse Anxious in Cross-Ties

Q I am looking to buy a seven-year-old Thoroughbred for my daughters to ride in hunter classes. When he is cross-tied for tacking up, he moves around nervously and bites at everything within reach. When the girls ride him, he seems to be fine and does not spook around other horses in the arena. The trainer says that if you are standing near him and attempting to tack him up, you should bump him in the head with an elbow to keep him from biting. My daughter claims that will make him head shy, but having been on the receiving end of his habit, I feel it is either him or me. By the way, he is a gelding and about 16.3 hh, so he is not small.

I can understand one ought not beat a horse, which will make him avoid people. But the question is, how do we keep him quiet in cross-ties? My other question is, why does he behave this way? Did the previous owner do nothing about the problem? Perhaps it would be best to keep looking and just find a quieter horse. The trainer seems to feel that manners can easily be taught. If so, why has he not learned already?

A Whenever I hear about a Thoroughbred that fidgets or acts up on cross-ties, my first thought is that the horse was bred for racing and started his career at the track. Racehorses are never cross-tied. At the track, horses are tied in their stalls by a single tie. The aisles aren't used for tying, and horses that are being bathed are simply held by the lead rope.

Racehorses and ex-racehorses don't understand what is expected of them in cross-ties, and they get anxious, try to move around, and are usually punished for moving. Then they become more anxious, move around even more, get punished again, and the cycle repeats. The only way to avoid or break this cycle is to teach the horse to stand quietly in cross-ties, and that takes time and effort. Since this horse is fine under saddle, the problem seems to be limited to his behavior on cross-ties, and that's something that can be solved.

The reason this horse hasn't learned good manners on cross-ties is that he hasn't been taught those manners.

Let me explain a little about why your horse may be doing what he's doing. At the racetrack, horses are confined around the clock, fed high-energy feeds in large quantities, and spend most of their time bored half to death. In addition to the boredom, and depending on the track, the trainer, and the grooms, the horses are often handled roughly. As a result, many racehorses don't expect kind, quiet interactions with humans. When they see someone coming with brushes or tack, they snap, snarl, and fidget, and they will often try to bite or kick. When they become "civilians," their new owners

An ex-racehorse isn't used to cross-ties and may have had bad experiences being tacked up.

often assume that the horses know more than they do about saddle-horse barn manners. At the track, being tacked up means that a horse is getting out of his stall — he's going to gallop or he's going to race, and in either case, he gets very excited. This habit of dancing with anticipation often carries over to life after the track. It's not bad behavior; it's a conditioned response. You can condition a new response in its place.

Tacking up is also an uncomfortable process for many racehorses. They're bursting with energy, and a good handler can manage to tack them up quietly even while they dance around. In most cases, someone slaps the saddle on, jerks up the girth, slams a bit against their teeth, and shoves the bridle over their ears. This is painful and frightening and sets up negative expectations. Again, it's a conditioned response. And again, you can teach the horse to react differently, by showing him that your approach is different.

Your trainer is right: Manners can be taught. The reason this horse hasn't learned good manners on cross-ties is that he hasn't been taught those manners.

If you, your daughters, and the trainer are prepared to take some time and use consistent handling, here's what I suggest: First, it goes without saying that your tack should fit the horse. You won't be able to convince him that a bit, browband, girth, or saddle won't hurt if it really does hurt. Second, don't cross-tie him to tack him up. Instead tie him to something solid (a tie-ring is ideal, but a thick post can also be useful) with a fairly short lead rope, leaving just a couple of feet between his nose and the knot. For safety's sake, *always* use a quick-release knot. This is the approach to tying that will make sense to him.

Now you can begin to work on the biting problem. Your trainer is right about the elbow — but so is your daughter. Hitting the horse in the head with anything, including your elbow, will make him nervous and head shy. You should never hit a horse in the head. I'm sure that what your trainer meant was not, "Hit the horse with your elbow," but rather, "Lift your elbow so that the horse runs into it himself." You won't have to do much; just be ready so that when the horse swings his head in a genuine attempt to bite, he meets your elbow or the end of a wood-backed brush instead of flesh. At the same time, bark "No!" at him or make a loud buzzer noise. Then immediately go back to talking calmly and doing whatever you were doing. The horse needs to learn that you are kind and that he is safe, but that biting has unpleasant results. Horses have very acute hearing and very sensitive ears and muzzles, so the combination of a harsh noise and a bump on the muzzle is very effective indeed.

> *Discipline — the same sort his mother would have given him when he was a foal — tells him, "This behavior is not allowed." Anger tells him, "You're a bad, wicked horse, I hate you, and you're in big trouble forever."*

Remember that if you do have to discipline him, teach him what's not acceptable by letting him run into something hard; don't punish him by hitting him. There's an enormous difference, and horses are quick to sense it. Discipline — the same sort his mother would have given him when he was a foal — tells him, "This behavior is not allowed." Anger tells him, "You're a bad, wicked horse, I hate you, and you're in big trouble forever." In the first instance, he'll feel more secure, knowing the boundaries. In the second, he will become frightened and resentful and eventually panic — and you don't want a 16.3-hh frightened, resentful, or panicked horse on your hands. Biting can't be allowed. Making faces *can* be allowed. Your horse should learn the difference.

By being kind and firm (not tentative; many Thoroughbreds are very ticklish!), and by moving slowly, talking in a low voice, and feeding an occasional treat while being very careful to tack up as painlessly as possible, you can teach this horse that he doesn't have to anticipate discomfort. If you wait for him to lower his head for the bridle, slide the bit into his mouth without hitting his teeth, and gently put the headstall over his ears — and then do it this way every time — you'll be surprised at how calm he can become.

Take a week to tack up the horse and simply take him out for a short walk in hand. Pat him, give him a few treats, and put him away again. You're creating a new set of associations in his mind: Tack doesn't have to mean excitement, speed, or going to work; it can mean going for a walk, eating some grass and an apple, and going back into the stall or back into the pasture.

Once you've worked with the horse on the single tie as described above, then you can begin to teach him how to stand on cross-ties — just as you would teach a young, untrained horse. In this horse's case, when he is calm about being tied with a single tie, you would do well to begin by cross-tying him in his stall, so that he will encounter a wall if he moves backward, before the ties tighten. If he is an ex-racehorse, being tied in his stall will seem entirely normal to him, and he will be mentally better able to accept the cross-ties. Keep everything calm, happy, and comfortable, build up a new set of associations with the process of cross-tying, and then when he's at ease with being cross-tied in his stall, you can begin again, carefully, in the aisle. Don't worry about starting over each time — it will take less and less time at each instance, and the lesson will stay with him for life. Do remember that someone should remain with your horse at all times when he is tied, no matter which method you use.

Ground Tying

Q I would like to teach my mare to ground-tie. Unfortunately, I think I've trained Molly in such a way that I may not be able to accomplish this. I've worked quite a while with her to get her to follow me at all times, and I love that she will do this without my asking. But now I want her to stay when I tell her, and she won't. I end up having to tie a rein to something, which I don't like

A horse needs a lot of training and experience before she can be relied on to ground-tie under all conditions.

to do. Is there a way to teach her, or do I need to content myself with the fact that I have a horse that tags along?

A You're right, you may have created a tag-along horse. Since Molly likes you so much, convincing her that she should not follow you may be a tough proposition, especially since she's been rewarded for following you in the past.

You're right to worry about tying her up by a rein; it's a bad idea. If she panics and pulls back, she could get hurt. Reins and bridles do break, but generally not until the horse has hurt her mouth, badly or very badly, depending on the bit you're using.

Ground-tying isn't always successful: Even horses that have been taught by one of the old cowboy systems (tying the rein to a fixed object, hobbling the horse and tying the rein to the hobbles, tying the reins to the saddle horn to pull the horse's head in) generally figure out when they are truly tied and when they are not, and if there's grass in the vicinity, or if something frightening pops out of a cornfield, that horse will be on the move. Here again, stepping on a rein can damage the horse's mouth. Although many horses will eventually learn to carry their heads to one side so that they can move along without stepping on their reins, this isn't necessarily something you want Molly to learn.

There's another option, though. It's one that the cavalry used and many trail riders use today. When you go for a ride, instead of removing Molly's halter and lead rope, leave them on and just put the bridle on over the halter. Leave the lead rope fastened to her halter, and tie the other end of it around the base of her neck in a loose loop. The loop won't bother her, the section of lead rope connecting the halter ring to the loop won't interfere with the reins, and you'll be able to tie her by the lead rope without risking harm to her mouth. In fact, if you want to stop for lunch and let her graze comfortably, you can take off the bridle. If you find that this works well, you may want to invest in one of the combination halter-bridles that are increasingly popular with trail riders. Whatever you choose to do with your mare, you are wise to realize that her following you is the result of her training. All too often, horses are punished by humans for doing precisely what humans have taught them to do.

CHAPTER 16

Herd Behavior
and Turnout

TURNOUT IS ESSENTIAL for horse health, happiness, and sanity. It's also a great help to owners and riders who want to learn how horses think and how to communicate clearly with their horses, because horses that understand herd discipline will quickly learn human discipline. But all turnout isn't equal. Suitable turnout means safe turnout — a group of compatible horses in a safe field of appropriate size surrounded by safe fencing. Horses are individuals, and even though all horses need exercise, freedom of movement, and companionship, not all horses are compatible with one another, so turnout situations must be carefully managed to keep all of the horses healthy and happy.

Mares and Geldings Sharing a Field

Q I've decided to give my six-year-old mare, Cassie, a vacation this summer. My husband and I recently bought some property that includes common land and equestrian facilities. I think it would do Cassie a world of good to run around on a section of land and simply go on trail rides once or twice a week for a month or so. She's been in her own paddock and box stall on cold nights for the past one-and-a-half years. Cassie has always been a little spooky, and I think more turnout might help settle her down, as it seems to have helped a very high-strung Arabian that is boarded at our barn.

There are presently ten geldings on the common property. Cassie would be the only mare, at least for now. What difficulties might this cause? I know a lot of facilities keep the mares and geldings separate, and I've never fully understood why.

A You are right to want Cassie to have as much turnout as possible; horses are designed to live outdoors and move about freely, day and night. The nervous energy that many horses build up when confined (what old-timers used to call stall courage) frequently disappears when horses are allowed to live out in a field, where they can walk off their energy a little at a time.

Some mares and geldings can share a pasture peacefully,
but more often it is a recipe for trouble.

Sharing a field with geldings, however, is another matter. Although there are individual mares and geldings that can share a field, it's generally better to keep them in separate fields. Many people do keep mares and geldings separated, and for good reasons.

Some geldings are very aggressive and will attack and injure mares. Another reason to keep them apart is sexually based: Many geldings will attempt to mount mares when they come into season, and this is dangerous. Although the geldings may sustain injuries as well, especially if the mare is shod (hind shoes should be removed from any turned-out horse, by the way), most of the damage is sustained by the mare. Even if the gelding doesn't manage to penetrate the mare, he can injure her back. And if he is successful, he can cause an infection that may render the mare sterile. Sometimes you can avoid the problem by putting the mare elsewhere when she is in season, but that's not always easy to arrange, and sometimes her pasturemates will notice her receptive condition before you do.

Talk to your veterinarian about this; she'll be able to advise you. She may know of a place where mares can be turned out together. Or the managers of the common property may wish to subdivide the common land. It's quite likely that this issue will arise again and again, since many people ride mares. Partitioning the common land now will make it possible for other mare owners to turn their horses out, too.

Wild-Horse Behavior

Q I just adopted a mustang mare, and she is in my back pasture right now. I got so caught up in the excitement of seeing wild horses and wanting to give one of them a home that I didn't stop to think about how I was going to train her. I have trained my other horses (two mares and one gelding), but I have no idea how to train a wild horse.

My gelding was a rescue horse. He was abused, neglected, and only two years old when I got him. It took six months before he would trust me, then he got to where he would do anything I wanted. If it took six months for him, will it take a year for a wild horse? More than a year? I really want to train my mustang mare and teach her to trust me, but I'm afraid that she will be much more difficult than my gelding was.

A If your experience is typical, you're in for a pleasant surprise. Wild horses, brought up in herds and having spent their lives on the move, are not only clever and strong, but extremely easy to train. You'll gain the trust of your wild horse in the same way that you gained the trust of your other horses — by being clear, consistent, and kind at all times.

Your new mustang will probably be much easier to train than your gelding was. His background included confinement and abuse or neglect, and he didn't learn anything that he needed to know until you brought him home. Your mare's background is entirely different. She is already well socialized. During her life as a member of a wild herd, she learned about herd hierarchy and discipline. Thus she'll understand the idea of cooperation, and she will have a very acute understanding of equine body language. Because she has already learned so much, she'll have no difficulty learning the things you teach her.

Spend some time watching her interact with your other horses, and you'll see how observant she is and how responsive she is to subtle signals. She will be just as responsive to *your* signals once she's learned to understand them.

Horses that have grown up as part of a herd will be well socialized
and ready to accept directions and discipline.

Herd Dynamics

Q I have a mare and a gelding, both ten years old, who have lived together for about nine months. They have a dysfunctional relationship by human standards; she is mean to him, and he likes it!

Flash, a Quarter Horse gelding, and Sydney, a Quarter Horse–Arabian cross mare, live in a several-acre pasture with a good-sized three-sided shed that is divided in half, with one open stall for each. They really do like each other, as far as I can tell. They are always together, and every now and again she will rest her head on his back. They usually lie down and sleep right next to each other.

The problem is that Sydney can be mean to Flash. This usually happens when we feed them or if I go out to chat with them. When I visit, Sydney will do everything she can to keep him away from me. Flash is such a people lover that I hate to see him just hang back and not come up to me. Also, sometimes when they are hanging out and doing nothing, she will walk up to him and bite him.

When the food comes out, Sydney is right at the fence. Flash, of course, hangs back. She pins back her ears, wiggles her butt, and kicks out, frequently very high. She also chases him away. Eventually, they will eat together, but not at first. They each have their own grain bucket, and I put out a pile of hay for each of them, plus at least one neutral pile. They are always fed in the same place, and Sydney is fed first. I couldn't feed Flash first if I wanted to.

Am I projecting human emotions onto normal horse behavior? Is my gelding a happy horse even though the mare is so mean to him?

In addition, Sydney paws the ground for her food. She has done this since we got her nine months ago. As I walk to the fence with the food, I stop every time she paws. When she stops, I continue walking toward her with the food. Don't you think that after nine months she should get the picture? What else can I do, or should I leave it alone? She was a sale horse, and we do not know anything about her background. She is wonderful around people, dominant over Flash, and aggressive over food. Is she a normal mare?

A I'm happy to tell you that this is a perfectly functional relationship, horse-style. Horses are not in the least democratic; every animal in a herd has a particular place in the pecking order. When you have only two animals in a "herd," one of them is going to be dominant. In this case, it's the mare. Sydney keeps reminding Flash that *she* is the number one horse, and that's quite

The dominant horse will warn off the lower-ranking horse.

normal. They haven't been together that long; wait another year or so, and I think that they will settle down more comfortably together. Sydney will still be dominant, but she won't have to make such a production out of proving it.

I'd be pleased with those two horses, if I were you; it isn't always possible to keep mares and geldings together, but these two are working out their differences. The fact that they eat together (after Sydney reminds Flash of his place in the herd) is a good sign. Hanging out together is also good, as is resting heads on each other's backs. These are signs of companionship.

If Flash were truly frightened of Sydney, he wouldn't go near her or allow her to go anywhere near him, much less eat with her or sleep anywhere near her! He knows that it's perfectly normal for Sydney, as Boss Horse, to make threatening faces, aim kicks in his general direction, and chase him away from attention from people and from food. This is not a problem for either horse and won't be, unless you notice Sydney keeping Flash away all the time and eating all the food herself.

You've already noticed that Sydney's fussing takes place when there's something specific to fight over — when a human arrives with food, or when a human arrives to do some petting or grooming. Again, this is normal. Her background may contribute to her behavior; she may have been in situations where she had to compete for food and attention. But it's entirely possible that this is just Sydney!

Pawing means eagerness, impatience, and a wish to move forward. Pawing at mealtimes simply means, "I want to get to that bucket now, so hurry up!" There's no reason to punish her for this; it's basically the equivalent of a hungry baby banging on the tray of his high chair. If Sydney paws while you are grooming her or tacking her up, that's another matter, and you'll be in a position to say, "No," and tap the offending leg with a whip or your toe.

It sounds to me as though you have two very normal horses that get along well with you and each other. Enjoy!

Companion for Older Horse

Q My 20-year-old gelding, Sam, hasn't had the easiest life. He's had 17 owners and was always "trained" with very abusive methods, until I bought him three years ago. Because of his past, any kind of change in his situation or routine is disturbing to him. For example, I'm the only human he wants to deal with on a regular basis, and he's also particular about the horses with which he wants to be friends. Despite all this, he's a brave and reliable mount and has become my favorite horse.

Sam is currently pastured with three other geldings (ages 9, 11, and 12) who all get along reasonably well. His best friend is dominant in the herd, and for the two years they've been together, this horse has aggressively kept the other horses from picking on Sam. I've noticed lately that this horse has started bullying Sam a bit — nothing too dramatic so far, just things like jostling him to the other side of the hay bales out in the field, but it concerns me. All the other horses are much bigger than Sam, and I hate to think about what might happen to him if he starts moving to the bottom of the pasture hierarchy. I'm contemplating buying an older, smaller pony so that he and Sam can share a pasture without facing so much competition. That seems like a way to keep Sam happy and stress-free for as many more years as possible, which is my main objective!

I've noticed lately that this horse has started bullying Sam a bit — nothing too dramatic so far, but it concerns me.

It's not an easy decision, though, since Sam adores his current best buddy, and it seems cruel to separate them, especially considering how much separation Sam's already had to endure in his life. I don't know which is the right thing to do.

A donkey can make a fine companion for an only horse.

Do you have any advice for me? I love the old boy so much that I'm afraid my judgment is too clouded to see the situation clearly.

A   Sam was lucky to have found you after so many owners and so many bad experiences. I can see that you're trying to make up for his earlier experiences. Good for you!

After two years of sharing a pasture with the other three geldings, Sam should be fairly secure in his position in the herd. If the pasture is large and there is plenty of grazing and/or the hay is always distributed in piles that total at least two or three more than the number of horses in the field, then even the bottom horse is likely to be healthy and well-fed. (The bottom horse isn't at all insecure, by the way — he always knows exactly what his position is!) The most secure horses in any herd are those at the very top and at the very bottom; it's the ones in the middle that push and shove each other to see who's number five or who's number six *today*. Being at the bottom of the pecking order in a well-managed pasture isn't a bad thing. It's the change in Sam's position that is worrisome. If his status is changing, then there may be a reason for it, and that's what you'll need to investigate.

Sam is much older than the others, but that's not necessarily a reason to get picked on. In fact, older horses are often the top horses in a group. Size isn't necessarily related to whether or not a horse gets picked on, either; there are herds in which a smaller, faster, more determined horse holds the top position above more passive horses that may be two or three hands taller.

It's possible that Sam may become a little more passive as he ages, but this isn't guaranteed to happen. If I were you, I would look for another cause, probably a physical one, for the changes you may be seeing. Physical changes are important, both in themselves and because of the underlying reasons for the changes.

Has Sam lost weight recently? If it's winter where you live, don't just look at him over the fence; be sure that you run your hands over Sam to check his condition. In winter, older horses can look like teddy bears, and a heavy winter coat can disguise a significant weight loss. If he has lost weight, you may want to have his teeth checked thoroughly, review his worming program, and perhaps make some changes in his diet.

There can be other physical changes, too. Older horses can become arthritic and stiff and find it more difficult to cope with cold weather and restricted movement. Many owners of older horses are reporting good results from feed-through products such as glucosamine and chondroitin sulfate; it can't hurt to try some if you think Sam is a little stiff and uncomfortable. Twenty is not old, but horses can age more quickly if they aren't maintained well, and not all 20-year-old horses are equal. (Think about two cars: same model, same age, one poorly maintained with high mileage, and the other well maintained and with half the mileage of the other.) Since Sam has had so many owners in his 20 years, it's quite likely that there has been more wear and tear on his body than would have been the case if he had belonged to one good owner all that time.

Sometimes the first clue that a horse isn't well is that his usual companions are treating him differently.

Sometimes a horse owner's first clue that a horse isn't well is observing that the horse's usual companions are treating him differently. If Sam's pasture mates' attitudes toward him are changing, it might be a good idea to have your vet give Sam a careful examination. Sam may need more dental work, different feed, a feed supplement, or perhaps some sort of medication. Horses that are healthy and feel good can continue to be active and cheerful into their twenties and thirties, and sometimes even longer. It's possible that a session with an equine dentist, followed by a more nutritious diet, might get Sam back to normal.

Also ask the vet to check Sam's eyes. Loss of vision can make a horse timid. Sam probably has perfectly normal vision, but it can't hurt to check; it's just one more possibility to investigate.

In addition to bringing the vet out for a look, it might be helpful to bring along a friend. It can be hard for a loving, hands-on owner to notice changes in a horse, simply because seeing the horse every day can make small, incremental changes difficult to spot. Vets usually see healthy horses twice a year, which allows too many months to go by between visits. If you have a friend who knows Sam but doesn't see him as often as you do, ask him or her to come out with you every few weeks and take a look. It's always useful to have another pair of eyes.

I wouldn't shift Sam out of his established group unless there's a clear reason for doing so. If he and his best buddy are still pals and the group works well as a whole, there's no reason to separate Sam from the others. If the group is no longer working well and if Sam is getting picked on, you could try putting him and his best buddy into a pasture that adjoins their current pasture.

It's always easy to find companion animals, and if Sam were alone in a several-acre pasture behind your house, it would make good sense to bring in another animal — a pony, donkey, burro, or goat. As it is, though, he has friends of his own and is a member of an established group. He's secure in the group and knows what to expect, so I don't think there's any reason to change that situation right now. If you do decide to bring in a new animal, put him in the pasture next to Sam's for a month or two so that all of the animals can become familiar with one another before you turn out Sam with his new friend.

CHAPTER 17

Mares and Foals

EVERY MARE OWNER will, at some point, have to deal with a number of issues from heat cycles to foal imprinting. For a perplexed rider or horse owner, understanding these topics can be the key to maintaining a good relationship with a mare — and building a good relationship with her foal. However, misunderstandings abound. Many behavior problems are wrongly blamed on heat cycles; many perfectly normal mare-foal interactions are misinterpreted (and some abnormal ones are accepted) by first-time owners; many problems are caused when owners misunderstand the meaning of "imprint training" — or just can't wait to play with the new foal. With patience, understanding, and solid basic information, owners can safely relax and enjoy their mares and foals.

Mare's Estrous Cycle

Q I have a nine-year-old mare, and I was just curious about a mare's heat cycles. She comes into season every four weeks or less and lasts about seven days or so. Does this time correspond to the ovulation cycle? If so, why does it last so many days? Do mares have a period of time when they shed the lining of the uterus when not fertilized, like humans do?

A What your mare is going through is simply her estrous cycle, which takes place more or less year round. I say "more or less" because the strength and predictability of the cycle is dependent on the length of daylight, and thus her cycles will be stronger and much more predictable during breeding season — from late spring through summer and into early autumn. Mares don't menstruate, so, contrary to the opinion of many riders, they don't get PMS.

In the winter, which is not a normal breeding season, mares tend not to show signs of heat or estrus. Even those mares that do show signs are usually not ovulating, and those that show signs and accept stallions during the winter months rarely become pregnant. Nature intends for mares to conceive during the spring and summer, so that foals will be born the following spring, when there is abundant new grass. It makes very good sense.

Your mare's cycle may seem erratic and odd during the early spring; this is normal. During the winter, it's typical for no follicles to develop on the ovaries. As the days lengthen into spring, follicles do begin to develop, but these follicles typically come and go without maturing or releasing an egg. Because of this, the cycle will be unpredictable. Your mare may not come into heat all winter and then become completely erratic in the spring! You might see one mare come into heat for two or three days, go out of heat for a week, and then come back into heat for another two days. Another mare might come into heat in early March and remain in heat for 10 days, two weeks, or longer.

By the time spring is firmly established, usually in early or mid-April, most mares will be ovulating, and their cycles will begin to take on a regular pattern. Most mares will continue to ovulate and show predictable heat cycles through the summer and sometimes through the early fall as well. As October approaches, mares typically show fewer and weaker signs of heat, and by the time winter comes around, they may show no signs at all until spring arrives and the cycles begin again.

The estrous cycle is the time from one ovulation to the next. For most mares, this cycle lasts about 21 days. If your mare's cycle lasts only 19 days, or lasts as long as 22 days, don't worry; she's still in the normal range. During the cycle, the mare will be in heat (estrus) for 5 to 7 days, then will be out of heat (diestrus) for the next 14 to 15 days. Breeders will often speak in shorthand: "Is she in? Is she out?" This is important information. While a mare is in heat she will accept the stallion; when she is out she will not.

During the five, six, or seven days of estrus, there is steady enlargement of a follicle (which contains a developing egg) on one of the mare's ovaries. When the follicle reaches its maximum "ripe" size, it bursts and the egg is released. This is called ovulation. Once the mare has ovulated, she will be in estrus for only one or two days more.

Hormones control the cycle. When estrogen is the predominant hormone, the mare is in estrus. After ovulation, another hormone, progesterone, takes over. When the mare has ovulated, a progesterone-producing structure called the corpus luteum (CL) will form on the ovary. As long as progesterone is produced, the mare will be in diestrus — out of heat. This period normally lasts 14 to 15 days, unless the mare becomes pregnant.

If the mare was bred while she was in heat and if she became pregnant, then the CL will remain on the ovary and continue to produce progesterone. Thus the mare will not come back into heat. If the mare was not bred while she was in estrus or was bred but did not conceive, the CL will last the usual 14 to 15 days and then regress, allowing estrogen to dominate once again and estrus to begin. Neither the buildup to ovulation nor the regression of the CL is instant; it takes time for the follicle to ripen and burst and time for the CL to grow and the hormone balance to shift. That's why the estrus period lasts 5 to 7 days.

Mares can be touchy and easily distracted by other horses — particularly stallions — when they are in heat. But many mares do not show any particular behavioral changes during their cycles. Some mares can be erratic performers in the show ring while they are in heat, but many other mares simply go on with business as usual. If you own a mare that shows strong changes in her performance while she is in, it would be a good idea to consult your veterinarian. Estrous cycles and "mareish" behavior are often blamed for changes in a mare's performance, but there are many other possible causes, including hormonal problems, cysts, and tumors. Some mares do seem to experience pain at the time of ovulation; others become very tight and tense in their backs at that time.

Most mares' cycles last between 19–22 days, with the mare in estrus for 5–7 days, then out of estrus for the next 14–15 days.

Be aware of your mare's normal cycle and her typical behavior, and consult your veterinarian if she begins to show unusual behaviors or changes in her typical cycle — for example, if she normally has a typical cycle, goes into heat early in July, and doesn't come out of heat for several weeks. There are treatable medical conditions that will cause mares to show some or many of the behaviors associated with being in heat, so don't just write this off as being "mareish." Always take steps to find out what is actually going on with your mare.

New Foal, Possessive Mare

Q Our new foal is almost a month old and is just as adorable as can be. She is strong and healthy, and the mare seems to have plenty of milk and is a wonderful and attentive mother.

The problem is that the mare is super possessive of the foal, and it's her second one. The filly seems to want to come up to us and check us out, but the mare just gets in between and turns her around. The mare's not mean to us nor does she try to harm us, she just moves her filly away from us. She's teaching her to be afraid of us. Is there anything we can do get the mare to trust us more, or will catching the filly now make things worse? We feel like we really need to get a halter on her and get her used to us, but we don't want to scare her even more.

The mare comes to us willingly and will eat from our hands, let us groom her, and whatever else we want to do, just as long as we don't make a move to catch the filly. If we do, she'll calmly turn her baby and walk away from us. We've tied her so that we could spray them with fly repellant, and we've held the filly once or twice with the mare tied and standing right next to us. The mare just fidgets a little, and the filly will calm down and let us pet her after a few minutes, but then the mare's a little harder to catch the next time we go out. We want to get close to the little filly and have her trust us enough to let us pet her and groom her.

A I know it's hard to stay away from your new filly, but don't worry. One month old is young, and the foal's mother is simply protecting her baby. It's quite natural. By trying to approach the filly, you put the mare on alert, so don't try. Instead, pay attention to the mare! She is *not* teaching the filly to be afraid of you; the filly will learn *that* only if the mare becomes afraid of you. This filly has one role model, and that is her mother. If the mare isn't afraid, the filly won't be either. Handle the mare the way you would like to be able to handle the filly, and be patient.

Don't worry about putting a halter on the filly. One month is really too young for leading — you could damage her neck — and you will be able to halter her perfectly well later on. If you push her right now, you will create problems that will be very difficult to deal with later. If it's any comfort, one of

A mare's job is to protect her foal. This mare is putting herself between her foal and any possible threat.

my mares was first haltered at two months; the other, at three years. Both will just about put their halters on by themselves now. You are not on a deadline, so take a deep breath and relax.

Here's my system for dealing with this sort of situation: Go out to the field with a pocketful of treats and a brush. Pay attention to the mare and ignore the filly. Talk to the mare, pet her, brush her, feed her treats, and then go away again. Don't try to catch the filly or even pet her — just focus on the mare, and then leave. Do this frequently, and it will have two very useful effects: The mare will enjoy it and will think you truly appreciate her for the wonderful creature she is, and the filly will watch the interaction and learn from it. If Mama always comes up to you and obviously enjoys your visits and the attention she gets, the filly will notice.

> *If Mama always comes up to you and obviously enjoys your visits and the attention she gets, the filly will notice.*

Foals are very curious by nature, but they are also often timid, especially at this age. Catching a foal in this situation is very much like catching a cat: You just shouldn't do it. Find a warm wall to lean against and just stand there, or bring out a muck bucket, turn it upside down, and sit on it. Don't do anything. Pet the mare if she comes to you, and if the filly comes to you as well, let her sniff you but don't try to grab her. If she finds you interesting and nonthreatening, she will come back. Move very slowly, and talk softly. Pet her if she comes close, but don't grab her or try to hold or confine her. And don't raise a hand toward her face: Pet her only on the neck, side, back, and withers.

Sometimes when you come out, put a halter on the mare and lead her around the field, stopping here and there to feed her a treat and brush her or scratch her itchy spots (if you don't know where they are, find them; halfway up the neck under the mane is a good place to start). She will start associating the halter and lead rope with treats and good times, and the filly will observe this peaceful exchange.

If you and your spouse are doing this as a team, one of you can keep playing with the mare and feeding her treats, and the other one can pet the filly *when she comes up to you.* Again — don't go after the filly. *Never* sneak up on her or try to pat her while she's dozing, or you may get an unpleasant surprise. Foals have a built-in kicking reflex, and if something touches them suddenly on the rump, they will let fly with both hind legs. When the herd is on the move, this reflex protects them from being run down by older, larger horses.

At the point when the filly comes up to you and allows you to pet her, don't spend much time on her face and neck; go directly to her withers and to the spot on her back right above her tail and scratch those places. This is sheer heaven for a foal, and she will form a very good opinion of you. Talk to her and scratch her withers and back first, then her rump.

You do need to get to the point where you can tie the mare while she gets her hooves trimmed and hold the filly while she gets *her* hooves trimmed. At her age, trimming will be just a matter of a few moments with a rasp, but it's important for her to be relaxed about this.

When you're at the point where the mare is comfortable with you handling the filly, you can begin to practice a little bit of leading, but not with a halter: Use a foal rope (a wide, soft cotton rope; you can also buy a long piece of cotton rope, unwind the strands, braid them into a flat braid, and tape the ends). First simply loop the rope over the filly's rear end, so that instead of pulling her, you are encouraging her to move away from the pressure on her haunches. Eventually form the rope into a figure eight, with one loop around her rump, the other around her chest, and the rest of the rope held like a "handle" over her back. This will give you more control but still not frighten the baby.

Take your time, and focus on the mare. It'll pay off.

Mare Won't Let Foal Nurse

Q My mare had her first foal three days ago, and I don't know if we will ever breed her again. She was horrible. We weren't there when the foal was born, but we were there just afterward and pulled the placenta out. The mare got in our way when we were trying to imprint the foal and made things very complicated. Then when the foal wanted to nurse, the mare squealed and stamped and moved away from him. We took him away for an hour and imprinted him some more in a different stall, but when we brought him back, he tried to nurse again and she tried to kill him. We had to take him away completely and call the vet.

The vet told us to get colostrum from the mare and feed it to the foal right away, but we didn't get very far because she got angry with us when we tried to

Maiden mares can react badly to nursing if their udders are full and sensitive.

touch her udder. I know she had milk because her udder was huge, and we had been looking under her every day for a month to see when she would get milk. Although she had plenty, she wouldn't let the foal have any. I didn't know there were mares that are just horrible mothers. But she is very pretty, and we would like to breed her again. Why was she so horrible to her foal, and will she do the same thing every time? I noticed that her nipples were very small; do you think that something is physically wrong with her?

A It doesn't sound as though there is anything wrong with your mare physically, and I'm not convinced that she was horrible, although the circumstances certainly were. If you do breed her again, there are a lot of things you should do differently the next time.

First, be prepared. Know what's normal and what isn't for mares and foals. Have your foaling kit ready, and when you see that the foal is about to arrive or has just arrived, let your vet know immediately.

During that last month when you were looking under your mare every day to check her udder, you should also have been touching and handling it so that she could become used to the sensation. It's not at all unusual for a maiden mare to have a negative reaction to having her udder pushed and pulled, especially if it is full, tight, and sensitive. If you spend some time every day getting your mare accustomed to having her udder handled, the foal will benefit in two ways.

If everything goes well, the mare will allow the foal to nurse immediately, as the bumping and tugging won't upset, frighten, or hurt her. If everything *doesn't* go well and you need to milk the mare to get the essential colostrum into the foal during those first critical hours (a feeding bottle and lamb's nipple should be part of every foaling kit), she won't object to the process; she'll be accustomed to the feel of your hands, and you will be gentle and skilled instead of abrupt and inept. Mares have surprisingly tiny teats, but it's not at all difficult to milk a mare unless you have enormous hands and huge fingers.

Unless there's a truly compelling reason to do so, you should leave mare and foal alone. By entering the stall and handling the just-born foal, you can interfere with the bonding process and even cause a mare to reject her foal. A mare needs time to get to know her baby.

If a foal is weak or if something has interfered with the normal mare-foal bonding process, the foal may have a hard time nursing when he finally stands and finds the mare's udder. If the mare's udder is *too* full, it can be impossible for the foal to suckle properly. The longer the foal goes without suckling, the tighter, harder, and more painful the mare's udder will become. The solution to this problem is for a human to enter the stall quietly and milk the mare, first transferring the milk to a bottle and then feeding the foal. After a few swallows of milk, the foal may be strong enough to try again. After a little milk has been removed from the udder, the udder will be flatter and softer, the painful pressure will be relieved, the foal will be able to suckle effectively, and the mare will be much more willing to allow the foal to nurse.

Unless there's a truly compelling reason to do so, you should leave mare and foal alone. By entering the stall and handling the just-born foal, you can interfere with the bonding process and even cause a mare to reject her foal. A mare with a new foal needs time to get to know her baby, and humans should interfere as little as possible. If it's necessary to help deliver the foal, do so, but then *leave the stall.* If you are worried that the mare might step on the trailing amnion and deliver the placenta too quickly, tie the amnion to the mare's tail and then leave the stall. You'll have plenty of time to play with the foal later. The time immediately after foaling is for just the mare and foal, unless something is wrong — in which case you'll need the help of an experienced veterinarian.

The problem with "imprinting" foals is that the process is not actually one of imprinting — it's desensitization. There's nothing wrong with doing this, but calling it imprinting makes owners believe that they need to interfere with nature and interrupt the mare-foal bonding process, all in the interest of having a foal that will be easy to train later. Don't rush into the stall to handle the foal; give him time to get to know his mother.

If after a few hours the mare and foal have bonded, both seem healthy and cheerful, and all of the foal's systems are "go" (in other words, he's drinking milk and you've seen him urinate and defecate), it will be fine for you — with the mare's permission — to pet the foal, lift him, carry him, hold him, lift his feet, and handle him. But don't begin your desensitizing program until the mare and foal have had an uninterrupted chance to bond. What *you* want to do with the foal can be done when he is two hours old, four hours old, or four days old. What the *mare* needs to do with her foal has to be done in the hours immediately after birth.

Filly with Bad Habits

Q I have a seven-month-old paint filly that I am trying to train. I have had a lot of problems and have come up with no successful solutions.

She is very big for her age — the vets say she should mature to be 17 to 18 hh — and she is very strong and loves to rear. She also bites. She starts out by licking, and then when you are least expecting it she takes a good bite. I have tried everything that everyone at my barn has told me to do, and nothing seems to work. I am starting to get more nervous, as she is getting very big and very strong.

For the rearing, I have been advised to pull her sideways and make her fall, and for the biting I have been told to hit her very hard after each bite. Both of these methods were very hard for me and took me a while and a lot of frustration to be able to do. Neither one of them worked! I am at the end of my rope. I feel like I will never be able to break her of these habits. She has done both since she was born, and everyone tells me it is because she is a baby and wants to play. I do not want to play with her like that. I feel unsafe handling her lately.

A. You do have a problem, but it's not so much a matter of what your filly is doing but rather *why* she is doing it, and what you are doing about it. At her age, she needs to be in a large field with other young fillies and adult mares. The lessons you want to teach her will be easy for her to learn from a human once she has learned them from other horses. You board her, but I hope that she isn't living in a stall, even a stall with a run attached; that's simply not good for her at this point in her life. Can you find someplace with a good mare pasture and safe fencing? You don't need a riding arena or jumps or barrels for a seven-month-old, and you certainly don't need a constant stream of bad advice.

Find someone who will keep your filly at pasture, where she should be, for the next two or three years, so that she can grow up mentally and physically healthy, and so that she can learn good horse manners. Meanwhile, you can focus on taking lessons from a good instructor who can help you learn about horses and training. That way, you'll both be on the right path, and you'll be able to go out and work with your filly for brief periods once or twice a week, which is all the human-based training she needs right now.

You can afford to take your time with this filly. If she's going to mature to a height of 17 to 18hh, she may not be ready to begin mounted work until she is four or five years old, or older.

As for the specific behaviors you mention, licking and then nipping is fairly typical baby behavior; baby horses are extremely oral. Just as human babies explore the world by picking up things with their hands and putting them into their mouths, baby horses use their mouths to feel, touch, and taste everything they can. This doesn't mean that you have to allow a baby horse to chew on you, but since you've already said that the biting begins with licking, your job is to pay attention and stop the licking when it starts. This filly isn't biting out of meanness, as she doesn't know it hurts you. To her, it's just a continuation of licking. Don't accept the licking by thinking it's cute and then get angry about the biting. Stop the licking, and you won't have to deal with the biting at all.

Hitting her is not a solution, and hitting her after she bites is just silly. If you want to affect her behavior, let her know you're unhappy while she is performing the behavior. In other words, don't let her lick your hand repeatedly, bite, and then hit her. That doesn't teach her anything except, perhaps, that you want to play a game with her. Teach her the word, "No," or make a very loud game-show-buzzer noise whenever she is doing something you don't like (and make the noise *only* when she is doing something you don't like). She will hate the noise and avoid doing whatever caused it. If she's a typical paint, she'll be clever enough to figure out what not to do.

Keep in mind, too, that this baby is doing something else that human babies do: She is teething. She will teethe for several years and will want to take things in her mouth and chew them. A tree branch, the handle of a Jolly Ball, a nylon bone meant for a dog, even a short piece of rope with a series of knots tied in it all make fine toys for her to play with in her field.

Rearing is normal, typical activity for a healthy foal in a pasture.

Rearing is another very typical baby activity. If she were in the field, she could do all the rearing she wanted and nobody would be annoyed with her. But if she reared and thumped her feet on another horse's side, the other horse would quickly show her why that isn't a good idea. Baby horses are extremely energetic. Babies that are forced to live in barns are always underexercised and usually overfed, and the combination of natural energy, too little exercise, and too much food will quickly create a youngster that seems out of control and dangerous to her handlers.

Pulling a horse over and making her fall is a very effective way to injure or cripple the horse and can also injure or cripple the person handling the horse. This sort of advice is something you will never hear from a true horseman.

Rearing doesn't just happen; just as biting begins with licking, rearing begins with stopping, then straightening, then shifting the weight to the hindquarters, *then* rearing. The time to stop the rear is long before it happens, and preferably right about the time the horse stops. If the horse is walking with you, she can't rear without stopping; if you don't allow her to stop, she can't rear. If a horse is turning, she can't rear without stopping and straightening her body. So if you suspect that your horse may be thinking about rearing, try leading her in curving lines. In practical terms, that means teaching yourself to think: "I'm walking, and the horse is walking at my shoulder. I'm walking, and the horse is walking at my shoulder. I'm walking, and the horse is slowing and beginning to stop. I'm encouraging the horse to move forward and turn left with me. I'm walking, and the horse is walking at my shoulder."

When you handle any horse, you must always be very aware of everything you are doing and everything the horse is doing. If you encourage the horse forward and around a turn as soon as you feel her drop back from her leading position near your shoulder, you'll stop an incipient rear before it gets off the ground.

I think that the main problems here are these: First, you've bitten off more than you can chew, and this is not the time in your life when you should be trying to train a foal. Second, you're in a situation that would make life hard even for the most accomplished professional trainer. Try to get this filly into a mare pasture somewhere safe, and leave her there until she is at least three. Keep an eye on her; go out and handle her; teach her to lead and stand for grooming, hoof trimming, and shots; and teach her to get in and out of trailers. Turning her out doesn't mean abandoning her; it means doing what's right and letting her grow up normally. Wear your helmet whenever you handle her — it's a good precaution when you're dealing with excitable young stock. Once you've had a year or two of lessons with a good instructor, you'll be much more confident about your own abilities, and you'll find it much easier to just say "No" when someone gives you bad advice.

There is nothing wrong with deciding that a certain horse is not for you, even if you went to a great deal of effort to buy that horse. In fact, it's a sign of maturity, clear thinking, and good horsemanship.

Here's another possibility you may want to consider. If you aren't desperately attached to this particular filly, you might consider selling her to someone who has a suitable place to let her grow up and the ability to train her when she's ready. You might prefer to find a horse that you can ride and enjoy now and for the next few years, instead of paying board to maintain a baby that won't be ready for under-saddle training for several years to come.

There is nothing wrong with deciding that a certain horse is not for you, even if you went to a great deal of effort to buy that horse. In fact, it's a sign of maturity, clear thinking, and good horsemanship to be able to look at a situation and say, "I made a mistake. This isn't what I wanted, this isn't going to work, and so I'm going to correct the mistake." We all make mistakes. The trouble with mistakes involving horses is that if we don't correct them, we can put ourselves, other people, and the horses in great danger. It's just not worth it.

Difficult Colt

Q I have a question about a 10-month-old male foal. I had a female foal that was very easy to train and learned everything without a problem. This male foal, on the contrary, has always been a little difficult.

It seems the foal does not have much confidence in humans. It took a lot of time for him to accept me touching him. In general, his eyes are quietly, confidently looking out to the side, with a little white visible. He is not mean at all but easily turns his behind, and he will kick his back legs at you. I leave him quietly when he is eating, but on a couple of occasions when I brought him food, he turned his rear to me and I had to move away.

I can often come quite close to him, even from the back (I don't want him to think I am afraid), and it is usually not a problem. (He also moves away when I tell him to by clearly holding my arms out to him.) I wonder if this is caused by the circumstances of his birth: He was born early in the morning, we weren't there, and the mare gave birth outdoors. Just after his birth, he fell down under the fence, pretty far away from his mother, and could not climb up again. We found him in the bramble bushes, and we had to carry him, with difficulty, up steep inclines and over a fallen tree. This must have been quite a trauma for him.

Meanwhile, his mother was looking for him all the time, as was his old "auntie." But they were all fine, and once they were reunited, we led them quietly to the stable, where they stayed for some hours and where he nursed.

This foal also has, from his early days, had the habit of biting. He says hello and then bites, as if he just wants something in his mouth. Now I give him a rope to bite, and then I touch him, lift his foot, and so on. But as soon as he drops the rope, he bites my clothes or my arm. I tell him strongly, "No," and he stops, but he'll do it again later. He also bites his mother. The more energy he has, the better he feels, and the more he bites his mother or other horses. They are patient with him, play, or are stern with him when they are fed up.

Is this typical male behavior, or is he simply a wild thing? Is he a particularly strong character? Could you say something about how to handle him? For instance, should I give him more discipline and stall time than average, or does he, on the contrary, need a lot of freedom?

I also have difficulty making him follow me. I tried with a rope around his hind legs, as I had read somewhere, but he resists a lot. I don't want to force him; this doesn't seem to be the right way for him. When he is in the right mood, he comes when I call him — he is always curious and sometimes whinnies to me — but that is not enough. I would like to lead him places sometimes.

Finally, what is a good age to have a male foal castrated?

A I don't think that there is anything wrong with your foal; he sounds like a normal 10-month-old colt. The behavior problems you've described — aggression toward other horses, resistance to leading, a desire to bite or chew everything within reach — are all very typical colt behaviors. They are also behaviors that tend to get much more noticeable and much more pronounced at puberty. At 10 months, your colt is probably reaching that stage.

His early trauma may have affected him, but there is nothing you can do about that now. You can focus on building a good relationship with him and that will be much easier for you when he is capable of paying attention and listening to you. Right now, it sounds as if he is listening to one thing only: his hormones.

To answer your last question first, a good age to have a male foal gelded is any time at all. The sooner, the better, because the process is easier and less painful and the recovery time is shorter. But now would be an excellent time. It's still early enough in the year that you shouldn't have a problem with flies. If you don't geld him soon, you may find that his mother and his "auntie" — and any other available mares — are pregnant, and that may not suit your plans. So why not separate him from the mares immediately and put him in a field with colts and geldings? If it takes a few weeks before you can get your veterinarian to come out to geld the colt, at least he'll be with other horses, and they may be less patient and tolerant than his mother and "auntie." Horses learn discipline best when they learn it from other horses, and some mares are too old, gentle, and patient to discipline their foals properly. Such foals will be better off if they are turned out with older geldings who can be a little more forceful with them at first, which will teach them some manners.

A month or two after gelding, he should settle down and his behavior should become less silly. But he will still be interested in tasting and biting everything, for two reasons: Since horses have no hands, they use their muzzles, lips, and teeth to investigate unfamiliar objects; and for the next several years, your colt will be losing baby teeth and growing permanent teeth.

Don't try to keep him from tasting and chewing objects; it's natural behavior. But do teach him that biting humans is not allowed. He needs to learn to stand quietly for the veterinarian, the farrier, the dentist, and you, too. And he should definitely learn to lead.

At 10 months, your colt is old enough to be quite strong. You will probably want to use a foal rope (see the New Foal, Possessive Mare entry earlier in this chapter for a description) until he leads well. If you use it in a figure-eight formation, you will have the foal in a sort of handy "suitcase," which may make it easier for you to lead him.

Standing next to his shoulder and facing forward, ask the colt to move forward by moving your hand forward so that the rope pressures his hindquarters. When you want him to stop or stand, just stop or stand quietly so that the foal's forward movement will be restricted by the rope around his chest. Talk to him. Teach him what you want and what the words mean; this way, he can

If you have a cheeky young colt, turn him out with other colts
and older geldings who can teach him some manners.

learn to go, stop, stand, and turn. Since there are no knots or clips anywhere on the rope, if the foal becomes tangled, you can let the rope fall to the ground and begin again later.

As he begins to understand this arrangement, you can start using a halter with a short lead rope. With the foal rope in one hand and the lead rope in your other hand, you'll be able to teach the colt to respond to light pressure on his nose. At first, use only the foal rope and just hold the lead rope loosely. Gradually begin to use a small amount of pressure on the lead rope at the same time that you use the foal rope, so that the foal will learn to point his nose in the direction that he is going. When this is comfortable for you both, you can begin to use the lead rope just before you use the foal rope; in this way, the foal will learn to respond to the lead rope (with the action of the foal rope coming immediately afterward to reinforce your request). Finally, the foal will come to understand and respond to the lead rope alone, at which point the foal rope can be discarded.

If you can't find a suitable flat-braided cotton rope, you can make your own. Buy a piece of three-strand twisted cotton rope, then untwist the strands. Fasten them together at one end, braid them, and secure them when you reach the other end.

Take your time, be patient, do not accept any biting (if he nips you, move toward him swiftly and make a disconcerting, loud noise — this tells him that he has made a mistake and that he should not do that again). Spend a lot of time talking to him and grooming him, and teach him to stand tied and to lead and pick up his feet. Take him for walks; he won't be old enough for formal riding-horse training for several more years, but he is old enough to learn good manners and how to be a good companion. Make his time with you enjoyable, praise him whenever he does what you want him to do, and don't be afraid to be strict with him and say no. He needs to understand exactly what you want and what you will allow. Young horses, like young children, are much more secure and comfortable if they know what the rules are and that they are not in charge of everything. You can make this clear to your foal. He won't be angry; he will be more at ease.

> *Young horses, like young children, are much more secure and comfortable if they know that they are not in charge.*

Above all, let him spend most of his time outdoors, in a field with other horses (preferably geldings). He will be physically and mentally healthier and much easier to train.

Imprint Training

Q My husband and I have done a lot of reading about imprinting foals and how you can almost train them right at birth — not riding them, of course, but teaching them so that they will do everything you want without any resistance later on when you want to ride them.

Last year when we bred our mares, we did everything we could to be there when they foaled so that we could imprint the foals. We missed both births! Both mares foaled very late at night, after we had decided they just weren't going to foal that day and we went to bed. In the morning, we found the foals with the mares. They were at least five hours old, but we did all of the imprinting anyway.

The problem is that although we did everything, the foals don't behave the way they are supposed to. They are six months old now, and both of them are pushy and act wild. We went to visit them yesterday and checked on their imprinting. They behaved as if they never saw us before, and they didn't act imprinted at all. They don't stand still for handling and grooming, you can't pick up their feet, they shake their heads when you put halters on them, and if you try to get near them with clippers, forget about it, no way.

We introduced them to *all* of those things when we imprinted them, but it seems that was just a waste of time. So does imprinting just not work, or did it not work because we weren't able to do it right after the foals were born? Or is something wrong with these foals? At this point, I dislike the word *imprinting*.

A First, "imprinting" isn't actually imprinting, so if you dislike the word, that's not a problem.

Unlike puppies, kittens, or human babies, foals are neurologically mature at birth. That is why a half an hour after birth, a foal can run alongside its dam. The idea of "imprinting" is based on the fact that since horses are not fearful in the first few hours after their birth, humans can take advantage of this short period of fearlessness and expose the foal to the sight, sound, and smell of humans — not to mention halters, ropes, clippers, blankets, and just about anything else. It is believed that this will enable the foal to remember those people and items later and perceive them as nonthreatening. In the several hours after the foal's birth, it's possible to hold him, handle him all over, lift and tap his feet, put fingers or other objects into his mouth, and generally introduce him to all the forms of equipment that he will otherwise meet gradually over the next three or four years.

The "imprinting" part of this early desensitization process comes from the idea that during the first few hours of the foal's life, the foal learns more quickly and more intensely than it ever will again, so whatever you teach at that time will have the most impact. The time frame is arguable, but you were probably still within that window of opportunity when you began working with your five-hour-old foals.

I don't think your present problems with your foals are a consequence of imprint training, but they may well be the consequence of *incomplete* imprint training. The problem with imprinting is that many people become so involved with checking items off their list of things to introduce that they don't actually complete the process of desensitizing the foal to the handling or to the objects.

It's essential that the foal become absolutely accepting and passive about each new object or process before the handler moves on to the next one. If the handler rushes through the process and doesn't allow the foal to become totally accepting, the result can be the exact opposite of what the handler intended: Instead of becoming desensitized and accepting, the foal can become sensitized, anxious, and fearful. That may have been the case with your foals.

Another possibility is that the lessons taught soon after birth weren't kept up. How often have you visited and handled these foals in the six months since they were born? Desensitization is not a one-time procedure. People who are successful at imprinting their foals take all the necessary time during the first lessons, working with the foal as soon as it has had a chance to bond with its dam. They also continue the lessons over the next few weeks, creating a foundation for the foals' future learning and for the foals' relationship with the humans. Then, over the next months and years, they continue to build on that foundation. By the time the foals are two or three, they've become thoroughly desensitized and have accepted humans as higher-up in the hierarchy.

The lessons that follow the initial desensitization are just as important as the initial imprinting. Handling the newborn foal, if you do it properly, can help him learn not to fear you, but there's a downside to that: He may come to think

*Early handling of a newborn foal takes advantage of his relative
fearlessness in his first few hours.*

of you as an equal. It's important that you complete the process over the next few weeks by teaching the foal that you outrank him, now and forever. If you don't complete the program, you can "create a monster" — that is, you can teach the foal that you are harmless and shouldn't be feared, and that you shouldn't be respected either.

In the world of horses, dominance is very simple — it all comes down to control of movement. If you can make a horse move his feet or if you can prevent him from moving his feet, you outrank him. If the horse can make *you* move your feet or prevent you from moving them, he outranks you. The horse world is vertical, not horizontal, so either you outrank the horse or the horse outranks you; as far as horses are concerned, there is no middle ground.

In this case, I suspect that you may have been in a hurry when you did the initial imprinting — after all, you were concerned that you might have missed your chance. You probably didn't follow up over the next several weeks, and the foals didn't learn to respect you or see you as dominant, so they see themselves as dominant.

You don't want your foals to be afraid of you, but you do want them to see you as dominant; otherwise, they may calmly accept handling but may then crowd you and push you around. They're not being bad when they do this, but this behavior is something you will need to change before you can hope to work with them and train them effectively.

It may help you to go back and review the writings and videotape of Dr. Robert Miller, the veterinarian who developed the concept of imprint training. That will help you understand what you could have done differently. One of the keys to success is that he calls his method imprint *training*; it's not, and was never meant to be, a one-time experience that would affect the foal forever.

Don't worry, your foals aren't doomed to be ill-mannered louts. Many foals grow up without any sort of training by humans and still become good equine citizens later in their lives. Enlist the help of a good trainer and start your youngsters' training again. By the time they're of an age to begin serious work, they should be ready.

If you have the opportunity to deal with young stock from birth, it's a definite advantage if you can handle foals early and often and take every opportunity to add to their education and to their confidence in you. If you don't like to think of this as "imprint training," just think of it as early, intensive training. All good breeders spend time with their new foals, getting them used to handling and teaching them that humans are kind and gentle and must be obeyed. What you choose to call the process is up to you.

CHAPTER 18

Stallions

HORSE OWNERS OFTEN BECOME very emotional about the issue of whether or not to geld their colts. For various reasons, many owners ask their friends, neighbors, and veterinarians, "Why should I geld this colt?" The problem is that they are asking the wrong question. The question shouldn't be, "Why should I geld this colt?" but, rather, "Why should I keep this colt intact?"

Should I Geld My Stallion?

Q I have a five-and-a-half-year-old Paint stallion. I bought him from a man who was just getting too old and wanted to get out of the breeding business after 40-plus years. I fell in love with this pure white Sabino stallion with blue eyes and awesome conformation, down to the flawless shape of his baby-doll head.

After careful consideration, I decided I really couldn't do all it takes to offer him for stud service. He is on a private pasture 24/7 and has two old mares to keep him happy. He practically catches himself; if I hold out his halter, he will walk right over and stick his nose through the cavesson. I can ride him bareback with just a loose hackamore and he is a perfect gentleman. He is even starting to steer with just a shift in weight and light leg pressure. He doesn't rear, buck, kick, or have any other typical stallion behavior. However, he is anything but placid.

He has a charisma that I have never seen in a gelding in my 11 years with horses. Stallions just have a certain flare and bold neck carriage that I don't want him to lose. He fears nothing, and I treasure everything about him. You had once said that stallions who are gelded lose some of their curves, which is something I love about him (that arched, not crested, neck). He knows he is a stud and shows it off. Is there really any reason I should geld him? Don't humans basically do that for safety and the economy of keeping a gelding?

A If you own a lovely stallion and can keep him in the way you've described— that is, in a big field, with stallion-safe fencing and two mares for his small "herd" — then there's no urgent reason to geld him. But I'd be curious to know how long you have owned the stallion. If you've never been around him when nature turns up the hormonal thermostat (late spring and all summer), then you haven't had a chance to see your stallion as a stallion. If he continues to have lovely manners and expresses no real interest in mares even when it's mid-June and they are experiencing strong heats, I'd be very surprised.

Most stallions aren't lucky enough to have the sort of safe setup that you offer your horse. If you were keeping your horse at a boarding stable or at home but without the big field, the stallion fence, and the mares, I would probably advise you to geld him just so that he could enjoy a more normal life.

Far too many stallions are kept as stallions only because their being intact is some warped projection of their owners' egos. Stallions locked in stalls or kept in tiny runs, isolated from other horses, unable to do anything that would be normal for *any* horse, have very unhappy lives.

The "economy" of keeping a gelding usually means that horse owners can allow their geldings to go out with the other geldings to play and walk and eat in the field. It means that the horse can go to shows and clinics and competitions

Even the most good-natured stallion needs a safe, well-managed environment.

without any special arrangements having to be made, and it means that the owner doesn't have to put up special fencing at home or elsewhere.

It sounds to me as though you have a lovely stallion with a great personality — and I'll bet that he would make a wonderful gelding. The physical muscling that you like so much is muscling that can be developed in geldings, and to some extent in mares, through correct work; upper-level dressage horses, for example, can look very stallionlike in their contours, even if they are geldings or mares.

As for the "showing off," this can last a lifetime, even after a stallion is gelded. In my paddock, I have a gelding who is 25 and blind and still "struts his stuff," arching his neck, dancing in place, and basically telling all the other horses just how wonderful and important he is.

If you do keep your horse intact, be aware that his behavior in spring and summer — prime breeding season — may be less controllable if there are mares in heat anywhere near. For a stallion with a superkeen sense of smell, "near" may mean "a mile or two from home." When the hormones take over, even the kindest, gentlest, sweetest stallion will still be a stallion, and you will need to be alert at all times. Liability may be a concern, and you might consult your farm insurer, and perhaps an equine law specialist, about this. Be sure that your insurance coverage is still active when you're keeping a stallion. Be sure that you understand any terms and conditions for coverage and that you meet any special requirements your insurer may have in terms of fencing and/or management.

From your description, I'd say that the qualities you like most in your stallion are there not because he is a stallion, but because he is a healthy, energetic young horse. There's a certain mystique to owning a stallion, but it's a mystique that causes far more harm than good, both to the stallion and to his owner. If you own a stallion that is not part of a well-thought-out breeding program, you need to ask yourself why this horse is still a stallion and whether keeping him intact is really to the advantage of the horse. In almost all cases, the honest answers to those questions are: "Because I think owning a stallion is cool" and "No."

> *Gelding a stallion isn't a punishment; it's usually a good decision made by a knowledgeable, caring owner whose priority is the good of the horse. It is often performed so that the horse can have a better life.*

The vices that young stallions develop are usually the result of mishandling, and the mishandling is often done by very kind, loving owners who simply don't understand what it means for a stallion to be a stallion. Gelding a stallion isn't a punishment; it's usually a good decision made by a knowledgeable, caring owner whose priority is the good of the horse. Gelding is often performed for the horse's convenience, so that he can be physically comfortable, mentally stable, have a better life, and experience more freedom and companionship of other horses.

There's a difference between fear of stallions and respect for stallions. Don't confuse one with the other. If someone says to you, "Stallions are unpredictable," this doesn't mean that you're talking to a fearful, ignorant person who just doesn't understand how sweet stallions can be. A carefully managed, well-trained breeding stallion can be a gentleman at most times, but the best stud grooms will tell you that it is never safe to sit back and take those nice manners for granted.

Talk to your veterinarian, explain that you are not going to be using the stallion for breeding, and ask for advice. Better yet, sit down with your vet and make two lists: one of the advantages of gelding and one of the advantages of not gelding. The length of the first list may surprise you.

Testosterone and Manners

Q I run a small boarding stable. As a favor to a boarder, I agreed to allow her friend to briefly keep his colt here until he could move the horse to his new farm. That was two months ago, and the colt is still here. He is a problem because he is totally out of control — even worse than when he got here. His owner, Brad, is the other problem. This guy is just about as bad as his horse when it comes to manners and behavior. The colt gets out once a day, for about half an hour, which I think isn't enough time, but we don't have a separate pasture with stallion fencing and the colt (two years old) is already a big, strong horse.

I don't think the colt is a mean horse, but Brad always makes a big deal out of putting a chain over his nose or through his mouth and yanking on it and yelling, "Out of the way, chicks, this here is a stallion!" I think that the chain makes the colt rear, because it probably hurts him, and sometimes when he rears he will paw at Brad with his front feet. I think that someday he'll strike at his owner and nail him, and, frankly, I won't be sorry, but I hope he's off my property when it happens.

My boarders are getting upset. They don't like to watch Brad's treatment of his horse, but it seems like the more people there are at the barn, the more this behavior happens. If five people are riding in the arena, that's the time when Brad will come in and act up.

There is some problem with the new farm, which is why the colt has been here so long, but his manners aren't getting any better. I've asked Brad to leave, but he really doesn't have anyplace to go except his new place, so I'm probably stuck with both of them for another month. I don't appreciate being told, "Look, lady, he's a stud. That's how they are. You have to get after them or they'll try and kill you. You can't ever trust a stallion; they're wild." I've known some darn nice stallions, and I think that Brad could teach his colt manners, but he just walks off whenever I suggest it.

Do you think it's true that stallions have bad manners just because they are stallions? I've heard that testosterone is the reason stallions can be out of control. Should I just refuse to have a stallion at my place ever again? Does this have anything to do with Brad being a guy? All my other boarders are women, and I haven't had this problem with them. I guess I'm not sure how much of this is male hormones!

A Let me answer your second question first: It's up to you whether you board stallions. It's your place. You know that you don't have enough turnout for a stallion, and you obviously

Sadly, there are people who own stallions because they want to show off their 'mastery' of a large animal.

haven't enjoyed having this one around, so perhaps you would be better off making a no-stallions rule. If you ever need to accommodate a nice person with a nice stallion, you can make an exception to the rule — but be sure to talk this over with your insurance agent first. Keeping a stallion on your property can cause your insurance rates to rise and might even require that you take out a new policy.

Now, in answer to your first question: Stallions have stallion behavior, just as mares have mare behavior and young horses have young-horse behavior. But *all* horses can have perfectly nice manners if someone bothers to train them well. And that, I suspect, is the problem with this particular colt — nobody has trained him well, and, in fact, someone is training him very badly indeed.

Testosterone isn't an instant chemical formula for bad manners, and it's not an excuse for bad manners in horses or humans. A female trainer who acted in an equally stupid and aggressive way toward a colt would provoke similar reactions; I've seen that happen. Bad training practices, ignorance, and attitude problems aren't gender-linked. There are many excellent male trainers and lovely, well-behaved stallions in the world. Don't judge the stallion's temperament by the trainer's stupidity, and don't judge the trainer by his testosterone level. Real men don't get their kicks out of keeping young stallions confined and provoking them to rear so that they can then "master" them.

For your safety and peace of mind, and for the sake of your insurance coverage, it might be best if you insist that Brad take his horse and leave sooner rather than later. It may be the best thing for the colt, too. Perhaps Brad can rent a field somewhere and the colt can go outside and be a horse instead of an extension of Brad's ego.

In the meantime, try this: Since you are clearly not set up to accommodate a stallion and need to make some strategic changes to keep everyone safe until Brad leaves, give Brad certain hours that are his time to come out and work with his horse, and assign him the hours when nobody else is likely to be around. This will accomplish several goals. First, Brad may get annoyed and be inspired to take his colt away sooner than he planned. Second, he may lose all interest in jerking his horse around if he can't do it in front of a group of women. Third, even if he stays for the rest of the month and continues to handle his horse badly, your boarders won't be put at risk by sharing the ring with him.

Young Stallion Won't Breed

Q I'm too embarrassed to talk to my vet about this, so I'm hoping you can help me. Two months ago, I bought a Paint colt off the show circuit, with the idea of making him my breeding stallion. He has just the coloring and the bloodlines that I want. I own five mares. It's going to be breeding season soon, and I thought I had better be sure that he was fertile. My vet checked him out and said he is.

A couple of days later, one of the mares went into heat and I took the stallion over to her paddock. But there was a real problem trying to get him to breed the mare. He seems sort of interested, and then he just shakes his head and starts walking backward. When I called my vet he said, "Well, he might be gay." I think that he might have been joking, since he's always cracking jokes and he'd just finished telling me a funny story, but now I'm really starting to wonder. I'm worried that he must have been serious.

Do you think it's possible for a stallion to be gay, and is there anything I can do about it? And if he isn't gay, what do you think is the problem? I can't believe I had him in a paddock with a mare in heat, and he wouldn't even try. I'm so worried that my new stallion isn't a real stallion after all.

A I think your vet was trying to be funny. Although homosexual behavior has been observed in all kinds of animals, it's very, very unlikely that your young stallion is gay. What is likely, though, is that he isn't sure what the appropriate response should be to the mare. As a young horse on the show circuit, he has spent his entire life in stalls, trailers, and show rings, where he was probably yelled at and hit whenever he expressed any interest in a filly or mare. That's not very conducive to the kind of relaxed focus and confidence that a breeding stallion needs. Don't worry; this isn't at all uncommon behavior with young colts just coming off the show circuit or off the racetrack. If understanding owners are willing to give these colts some time to let down and become typical horses again, preferably while watching other horses interact, the youngsters eventually realize that they won't be punished for nickering at mares, and then their natural instincts will begin to reassert themselves.

The act of breeding is probably, at least to some extent, a learned behavior. It's easy for a colt in a herd to know what to do; he'll have seen it often. For a colt that has never seen a stallion breeding a mare, some assistance may be required the first time or two.

Horse assistance is the best, and the ideal teacher would be an older mare who knows just what she wants and can convince your youngster that sniffing, "talking," and generally feeling and expressing sexual interest is perfectly acceptable, and that breeding is equally acceptable. It will take some time, but she'll probably teach him what he needs to learn, including how to tell when a mare is ready and when she isn't.

> *It will take some time, but she'll probably teach him what he needs to learn, including how to tell when a mare is ready and when she isn't.*

Human help can also be useful and is essential when dealing with very expensive young stallions or maiden mares. But the help needs to be from an experienced and calm, not a nervous and excited, person. If you weren't so embarrassed about discussing it with your vet, I'd suggest that you ask his advice about helping your stallion the first few times. Have you considered talking to your vet's wife about this? I know several horse owners who use their vets' wives as intermediaries when they want to discuss a subject they don't feel comfortable discussing with a man.

A good setup for breeding: The mare is ready, the stallion is interested, and the handlers are quiet and calm.

Don't write off your colt's ability to become a breeding stallion. Apart from lack of experience and the expectation of punishment, there may be other possibilities to consider. Your colt has been in the show ring. You didn't say what classes he was in, but as a Paint, his winning (or not) would have had a lot to do with his musculature. There's a tendency among many trainers to try to give their young Quarter Horses and Paints a bit of an edge by injecting them with various muscle-enhancing substances; steroids are among the most popular drugs. One of the side effects of steroid use is loss of libido. It isn't permanent, but if your colt has been pumped full of steroids for a year or two, he may need a year to get all of the drugs out of his system. One reason steroid use is prevalent is that lab tests don't distinguish between a horse's own testosterone and artificial versions, so time is really the only test if this is the case with your colt.

If you aren't in a hurry to begin your breeding program, I suggest that you let your colt grow up a little more. Work with him, get to know him, find out whether he's really exactly what you want. You know that you love his color and bloodlines — now take some time to find out about his intelligence, personality, and athletic ability. And while you're at it, reinforce all of his good ground manners. A breeding stallion should lead perfectly; he should stay at your shoulder and accept your directions to go, stop, stand, and turn. A horse that just follows you most of the time, one that has to be pulled around by his halter, or one that pulls you around by the lead rope is not trained to lead, and that's very dangerous behavior in any horse, particularly a breeding stallion. Manners are very important. See that your youngster keeps his.

If you can keep him turned out with one experienced older mare whenever she's in season, you may find that by the end of summer, he's figured out what to do. We make it very hard on horses when we ask them to breed at a time of year that is not natural for them. Horses are meant to breed in the summer; that's when mares are most likely to conceive, and that's when both the mare's and the stallion's sex hormones are running high. It's a sensible plan, from nature's point of view, since it means that foals will be born the following year when the weather is warm and the spring grass is at its best.

Inept or inappropriate handling can cause pain, fear, and confusion in a young stallion, and all of these lead to vastly decreased libido and sometimes to an inability to breed. If you do hand breed your youngster, be sure that everything is set up for success.

It's also important that your youngster's first experience be a good one for him. If you and your vet can arrange to work together, spend the next few weeks following the first breeding by quietly and calmly training your colt to understand and accept everything that comes with breeding. He'll need to learn about the washing routine, the teasing routine, and the breeding procedures. A special halter that's used only on breeding days is a good idea; it lets the horse know what today's job will be and provides a positive signal that is probably the best way to help you discourage him from showing too much interest at other times.

Inept or inappropriate handling can cause pain, fear, and confusion in a young stallion, and all of these lead to vastly decreased libido and sometimes to an inability to breed. If you do hand breed your youngster, be sure that everything is set up for success. You already know that the handlers should be experienced. In addition, the floor in the breeding room should have a nonslip surface. The mare should be experienced, patient, and strongly in heat — you should verify the latter with a teaser. The mare's tail should be bandaged, and the mare and stallion should both be clean. The stallion handler should keep your youngster in position behind the mare — over-enthusiastic youngsters can try to climb mares' shoulders or sides, which is a bad idea — and should be calm, encouraging, and willing to take as long as necessary for the stallion to mount and complete the act.

Handling breeding stallions is a specialized area of horse management. Hand breeding is an endeavor that involves two adult equines, extremely strong natural insticts *and* learned behavior. The process can be physically dangerous to the horses and the humans involved, so do everything in your power to ensure that it goes well. Please don't be embarrassed to ask your vet (or his wife) for advice, help, or a recommendation for someone else who can help. Until a stallion has learned what's acceptable, what's allowed, and how to do his job, he will need educated, experienced assistance. You don't want anyone to get hurt. You don't want your young stallion to become discouraged, but you must keep him under control. This is really a job for a professional. Find one who can help this colt — and who can teach you how to help your next colt.

CHAPTER 19

Geldings

"Neutered" doesn't mean "without personality" — nor does it mean "everyone's little friend." Geldings, like mares and stallions, are individuals with unique personalities of their own. Mixing geldings and mares in turnout can be risky, which is why many barn owners make it their practice to maintain separate pastures for mares and geldings. Some geldings are aggressive toward mares; others are amorous, and few pastures are sufficiently large enough to permit one horse to avoid or escape another. Every horse owner knows of individual mares and geldings that get along well, but as a general principle of horse management, it's best to avoid unnecessary injuries by maintaining separate, designated pastures and turnout areas.

Using a Gelding as a Teaser

Q My horse, Sam, is a gelding. He is ten years old, and according to the lady I bought him from, he was gelded late, when he was about four. He behaves better than he did when I got him, but some days he thinks he is a stallion. He gets very excited by the mares, and I have to yell at him and sometimes whack him with my crop to get his attention. Now I am keeping him at a boarding stable where he can be turned out with other geldings, so he is having a good time. He still notices the mares, but not as much as before.

The lady who owns the stable has three mares that she breeds. She wants to use Sam as a teaser because he gets so excited over mares in heat. But I am worried that he will carry over this behavior when I ride him and we see mares. Also, won't it confuse him when I always tell him to shut up and behave when he starts "talking" to mares, while she says it's okay for him to get excited?

I've owned Sam for two years, and just this last year he has started to listen to me about this. I like the barn owner a lot, but I am really worried about using Sam in this way. I don't want him to start misbehaving and not listening to me, but I don't want to make the barn owner mad either. I tried to tell her why I don't want to do this, but she says it won't hurt Sam because he won't actually get to breed with the mare. My instructor says I should not do this, but she is only out at the barn once a week, and I am there every day — and so is the owner. What should I do?

A You're going to have to be strong and say no. It's not a good idea to use Sam as a teaser. Breeding barns usually keep a stallion — often a pony — or a "studdy" gelding as a teaser, but it's for the convenience of the owner and to keep the valuable breeding stallions safe. A teaser's job is to investigate whether a mare is sufficiently in heat to breed, and the teaser gets very excited in the process. If the mare is not ready and she kicks, it's the teaser, not the valuable breeding stallion, that gets hurt. If she *is* ready, the breeding stallion is brought out and the teaser is put back in his stall. It's not much of a life. At the best breeding barns, the teaser stallion spends a lot of time in turnout with one or two barren mares so that he doesn't spend all of his time alone and frustrated, locked up in a stall.

Teasers are not used for riding or driving; they have a specialized job, and that's all they do. The nature of the job makes them unfit for riding and driving.

Horse-breeding and horse-boarding activities should be separate. Boarders' horses should not be used as teasers.

Teasers are encouraged to get as excited as possible and to try to excite the mares as much as possible. These are useful habits in the breeding shed, but not at all useful in the riding arena, in the show ring, or on the trail.

Be polite about your refusal (show the barn owner this letter if you think it will help her understand) but tell her no. This won't do your horse any good, and it could get him (or you) hurt. If you need more support, enlist your veterinarian. Your vet's advice should carry some weight, and you could even ask him or her to talk to the barn owner for you. Your vet may also be able to help the barn owner by suggesting other methods of monitoring her mares.

Gelding Attacks Mare

Q About 18 months ago, I purchased a wonderful grade gelding who is about six years old. I boarded him close by, where he got daily turnout and I took a lesson on him once a week. My husband and I were able to purchase about five-and-a-half acres with a barn and a fenced pasture of about one-and-a-half acres. So I brought my best friend home. The property is not fancy, but serviceable. We made minor improvements to the stall and fence as needed. I have neighbors with horses on two sides, so I was even able to get on their farrier rotation. I've had the vet visit. I have a manure-management plan, and I will put in a second pasture this spring. I would also like to get a second horse, but I don't want to rush and get something I can't handle.

My horse is out 24/7 with free access to his stall and run-in area. I supplement grass with around one pound of 12 percent sweet feed and give grass hay when the pasture isn't producing. My horse is doing light riding around the fields here, although he likes to run the fence line with the neighbor horses.

A wonderful opportunity presented itself when another neighbor had a nice mare for sale. She's around 15 years old and trail safe, even for little kids. I know her history: no bad habits, current on shots, and so on. My neighbor and I worked out a deal because she really wanted me to have the mare. This way, she will have a nice home, and her former owner would still be able to see her.

Here's the problem: My gelding hates this mare. We walked the mare over and let them sniff through the fence and over the stalls. We walked them side by side on the lead lines. They showed some curiosity, but neither my neighbor nor I tolerate bad manners when leading, so that wasn't a good indicator. But when we turned them loose, my horse pinned back his ears, swayed his head, and chased the mare like he wanted to kill her. The mare was terrified. We separated them and started over. The same thing happened, but this time he knocked her to the ground. I managed to get him away from her before injuries occurred. He does have enough respect for me not to run me down.

My neighbor was kind and took her poor mare back home. My gelding was not aggressive at the boarding barn. He's very friendly to me and my family, always coming up to the barn when he sees us. What happened? What can I do about bringing another horse home? Currently, I do not have the opportunity to have separate pastures. Is my horse doomed to a single life?

A Your gelding's behavior isn't a reflection on you or your farm, but it is a fairly typical illustration of why not to put mares and geldings in the same pasture. Although the introduction seemed far too quick, I don't think that was the main problem; it's the basic mix-and-match idea that's at fault. At good barns where safety is a priority, you won't find mares mixing with geldings. There is a mare pasture and a gelding pasture — end of story.

*Mares and geldings often don't mix well. An amorous or aggressive
gelding can seriously injure a mare.*

Some geldings, even otherwise perfectly peaceful ones, simply go mad when
they see mares in the field and are determined to kill them. Every year, at farms
where people don't know what is safe, don't observe safety precautions, or can't
be bothered to follow the barn rules, there are injuries, sometimes very severe or
fatal, when mares are turned out with aggressive geldings. Even when geldings
aren't aggressive, they still aren't necessarily going to be suitable candidates for
turnout with mares. Some geldings become amorous instead, and that can cause
different kinds of physical damage to the mares.

A one-and-a-half acre enclosure makes a nice grass paddock, but it's not
really large enough to allow one horse to escape from another, aggressive,
attacking horse. Even if you had a ten- or twenty-acre field with very strong,
horse-safe fencing, the problem would still exist, and although it might take a
little longer, there would come a time when one horse would be caught between
the other horse and the fence and probably be badly injured. It's just not worth it.

Everyone knows of one gelding who can be safely turned out with one particular mare. But by and large, it's not a good idea or a safe barn practice. If you
plan to bring another horse home and keep it in the pasture with your current
horse, get another gelding. They'll play gelding games, do a lot of rearing and

biting, and probably remove strips of skin from one another on occasion, but overall it will be much safer for everyone concerned.

Meanwhile, you might just want to allow your current horse to be a "lonely only" until you can fence another enclosure. Since he has fence line contact with other horses, he isn't likely to be really lonely. Fence line neighbors can become quite good friends. Don't worry that you're depriving him of companionship; there are other horses he can see, smell, hear, and talk to, and he has your family for companions as well. The horses who desperately need a pasture companion are the ones that find themselves alone all the time, with no other horses for miles around. A horse in that situation would need to be provided with a companion — another gelding, a mule, a donkey, a goat — for company.

The mare sounds very nice. If you really want to bring her home, perhaps your neighbor will be willing to keep her a little longer, until you can provide her with a safe turnout with a strong fence between her and the gelding. Or perhaps this neighbor might have an equally nice gelding for sale or lease? It can't hurt to ask.

Good luck with the place. You have good ideas and good plans, and I'm impressed that you not only lined up the farrier and vet so quickly, but also have a manure-management plan in place. But when it comes to the horses, unless you know that a particular mare and gelding get along well and can safely be turned out together, you'll need to make it a policy to keep the boys and girls in separate playrooms, for safety's sake.

PART IV

Away
from Home

CHAPTER 20

Trailers:
Getting in, Staying in, Getting Out

MANY HORSE OWNERS COMPLAIN of problems involving trailers. Their horses won't go near trailers, won't get into trailers, kick and scream while they're in trailers, or refuse to get out of trailers. Some horse owners deprive themselves of the pleasure of participating in group activities away from home because they don't think they can get their horse into the trailer for that trip to the fair, competition, or trailhead. Others worry about getting to the vet clinic in an emergency. Most "trailering problems" begin with an uncertain horse and a human in a hurry, and any horse owner who wants to give his horse a new attitude about trailers will need to bring skill, understanding, and infinite patience to the task.

Getting into the Trailer

Q We've been trying to get our new mare to learn how to trailer. So far, we've tried food bribes, brooms, and running a long lead rope through the trailer window to try to pull her into the trailer. We've been trying for a week. So far, we've managed to get her onto the trailer just once. When we did, we closed the door as fast as we could and just let her stay in the trailer for half an hour so that she would get the idea. But now she won't get in the trailer at all. One of my friends says we should have left her there all night and fed her in it so she would get used to it. Another friend says we shouldn't have closed the door, and we should have just let her get off the trailer. Who is right? I'm leaning toward the all night in the trailer idea, so that she can learn to feel safe there. If we let her get out of the trailer, wouldn't that just teach her to get out as soon as she gets in?

A What you need to ask yourself here is, What am I trying to achieve? If you have to get a horse in the trailer once, and you don't care whether she ever gets in another trailer as long as she lives, getting her in the trailer once and slamming the door behind her would work very well. If, on the other hand, you want to train her to accept trailers and trailering, and you want her to learn to relax and get in the trailer calmly whenever you ask her to, you'll need to take a different approach.

I know that it seems contradictory to go to all the trouble of coaxing a horse into a trailer, only to allow her to back right out of the trailer again. But here's the reason: Horses are instinctively afraid of confinement in small spaces. When you ask a horse to get into a trailer, you are asking the horse to go against her natural instincts. She will do this if she trusts you, but you have to be trustworthy *all* the time, not just until the horse gets into the trailer.

If you shut the door behind her and say, "Ha, we've got you now!" she will have all of her natural fears confirmed — against her instinct, she got into the little dark place, and then she couldn't get out. As far as she knows, she is trapped there permanently. Slamming the door and leaving her in the trailer all night, even with food, won't make her feel safe there and won't make her any happier about getting in the trailer. In fact, there's a good chance that you'll find the food still there in the morning.

On the other hand, if you ask her to get into the trailer, leave the door open, and allow her to back out whenever she likes, at whatever speed she likes, and if you remain quiet, never yelling or hitting or trying to prevent her from getting out of the trailer, she may fly out backward the first few times or even the first ten or twenty times, but each time she comes out, she'll be a little less frantic and she'll be more likely to go back in when you ask her to. Why? Her fears are not being confirmed; since she can get out easily, getting in obviously doesn't mean that she's trapped. The more often she gets in and gets out, the more she'll relax about the whole idea.

Horses like familiar situations, and getting in and out of the trailer fifty times will begin to make the trailer very familiar to your mare. She'll come to see the trailer as just another place, not as a terrifying trap.

When she becomes more relaxed about getting in and out of the trailer, and she's doing everything more slowly, with a lower head, you'll be able to begin expanding her "comfort zone." Do this gradually, by asking her to stay on the trailer a few more seconds each time. Don't force her to remain in place until she panics, but use praise and your own calm demeanor to keep her calm and in that trailer for a little longer each time. By now, you should be able to "read" her quite well, so watch her carefully — now, instead of *allowing* her to back off the trailer, you need to start *asking* her to back off the trailer just before she decides that it's time to leave. Once she realizes that you will eventually give the signal to get out of the trailer, she'll be able to relax even more. Eventually, she may stand there dozing until you get around to telling her, "It's time to back out now."

Trailering Trauma

Q I have a seven-year-old half-Arabian, half-Mustang pony mare named Precious. We have had her for almost nine months, and she is a pleasure to handle on the ground — gentle, well trained, and obedient. She was raised by one family since she was 11 days old (they also had her mother, who was caught from the wild, and Precious was raised with her) and handled extensively, which shows in her trusting attitude toward people.

Temperamentally, she is spooky and very quick to react when something frightens her. She can spin around and run awfully quickly, and tends to get light in front if pushed when she is scared of something, but she tries very hard to be good. However, I know her mother rears.

Last week, we had a trailering disaster. We have trailered Precious once before, in an inviting stock trailer with her buddies who trailer well, and had no problems at all. She just looked at the trailer, then hopped right in. I followed her the whole journey and could see her the whole way, and as far as I could tell, she had a fine trip, and even seemed to enjoy herself. She also loaded fine coming home. This fits with what her previous family told me. But when we trailered her again, this time with a com- mercial shipper in a slant-haul trailer, we had problems. The other horse loaded first, and up to that point Precious was fine. Unfortunately, once the other guy was in, he started to snort and bang around a bit, and at that moment, the shipper shut the divider. Looking back, I think the other horse acting up and the slammed door alarmed Precious more than I realized. When I started to load her, she came forward willingly, but balked at stepping up into the trailer. Then she reared, and kept on rearing. The shipper took her away from me, saying I was going to get myself hurt. He put a chain on her, which I'm sure she's never experienced before, then started to load her. Of course, she was really scared and she reared again. This time she hit the chain and panicked. The shipper loaded her eventually, but it was a horrible battle, and once she was in the trailer, he completely lost his temper and yelled at her, hit her, and kicked her.

Your mare will come to see the trailer as just another place, not as a terrifying trap.

On the way to our event, I had plenty of time to think over the situation. Should I just have taken my upset pony home? Would I have taught her that rearing is acceptable if I let her get her way? Should I have made the other people late by insisting on loading Precious myself, in my own way? I decided the shipper wouldn't ever touch her again. Coming home, I disregarded all his "helpful" advice to get tough with her and show her who's boss, refused to let him touch her, and ignored his predictions that I'd get myself killed. Precious snorted and backed up when she saw him but she trusted me and came up to the trailer. Then she started to shake and she reared. I tried to just let her go up and hit herself on the chain (yes, I used the chain, as I felt I needed to have some control) and stay in front of the trailer, which was all I was asking her to do. Eventually, she calmed down a bit and walked into the trailer at my request (she was shaking all over, but she did it).

This last week, we have been having remedial trailering seminars, using the stock trailer, her best buddy, and breakfast. On the first day, she stood in front of the trailer for half an hour, watching her buddy eat her breakfast in peace and comfort while she stood in the rain. Precious eventually loaded voluntarily. The second day it took 20 minutes, and the third day it took 15. Tomorrow, I'll try another friend's slant-load for practice. Personally, I think it's amazing how quickly she's forgiven me for being such a ninny and getting her into that situation in the first place.

How do I handle rearing if it should happen again? Other people say I should "beat the daylights" out of her if she does so she'll never do it again, but I'm sure she's doing it because of fear, and I don't think beating her up will do anything but make her sure she was right to be afraid. Better yet, how can I make sure it never happens again?

A In a lot of ways, you've really answered your own questions in this letter. I'll fill in a few blanks for you, but your own instincts are obviously good, so I doubt you'll find any surprises here.

Your mare sounds lovely — and yes, very forgiving. Horses *are* forgiving, and aren't we lucky, because if they weren't, they would never allow us anywhere near them.

Your mare reacted out of fear, and you were right that beating her into the trailer was not the correct procedure — and beating and kicking her once she was in the trailer was utterly unconscionable. I would let the owners of this shipping company know about the behavior of their driver, because it was entirely unacceptable. If he couldn't get her calmly loaded into the trailer, he should have refused to take her. As it was, you are lucky that the mare wasn't injured, and even luckier that she is still willing to trust and listen to you and get into trailers when you ask her to.

Yes, you should probably have taken her home. When a human is determined to have a physical battle with a horse, sometimes all you can do is safeguard your horse by removing her from the scene. It's difficult to go up against a "professional," but this will be an excellent lesson for you: Whether the person in question is a shipper, a farrier, a vet, a trainer, an instructor, or a clinician, you are still responsible for your horse's welfare, and you have an obligation to say no and take your horse away from that person when things go horribly wrong. *You* are the person who is going home with the horse, and *you* are the person who will have to deal with the consequences of whatever the other person did wrong. It won't matter whether the abuse resulted from hurrying, ignorance, or any other cause — what will matter is the effect on your horse and the subsequent effect on you.

No show, competition, clinic, hunt meet, or Pony Club mounted meeting — even a rally — is important enough to force a horse into a trailer using those methods. As you've found out, the only guaranteed result is a fearful horse. Luckily for you, your mare likes and trusts you, and is willing to let you prove to her that this incident was unique — and never to be repeated.

Your remedial seminars sound like just what your mare needs. Show her, by frequent, calm repetition, that getting on and off trailers is not bad in itself. Show her, by good, careful driving, that trailering is not bad. Many horses dislike slant-load trailers because the stalls are narrow and short, but your mare is small enough that she should fit comfortably into a slant-load, so that shouldn't present a problem. But always handle her slowly and carefully, remembering that she now has a very unpleasant experience that she may remember if the sights and sounds and sensations trigger the memory.

Create a horse that trusts you so much that she rears only when she is badly startled, and then calms down quickly. That's as good as it gets with sensitive horses; you can't take away their instincts, but you can teach them to react less extravagantly to moments of surprise and fear.

"Beating the daylights" out of a horse will only teach her to fear you. Feel confident in ignoring the people who offer you that sort of "advice," and don't ever leave them alone with your horse, lest they take it upon themselves to "teach her a lesson" for you. People like that can quickly create a horse with a chronic rearing problem, and the last thing you need is a horse that is so frightened of you that she will rear when she sees you. Instead, create a horse that trusts you so much that she rears only on rare occasions when she is badly startled, and even then calms down quickly and stays on the ground. That's as good as it gets with sensitive horses; you can't take away their instincts, but you can teach them to react less extravagantly to moments of surprise and fear.

Keep training your mare as you are doing now. Teach yourself and whoever else handles her to lead her forward on a curve if she thinks about rearing, and to talk to her gently and loosen the lead rope instead of tightening it, as yelling and pulling can trigger a rear. Teach yourself and whoever else rides the horse to send her forward on a curve or circle if she thinks about rearing under saddle, and to talk to her gently and relax the reins instead of pulling back or up on them. Learn to recognize the moment when your mare has been pushed too far and can't handle the pressure — and then learn to recognize the moment before that moment, back off, and help her stay calm.

Loading Horse into Trailer

Q I have hit a trailering glitch with my horse. I have been teaching him to "load himself," with me standing outside the trailer and sending him in. He will go in a hundred times. But as soon as he gets almost all the way in, he lowers his head to stand in front of the chest bar. I am concerned that if I leave the chest bar open he will keep going and get hung up in the front of the trailer, but with it closed, he stops too soon (I think he thinks he can't go any farther.).

If I gently swat him on the rear, he gets worried and backs out. I can send him right back in again, but he lowers his head on that last step and then doesn't want to go any farther. If I go to the front and pull him forward, he steps right up and I can hook him up, but I want him to walk in all the way by himself. How do I get him to pick up his head and take that extra step?

A You're obviously doing a great job of teaching your horse to load. Now let's find a way to persuade him to take that last step up toward the chest bar by himself.

I agree with you that swatting him isn't the answer; neither is pulling him in. There are two different ideas I'll suggest.

First, he may not realize until you remind him and he lifts his head that he *can* lift his head and take that additional step. One time-honored way to teach him is simply to have something there that he likes — tie up a hay net or hay bag in front of the chest bar, and let your horse figure out that taking one more step is worth the effort. This works well because he will do it for himself, and then when he is in the habit of doing it, he will do it whether or not the hay is there.

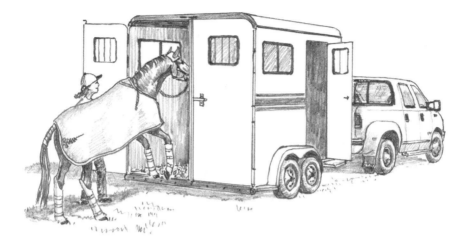

Every rider's dream — the "self-loading" horse.

Second, I suggest that in addition to this, you focus on teaching him to go forward when asked. If you can teach him to move forward (or backward, or sideways) one step at a time, he'll always be easy to load, easy to unload, and easy to put into strange stalls, wash stalls, stocks, and the like.

One of the easiest methods to teach a horse anything simple is clicker training. Don't be put off by the name: It's simply applied operant conditioning, originally designed for use with dolphins, very successful with dogs, and quite useful with horses, especially horses who belong to owners who are new to horses and not very fluent in horse language. Using this technique, you'll make a clicker noise as a "bridge," or marker, between the horse's action and your praise or reward; you will click instantly when the horse shows any sign of doing what you asked. In your horse's case, leaning forward or shifting his weight forward would both be signs of moving forward, and should be rewarded. The clicking sound lets the horse know, instantly and very clearly, when he has done what you wanted him to do. The click says, "Yes, that behavior is exactly right!"

Later, when you and the horse are both familiar with the clicker system of training, you'll be able to replace the clicker with a click of your tongue or a simple verbal command. These are useful because you may not always have the clicker in your pocket, but no matter where you go or what is happening, you'll have your voice with you.

Forcing Horses into Trailers

Q Is there any circumstance where you personally would force a horse to do something, like get into a trailer? Or do you think that this is always wrong and that there is never a valid reason for it?

A Yes, there are circumstances under which I would force a horse to do something, even though, as you can tell by many of my previous answers, I strongly believe that force is not a valid method of training. Sometimes, however, a situation can arise in which the issue is one of safety and survival, and this takes precedence over everything else, including training.

If I'm in a hurry to get to a show and I haven't trained my horse to get on the trailer, will I beat him to make him get into it? No. That's not for *his* benefit, in the short or the long term; it would only be for the benefit of *my* ego, and that's something that has no place around horses.

If I desperately want to get to an organized trail ride or if I'm on my way to the vet clinic for a non-emergency appointment, will I beat the horse to make him get into the trailer? No. Every time you work with a horse, you are training

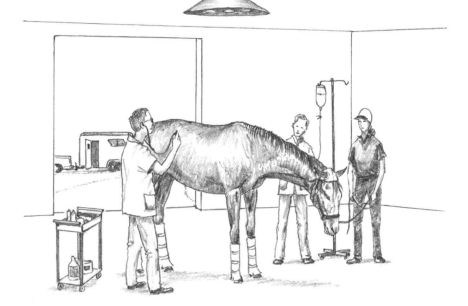

Sometimes getting a horse loaded into a trailer can literally be a "life-or-death" matter.

not just for that day, but for the next day and all the days to come. You need to begin as you mean to go on, and treat the horse well from the very beginning.

But there are circumstances under which I would do whatever was necessary, regardless of the effect on the horse or its training. In the past 20 years, I've seen some things that changed my original hesitation on this topic. For example, I've seen people frantically trying to load horses so that they can get out of the way of an oncoming canyon fire. In this case, there is no time to train and no time to explain or apologize. In such a situation, I'd use longe whips, longe lines, two brooms, and a winch if that's what it took to save the horse's life, and I'd worry about the other issues later. Similarly, if I had a horse with an acute surgical colic and I hadn't trained the horse to get into the trailer when asked, I would do whatever was necessary to get the job done.

The key question is, What matters most? If the horse's life and health will not be threatened if you don't get him into that trailer, then you should take your time and put in the training. If the horse's life or health *will* be threatened if you don't get him into that trailer, then you establish your priorities and do what you need to do. You can apologize to and train or retrain a *living* horse. You can't do anything at all with a dead one.

Step-Up vs. Ramp

Q I'd like to know about the advantages and disadvantages of a step-up trailer versus a ramp-load trailer. I would think that there might be safety and horse psychology issues to consider with both types.

A There's no definite answer to this question; the type of trailer you prefer is the type of trailer you prefer. Horses can do well with either or both.

There can be problems with both ramps and step-ups, and there are ways of making each one safer. Perhaps that is a logical place to begin.

Look at the main difference between the two trailers. A step-up is just a trailer without a ramp. Instead of walking up the ramp, the horse walks up to the trailer and steps up into it. Even when the elevation of the step is 18 inches, horses manage very well. It's not difficult for them, and although most humans would prefer to walk up a ramp, most horses are quite happy to climb into a step-up trailer.

The difficult part comes when the horse is asked to step down, backward, off the step-up trailer. With a ramp, the horse can move backward slowly, feeling the footing at each step. With a step-up, backing out means stepping out into empty space. The horse can't see behind himself and has no idea how far away the ground is, or even if the ground is there. Stepping backward blindly is a huge leap of faith for a horse.

Horses will step off these types of trailers, though. The secret is trust and confidence in their ability to rely on the handler to tell them what to expect. Verbal cues are very useful — on a ramp, a simple "Back" will do, but when exiting a step-up, especially a steep one, the horse will benefit from being taught the command "Step down." Some horses become much more confident when they understand that the handler will warn them whether to expect a step straight back, or back and down.

So which design is better? If you live in a very wet, rainy area, you may prefer a step-up because this type avoids the danger of a slippery ramp. Or you may choose to put something like coconut matting on your ramp to guarantee good traction, even in the rain. If you're not very strong, you may find it difficult to lift some ramps; if you find a very light, easy-to-lift ramp, you'll need to be sure that it's solid and steady enough for your horses to use with confidence.

Any horse can become reluctant to climb up a ramp that is flimsy, bouncy, or not placed firmly and solidly on the ground.

If your horses are elderly and somewhat stiff or infirm, a ramp will be easier for them. A trailer with a ramp may also be more practical if you intend to use it for very young horses — for example, if you plan to use your trailer to take your mares to be bred on their foal heats, you'll want to make it as easy as possible for a nine- or ten-day-old foal to get into and out of the trailer. For other horses, as long as they're active, healthy animals, it probably won't matter. A ramp can be a convenience, but it gives you more to clean and more hinges and latches to maintain.

From the horse's point of view, the easiest type of trailer would probably be one with dual ramps, so that no backing out is necessary; the horse enters the trailer by walking up the rear ramp and exits by walking forward and turning to walk down the front or side ramp.

If your horse leads and loads well, neither a ramp nor a step-up should be a problem.

There is potential for severe injury, so it's best to take a few precautions in *any* trailer. Even in wide, tall trailers, horses are safest if they wear head bumpers to protect the delicate poll area. Some horse owners routinely use bell boots and shipping boots or wraps, and these can protect the horse's lower legs from a close encounter with the front edge of a step-up trailer or the side of a ramp — two common sources of damage.

A horse that's reluctant to get onto a ramp trailer may walk around the side of the ramp and injure a leg on the edge or on the latch, and a horse in a hurry to get out of a ramp trailer may step off the side of the ramp and slide underneath, so it's best if the sides of the ramp are smooth and the latches don't protrude. The quality and position of the ramp matter, too. Horses need secure footing. Any horse can become reluctant to climb a ramp that is flimsy, bouncy, or not placed firmly and solidly on the ground. Trailer ramps should be heavy and solid, with some sort of mat or other heavily textured surface so that horses can step on them without slipping.

A horse that's reluctant to get into a step-up trailer may bang his front legs against the edge of the trailer or may find his hind legs sliding under the edge of the trailer, especially if the trailer is parked on a slick surface (tarmac, wet grass, mud). If the edges are sharp — or even just straight — this can peel the hair and skin off the horse's cannons. To guard against this sort of injury, step-up trailers should have rounded tubing welded under the edges.

That said, I should also point out that injuries that occur to horses getting into and out of trailers are rarely due exclusively to the design of the trailer. More often, they are due to a combination of factors, including trailer positioning and stability. A horse entering a trailer that shifts or starts to roll forward is likely to try to get away from that trailer in a hurry and can become injured on the way out. Handler error, usually compounded by the handler being in a hurry, is the cause I see most often. A horse's reluctance to enter a trailer is — assuming that the trailer is stable and of a suitable size — unlikely to have anything to do with the type of trailer used. It usually means that either the person attempting to load the horse on this occasion is causing a problem, or that there is a more fundamental problem with the horse's basic training.

> *A horse's reluctance to enter a trailer usually means that either the person attempting to load the horse is causing a problem, or that there is a more fundamental problem with the horse's basic training.*

Some horse owners insist that their horses' preferences are so strong that they will only consent to enter one type of trailer. Some even limit their activities: "I'd love to go to the show, but the only person from my barn who's going is Marlene. Her trailer is a step-up, and my horse will only get into trailers with ramps," or "Oh, I wish I could go with you, but my horse won't get into your trailer. He doesn't know about ramps; he only understands step-up trailers." This puts too many limits on what they can do and where they can go. Similarly, some horse owners are in the habit of leading their horses out of stock trailers or large slant-load trailers and don't feel comfortable with the idea of asking their horses to back out of a trailer. This, too, is limiting.

Horses should be taught to load and unload. Most of us trailer for pleasure — we take our horses to the trailhead or to a competition. It may not matter terribly if we're late to a competition or trail ride because the horse is reluctant to get into the trailer; those situations are certainly not matters of life and death. But what if we're on our way to the vet clinic with a horse suffering from injury or colic? What if there's another emergency, such as an oncoming hurricane or a fire? Those would be very bad times to spend half an hour dithering behind the trailer, wondering whether your horse will get in because he isn't used to that kind of trailer.

The type of trailer shouldn't matter, but the commands — such as "Go forward," "Go up," "Get in," and "Go backward," "Go down," "Get out," should apply to stock trailers, horse vans, trailers with ramps, and step-ups. Assuming, of course, that a trailer is large enough and solid enough to warrant asking the horse to enter, the issue in most cases is not whether it's the right sort of trailer, but rather whether the horse is well trained.

If you're buying a new trailer, you can choose the type you prefer; if you're buying a used trailer, find the biggest, sturdiest, and airiest trailer available, and don't let the presence or absence of a ramp keep you from purchasing the trailer you want. If he leads well, you can put your horse into whatever trailer you choose. He'll walk up the ramp if there is a ramp, or climb into the trailer if there is no ramp.

Hauling One Horse

Q I live in the United States and have a very ordinary trailer — a two-horse pull-along. I am going to start taking lessons with a woman who lives about half an hour from me, and I need to haul my horse over to her farm for the lessons. This is not a problem; my horse loads easily and the roads are very good. But I don't know something really important: Which side of the trailer should my horse ride on? I've been told that the horse should be on the left side, and then someone at the feed store said he should be on the right side, in case there is an accident. What is correct, and why?

A In the United States and Canada, where you drive on the right-hand side of the road, a single horse goes into the left side of a two-horse, straight-load, pull-behind trailer. If you live in the United Kingdom, where you drive on the left-hand side of the road, you would put the single horse into the right side of the trailer.

Roads are generally slightly higher toward their center and lower toward their edges, and you want to keep the weight in the trailer toward the high inside of the road. One horse in a two-horse trailer can destabilize the trailer if you go

A single horse should ride on the same side as the vehicle's driver.

up and down ramps and around turns with the heavy, tall weight of the horse on the low side of the turn. There have been some horrible trailer accidents as a result of people hauling one horse on the right side of their trailers and then making a tight turn to the right or getting a right wheel into a ditch.

Your horse will be most comfortable, and his ride will be easiest, if he is able to balance himself in the trailer. You can help him by giving him as much room as possible so that he can spread his feet. Horses also generally prefer to ride at a slight angle, with their heads more toward the center of the road.

If you'd like to give your horse relative comfort and freedom of movement, remove the center partition of your two-horse trailer and tie your horse on the left side. He'll be able to spread his feet wide for balance and shift his body toward the right, but most of his weight will be just where you need it to be — forward and on the left side of the trailer. Give your horse as much room as you can; he'll travel more comfortably and be less stiff and sore when he arrives.

CHAPTER 21

At the Show or Clinic

"SHOW NERVES" aren't just a human phenomenon — horses get anxious, too, but for different reasons. At competitions and other exciting, unfamiliar venues, even well-trained, experienced competitors — both equine and human — can become anxious and overstimulated. Whether a horse is nervous because he is reacting to his rider, or whether he is remembering previous experiences with another rider, it's essential that his rider take full responsibility for maintaining or changing the horse's attitude. Riders who are bringing their horses to a clinic or a competition primarily to expose them to new situations will need to remember that and not get too caught up in the excitement of the event.

Nervous Wreck at Shows

Q I have a 10-year-old German warmblood horse, Garfield, who is by nature very excitable and suspicious of his environment. He is and always has been spooky, in spite of a three-year campaign of mine to ignore and cure most of his fits, some of which are play acting and some of which are real (I have learned to tell which is which most of the time). He is naturally very forward-going, he is very obedient to the aids when in a quiet environment, and he thrives on work.

However, this attitude changes as soon as he is in unfamiliar surroundings and is aggravated even more if he is at a show. I have only now started to take him to very small unaffiliated shows where I know that there is very little fuss. If I get nervous, he is ten times more so. I have had to work on myself as well as on a gentle program of introducing Garfield back to the competition environment. I go to a small, local show every two months and just do one novice dressage class. I make sure he is comfortable and has a good time — nothing too stressful. But it is not getting any better!

He goes like an angel when schooled at home and in the warm-up area. Then, as soon as we enter the ring, he freezes and goes hollow, then becomes as stiff as a board and rushes through the test. He has been in competition at the same indoor school four times now, and it is the same every time. I don't think it was my nerves setting him off, as I was quite relaxed.

There is a similar problem with his jumping. He will jump happily at home but breaks out in a sweat at a show and naps [freezes] constantly if he sees jumps built up, for example, in the working-in area. I have never entered a jump competition with him so he should have no reason to distrust me.

Garfield was upset by his previous owner, who had him until he was six years old and tried to take advantage of his talent by pushing him too hard as a youngster in show-jumping competitions, until he was so frightened that he refused to jump a matchstick. He also had a very high head carriage when I got him, and I was told that he would not let himself be bitted. His previous owner claimed he was unridable because he had developed other vices such as rearing and bolting, which I have been able to cure. For the first six months, I worked him gently in a hackamore. Then I bitted him with a normal snaffle bit with no problem at all. I did not jump him for the first year; instead I took him right back to basics. He has fantastic paces, learns well, and finds dressage movements naturally easy. I have made lots of progress with him except for this one point. I am wondering whether aromatherapy or something similar would help his nervous disposition. What else can I do to produce a calm dressage test?

A I think that you have already defined and explained your problem quite well. Your horse has been overworked and abused at shows and has no positive expectations about any form of competition.

You're on the right track. What you are trying to do is give him a new set of experiences that will eventually outweigh the old, bad experiences. You are, effectively, trying to rewire his brain! It's the right approach to take, but it may take a very, very long time.

You know enough about Garfield's history to understand why he is so terrified of the show environment. There are probably many "triggers" for his fear — noise, crowds, the judge's box, stewards, other anxious horses. With a normal young horse being introduced to an exciting, stimulating show environment, it might take two or three such shows before he would be calm enough to do well at competitions. In your horse's case, it may take twenty shows or more. If you have the patience, you may be able to convince him that shows are not horrible, but it will take time.

The bustle and noise of the showgrounds take some getting used to.

Start imposing on your friends and neighbors. Take Garfield to as many different places as you possibly can, not necessarily with the intention of riding him. Take him down the road to a friend's farm, unload him, walk him around, hand graze him, give him treats, hand graze him some more, and take him home again. Make every experience positive, so that he can build up a set of good away-from-home experiences that may eventually outweigh the bad ones. Once he is calmer about the process, start riding him as well — again, schooling must be very calm and positive, with lots of rewards.

> *Make every experience positive, so that he can build up a set of good away-from-home experiences that may eventually outweigh the bad ones.*

After a couple of months, start going to every competition you can find — not to compete, but to simply go there and create a positive experience for your horse. Prepare as though you were going to compete, but once you are at the show, take Garfield for a walk in hand, take him into a quiet corner and longe him (if you do this at home), hand graze him, and hack him around. Do what you've been doing elsewhere. Show him the sights, talk to him, and carry a large bag of treats. Make the entire experience pleasant, so that the only things he associates with the process are treats, praise, and petting.

After a few such experiences, take him to a competition and enter him in a class or two, but with no intention of competing. I don't mean that you will scratch him from the tests, but that you will go into the arena and ride your horse and not do the test. Your only goal will be to keep him calm and happy, and if that means performing a few unscheduled halts and giving him treats — and using your voice and patting him — then do it. Because this is part of the retraining process, not a proper competition, you should arrange to show *hors concours;* you won't be eligible for a ribbon and so won't be tempted to perform instead of doing what you are there to do. If it isn't possible to show *hors concours,* have a word with the judge as you pass the stand and just tell her or him what you are there to do so that the judge won't ring the bell constantly or think you have lost your mind. Most judges will understand your goals exactly.

Ride the horse, and keep your breathing synchronized with his gaits. Don't worry about precision and accuracy and focusing on the test; do the best you can, but keep your mind on your business, which is helping your horse learn to relax by keeping yourself relaxed.

If this goes well, do it at a couple of competitions. If the positive experiences continue, you should be able to enter him in a few classes and ride them a bit more seriously. But again, your focus must be on the horse and on his relaxation. Focus on how your horse is feeling and on how you are riding and helping him, not on how you are doing. Smile, breathe, and keep thinking that you are doing this for fun. When you are thoroughly convinced of this and acting on it, it will be much easier for you to convince your horse.

At a competition, it isn't you he's reacting to, and it isn't you he distrusts. He's reacting to experiences he had before he ever knew you. Pain and fear are hard to overcome. You will only be able to help him overcome his fears if you are calm and positive and if you pay complete attention to him and ride each step. He won't rush through a test if you are breathing deeply and slowly and riding in the moment, constantly asking him for something (position, bend, straighten, etc.) and then rewarding him for trying (pat, scratch on the withers, murmur, praise). He can't think about two things at once; if he is focused on his fear, he can't focus on you. But if he is focused on you, he can't focus on his fear.

It can be desperately hard to reclaim a horse that's been abused at competitions. Garfield is carrying a lot of emotional baggage, and you must do everything you can to help him get rid if it. But you can't do it on a schedule, and you must realize that if there is enough baggage and it is heavy, he may never be able to put it all down. Still, he sounds talented, and it's certainly worth trying to create a new set of experiences and associations for him.

Horse Frightened of Stall at Show

Q I've just started competing my horse, Hawkeye. He is 10, and I am 43. We enjoy our rides at home, and he is very confident there. At shows, he's a different animal. I've always wanted to have a horse I could take to horse shows, but now I don't know if this is going to work out. I could never give up Hawkeye, but I don't want to give up showing either. I'm still so new to it, and I want to do it for a while and find out how much I like it.

Hawkeye is good in the trailer, but when we get to the show grounds, he panics when I put him in his stall. I've tried using a stall between two horses, a stall on the end of the row, and a stall on the end of the row with an empty stall on the other side. But no matter what, he panics, gets sweaty, and paces around and won't relax. He hardly eats either. He gets a little bit better on the second day and is usually not sweaty anymore by the end of the show, and by then he will also eat.

This makes me so anxious and upset! By the end of the second day, I'm exhausted. Why is he so frightened of the stalls at every show and is there anything I can do to make him relax? Will he always be this way? Please don't tell me to use drugs, because I really don't want to. Sometimes I wonder if he is afraid he has been sold, and if that's why he doesn't relax until he knows he'll be going home again. He is very calm in his stall at home.

A I can't promise an overnight cure for this kind of nervousness, but if you'll think like a horse and work with your horse's nature, you should be able to help him relax much sooner whenever he goes to a show.

Your horse's stall at home means security, peace and quiet, food, and familiar companions nearby. Your horse's stall at a show isn't really *his* stall; it's unfamiliar, there's no security associated with it, and there's certainly no peace and quiet. There's food, yes, but a nervous horse can't really take time for his food until he calms down. The horses next to him are strangers, so their presence doesn't help much. You are there, of course, but you're different, too. You're anxious and upset, and that just adds to your horse's nervousness.

It's very unlikely that your horse is worrying about the possibility of being sold — that's not a concept that horses understand. He *is* worried about having to stay in an unfamiliar enclosed space, and this is a concept that humans don't generally understand. To us, one stall looks very much like another, and as long as it's clean and safe, we find nothing scary about a stall at a show. But for your horse, this is a complete change of environment. He's somewhere different, and as a prey animal, he has to be on his guard. For a horse, "different" means, "this is bad," or, "this could get bad."

There are two ways you can help your horse relax in his stall at the show. The first way is to control your own emotions. *You* know that you're apprehensive and concerned because you're sure that Hawkeye will be anxious and agitated in his new stall, but Hawkeye doesn't understand that. He's already anxious, and your anxiety just makes his stronger. When prey animals are nervous, it's about potential predators — obvious or lurking — that could be dangerous. As far as

Be patient with the horse that needs time to adjust to unfamiliar surroundings.

he knows, you're anxious because there's a tiger hiding in the bushes or in the barn aisle, just waiting to pounce on both of you. If you're tense, he'll be tense. If you're relaxed, he may not relax completely, but he'll be less anxious.

The second way to help your horse is to make the unfamiliar stall more familiar. There's a very simple way to do this: Just take him out of it, walk him around a little, and put him back in. Do this five, ten, or even fifteen times, and you'll see him relax. To a human, this seems silly; it's the same stall, no matter how many times the horse goes into it. To a horse, this isn't silly at all; each time, the stall will be more familiar, and the horse will register, "Oh, yes, I've been here before, and nothing bad happened to me."

Horse Too Smart for Hack Classes

Q Squeak, my nine-year-old three-quarter Arabian gelding, is very pretty, and when he was four and five years old he did extremely well in class A Arabian shows (and open shows) in show hack and hunter pleasure classes. Unfortunately, he clued in very quickly and started anticipating every move, getting to the point where he would enter the ring and then just fight to go to the center to line up. Consequently, we gave up on flat classes for a while. Since then we've been doing dressage (which is harder for him to anticipate, but he still memorizes the tests better than I do!). I thought that he was just bored in the flat classes and that if we didn't do them for a while he'd get over it.

Last year, I put him in one flat class at a class A show. As soon as he made it halfway around the ring it was almost as if he realized this wasn't a dressage test but one of those evil flat classes, and he literally had what seemed like a temper tantrum. He wouldn't walk, he tried to head for the center, and when I wouldn't let him he just became uncontrollable. It was so bad I almost wondered if he had something under his saddle. We persisted through the class — came in last place, of course — and left the ring. It didn't seem to make any difference how mad I got or how I tried to appease him; he just wouldn't listen.

I checked him over after the class to make sure there was no physical reason for his reaction. Then I worked him in the holding ring, and he was fabulous. So good, in fact, that I got appreciative comments from others.

This is so frustrating. This horse is very pretty and would be virtually unbeatable in the show ring if he would behave. I know he isn't afraid — I thought perhaps it was the other horses in the ring or something — but he has

Find the work that your horse enjoys; some do not care for the show ring.

done this since he was four years old and has never had a bad experience. Plus, he is fine in the holding ring, where no end of wild and crazy things are happening (especially at an Arabian show!). Why does he hate these classes so? Shouldn't he do what I ask him, regardless of what he wants to do? Can an animal actually have these kinds of emotions? It isn't that he is picking up on any nerves from me; I showed his mother for ten years, so this stuff is truly old hat to me.

I would love to do some flat showing with him again, and hope to do so with his brother, Wilfred, but Wilfred is much smarter than Squeak and I wonder if he won't go "stale" even quicker. Do you have any solutions or suggestions for me? Squeak is smart enough to know that I can't get after him too much in the show ring. Should I just take him to schooling shows and battle it out once and for all? I really hate the idea of duking it out with him, but I just don't know what else to do.

A It sounds as if Squeak is just not very interested in those hack and pleasure classes. When you put him in a different sort of class, one that requires you to pay attention to him, and him to pay attention to you, he's fine. But when you put him in autopilot classes, you pay less attention to him, and he loses interest.

I'm afraid that there are really only two obvious choices here: You are either going to have to forget about those classes and focus on dressage instead, or you will need to figure out a way to ride him every step of every class, so that he is never expected to go on autopilot. You should also consider whether he simply doesn't like working in a group. Some horses are wonderfully suited to trail riding or pleasure classes because they love being in a crowd, but can't deal with the solitude of the dressage arena or the show-jumping ring. Others are great when they're alone but can't adjust to group classes. Squeak may just not like the atmosphere in those classes or the tension he feels from you because you're wondering whether he's going to do well or not. You may as well figure out what works for Squeak and then do that.

Duking it out with him isn't going to make him any happier about pleasure and hack classes, and it isn't going to make him enjoy them any more. It also won't help him enjoy *you,* so it's really a counter-productive idea. If you can't persuade him that the classes are fun, fighting with him certainly won't get that message across.

Yes, animals have emotions and preferences — and sometimes their preferences don't match ours. When that happens, try to convince them that what you want to do is fun: Set them up to succeed, talk to them, and reward them. If that doesn't work, find out what they do well and enjoy, and then do that instead! It's not the horse's job to do what you want to do and like it, regardless of his own preferences; it's the rider's job to enable the horse to enjoy his work. If he can't enjoy a certain type of work, you have to find the work he can enjoy.

If Squeak has been doing this since he was four, he's had plenty of time to get to like it — or get bored or annoyed. But before you decide that it's all a matter of attitude, check a few other things.

Do you use different tack for these classes? If he's fine in the dressage arena, he obviously doesn't have a problem with that bit and saddle, or with whatever spurs you may use. Go to a less expensive schooling show and try using the same tack and equipment in a pleasure or hack class. If he seems normal, then maybe it's the equipment that bothers him. Sometimes something perfectly innocent, like an extra-thick saddle pad or a show girth, can make a horse miserably uncomfortable, and the result will be bad behavior in any class he's entered in.

Animals have emotions and preferences, and sometimes they don't match ours. When that happens, try to convince them that what you want to do is fun: Set them up to succeed, and reward them.

If the tack checks out fine, you may just have a horse that doesn't enjoy those classes. Some do, and some don't. The ones that do aren't necessarily the most interesting horses. For example, years ago, I had a little Quarter Horse gelding, Moneyline, who won Western Pleasure classes all the time, and probably would have won them whether anyone was riding him or not. He certainly wasn't affected by anything I or any other rider did. This was the exact opposite of dressage. Here, the horse was in charge. He would go into the ring and "show" himself, and whenever the announcer picked up the microphone to ask for a jog or a lope, Moneyline would change his gait when he heard the microphone rattle. All the rider had to do was sit there and smile. He did wonderfully — although we would have lost every class if the announcers ever changed the order of gaits — but he was strictly a show horse. That was his job, he liked it, he did it well, and he didn't want to do anything else. He didn't like trails, and he didn't like working alone, so when I wanted to do those activities with a horse, I got another horse.

Maybe Wilfred will be your show horse, and maybe Squeak would like to be your dressage horse. It won't hurt if you only take him to dressage shows for a year or two and then put him back in a pleasure or hack class to see what happens. The dressage will only improve his performance, and if he still doesn't like those classes, you may not mind so much if he's good at his other job.

Show Anxiety

Q I am worried about going to only my second show in my life. My trainer has been working with me for two years, and I had been riding for seven years before that. I've gone from Tennessee Walkers to Quarter Horses to Arabians — you name it! But I just started riding a new horse. He is a Thoroughbred-Paint cross and is drop-dead gorgeous, but he has a little problem with spooking.

The show is going to be major: There are 70 to 80 stalls, a huge arena, and at least 20 people in each class. All I'm used to is the schooling show I went to for my first time and I only entered in one class! I'm scared to death. My trainer asked me to enter "at least" six classes, but because it's such a big show and so many people are going to be there, my horse will have so many things to spook at. The last thing I want is to be lying there on the ground with a horse bucking around, scared to death of a crumbling potato chip. Is there any way that I can get both my horse and myself comfortable in a show ring?

A It sounds to me as though you may be too nervous to have very much fun at this show. My suggestion is that you start with a much smaller show, where you can be more relaxed. I can guarantee you that your tension will become your horse's tension instantly, and if you aren't able to be calm, stay calm, and retrieve your calmness quickly after a spook or buck, this show is not going to be fun.

If it's the only show in your area for the next umpteen months and you're determined to participate, why not go early and spend the morning just walking around leading your horse? That way you can both get used to the atmosphere,

When both horse and rider are new to showing, it pays to start small.

and when you go into the ring for a class, it won't be totally unfamiliar. If your horse has a great time walking around with you, seeing the sights, getting groomed, eating treats, and generally thinking that the show is a good place to be, you'll both be able to relax and enjoy one or two afternoon classes.

I think it would be a big mistake to sign up for a lot of classes at your first big show. It's exhausting for you and the horse, not because of the physical demands of the classes themselves, but because of traveling to the show, being in an unfamiliar place, working in large groups, working on new footing, and the like.

If your horse had done this all his life, enjoyed it, and could "baby-sit" you through the experience, you could safely sign up for three or possibly four classes, although that's a lot to ask of both of you. Or if you had done this all your life, enjoyed it, and could "baby-sit" him through the experience, then you would automatically put him in one or two classes. If you want to get a horse started on the right path for a show career, you have to keep things pleasant and low-key. This means giving the horse a chance to go to a couple of shows and learn about the show atmosphere and then going in the class *or not,* depending on his degree of relaxation.

It also means participating in that class with a different goal. The others may be there for ribbons, but you have to be there for your horse, and your goal must be to show him that he can work in that ring, safely and comfortably, even with the other horses present and the crowds watching and the microphone rattling. This may mean coming into the middle and stopping during the class to pet the horse and let him stand and relax — and thus waving good-bye to any hope of a ribbon. If you need to do this, do it.

If you participate, don't fight with the horse and don't expect him to act like a seasoned performer, because he isn't. What you can fairly expect from him at a show is this: Whatever the two of you do easily and reliably at home, he will be able to do about 50 to 60 percent as well at this show. *Both* of you will be nervous and distracted. Keep this in mind, and select a couple of classes that are likely to be very easy for you both. Focus on enjoying the day. Then you can have a good time and look forward to your next show.

Standing Quietly at Halter

Q I have a four-year-old Paint filly that I'd like to show this year in halter and showmanship classes. My problem is that I'm not sure how to ask her to stand quietly when there is so much for her to see, hear, and explore at the show grounds. When we try this at home she pays no attention to me, and while she won't pull away from me, she will push me out of her way if she wants to turn around and see something or call to another horse.

A What you have to do is get your filly's attention and keep it on you for a reasonable amount of time. You can't make her stand and expect her to pay attention to you when you, too, are looking around at other horses, people, and events.

Go to some shows with your filly, but don't enter her in any classes. Groom her, band her mane if you want to, and walk her around the grounds for a couple of hours. Let her graze here and there and get used to a lot of commotion, including trucks, trailers, tents, dust, other horses and riders, and the noise of the PA system. If you aren't competing you won't get tense and worried, and you'll be able to use those first few shows as teaching time for your mare.

I think that you and your mare would probably enjoy doing some clicker training, which will help you learn how to get and keep your mare's attention, keep her focused and happy, and, most importantly, keep *you* focused on *her*.

Timing is key in halter classes. A horse asked to hold a pose for too long may become agitated.

Don't try to teach her to set up or do showmanship patterns at first. The lesson you want to teach her is very simple: Show grounds are nice places. Once she's relaxed and knows that the commotion isn't going to hurt her, you can start to use your clicker training to put her through her setting up and patterns. Use lots of praise, lots of treats, and lots of clicking, and then take her home.

Go to some shows without your mare and watch the classes you plan to compete in. Watch the handlers, the horses, and the judge. Don't try to watch everyone at once. Take notes. Then go home and practice what you've learned. *Now* you can start to get ready for a competition.

Here's one showmanship hint: Remember that in a halter class, horses are not asked to hold the pose forever. When you've posed your horse in the lineup, look at the judge and notice where he or she is. If the judge is seven horses away from you and you try to keep your horse perfectly posed and totally attentive until it's her turn to be inspected, she will become bored, frustrated, and cranky. Amateur handlers tend to make this mistake, and it costs them ribbons.

Watch the professionals. They let their horses relax while the judge is looking at the other horses, and then ask for the pose and focus while the judge is finishing writing up the previous horse. If you learn to let your horse relax when she can relax and then ask her to be alert and focused only when she needs to be, she'll always be fresh, eager, and interested whenever the judge is looking at her.

Nervous Horse Loses Weight at Shows

Q We bought a five-year-old Thoroughbred gelding, "Skinny" Binny, four months ago. He raced five times when he was three. He had a year off in a big field in Virginia and was only occasionally hill-topped and lightly trail ridden. Then he was professionally trained for three months.

My 13-year-old daughter and her instructor are trying to turn him into a hunter and show horse. At his first show, he was fine during the morning warm-up, until the loud speakers were used. He got very nervous and afraid. He broke out in a sweat, shook all over, and wouldn't stand. We suspect it is a flashback from his racing days. We decided not to do any classes and just get him used to everything, so we untacked him and grazed him. He eventually calmed down, until we could walk him right near the speakers without a reaction.

We were there for six hours, and his trainer says he looks like he lost about 100 pounds that day! He wouldn't drink at the show, but he drank a lot as soon as he was in his stall, and we gave him a bran mash that night. Binny is about 300 or so pounds underweight as it is. (He gets rice bran, coco soya, and a huge bucket of beet pulp every day in addition to the normal hay and grain that the other horses get.)

We knew that this show season would just be for getting him happily adjusted to showing, without pressure. The weight loss is my main concern. It has taken us four months to get him to gain even a little weight; we were shocked to see how quickly he could lose it. Do you have any suggestions for minimizing the weight loss during shows?

A If you want your horse to relax at shows, you're going to have to make that your focus for at least the next few shows. He might well have had a flashback to his racing days. What you did was exactly right — you took off the tack, grazed him, let him calm down, and generally gave him the impression that the show was not quite as scary as he had first thought. Well done!

Now, go out and do it again and again. Take him to shows, all kinds of shows — Western, hunter, jumper, dressage, local schooling shows. Take him to other people's barns, hand-graze him on the grounds and ride him in their arenas. Be so quiet and calm and nice that he knows he isn't in trouble and that he can always count on you.

Hand grazing is a good way to help calm a nervous horse.

You're on the right track as far as his training is concerned; this time next year, he should be happy to go to shows, because he'll be convinced that they're really nice places where horses have a good time. Follow the example of his previous owners, who began his training as a field hunter by hill-topping (observing the hunt, but not actively participating). The gradual approach is the best approach.

The weight loss probably isn't cause for concern. After all, it's not muscle weight that he's lost. Six hours of nervous sweating and not drinking can take an immense amount of weight off a horse, but most of that weight will be water weight, and it will come back as soon as the horse is drinking normally again. As he learns to relax away from home, he'll be more willing to drink.

You can try some of the old tricks like putting some kind of flavoring in your water at home (peppermint, Kool-Aid powder, or apple juice — whatever he likes) and adding the same amount of the same flavoring to his bucket at the shows, so that the water will seem familiar. You can even bring your own water to the show, but it's really much more useful to teach him to drink the water that's available wherever he goes.

Horses that are frightened are often unwilling to drink because dropping their heads and swallowing water puts them in a vulnerable position. They can no longer see things that might be sneaking up on them, and swallowing makes it harder for them to hear things. Again, as he relaxes, he'll find it easier to drop his head and take a drink without worrying.

When he's less tense, he'll be able to think about eating — and he'll relax even more. Chewing is relaxing for horses. Hand graze him, bring hay with you to the show, and don't forget that if you want him to gain weight, lots of grazing and lots of hay, salt, water, and possibly rice bran should be all he will need at this stage. If he needs more calories, you might consider offering him a good-quality complete pelleted feed instead of grain. Unlike grain, complete pelleted feeds aren't conducive to the development of gastric ulcers. Such ulcers are common in racehorses, show horses, and grain-fed horses, and one of the problems caused by ulcers is a reluctance to eat.

You've only had this horse for four months, and he hasn't had much experience out in the world. He knows a little about racing, not much else, and he doesn't know you very well yet. It takes time — quality time *and* quantity time — to build a relationship with a horse. Take your time, be very patient, and just keep showing him, over and over, that he is always safe with you. Thoroughbreds are intelligent animals; he'll figure it out. Right now he's basing his expectations on assumptions you can only guess at. Your job is to start creating new routines, new habits, and a whole new set of assumptions in your horse's mind.

To stay on the right path, just remember that you need to be consistent, kind, and take everything slowly. An old horseman once said, "I have to go slowly — I'm in a hurry!" This is one of the great secrets of horsemanship: The quickest way to get where you want to go is to take as much time as it takes to complete each step. If it helps, put up a banner over your stable door that says *Festina Lente* — Latin for "make haste slowly." That's the only way to work with horses.

CHAPTER 22

Moving to a New Home

MOST HORSE OWNERS have dreams of keeping their horses at home, where they can see them and interact with them at any time, and where the horses can be kept under exactly the conditions that their owners prefer. At least, that's what the owners think, up until the day when they're ready to bring their horses home. At that point, most people are assailed by doubts: Is the pasture grass good enough? Is the fencing safe? Will my horse miss his friends? Will he like it here? As in so many other cases, success is largely a matter of proper preparation. Your facilities don't have to be beautiful, but they should be safe. Remove toxic plants from the environment; put up a solid, horse-safe fence; and provide some sort of shelter before bringing your horse home.

Am I Ready to Bring My Horse Home?

Q I am about to close the deal on the purchase of a home on a little more than three acres of land. I think my dream of having my horse at home is finally going to become a reality, but now come the worries!

All of a sudden I'm realizing all kinds of things that I didn't worry about with a boarding stable. I plan to get a second horse, but maybe not right away. The neighbors have goats on the other side of a fence adjacent to where my horse would be. There are also other horses, not beyond an adjacent fence, but in sight. Would this be enough company for my horse for a month or so until I get him an equine friend?

Also, how tall do fences need to be? I've read a bunch of different things about types of fences, but nobody seems to be able to tell me how tall the fence should be or to even give me a guideline. The property already has a small shed/barn area. I plan to leave the doors open and just let my horse have access to the land. Eventually, I hope to be able to cross-fence the pasture to save the grass, but I know we won't be able to do that immediately. The pasture area is already fenced with wood posts and wire mesh. I think the wire mesh is thick enough to be sturdy, and the holes should be small enough that a hoof couldn't fit through. My big concern is the front of the pasture, which has a chain-link fence. I haven't measured it, but I think it is only about 4 feet tall. Is there a way to raise the height of a fence without replacing the whole thing?

My other problem is that there are a lot of thorny bushes in the pasture. Should I shred them? Is there a good source of information about dealing with the pasture?

A How exciting to be bringing your horse home — and how lucky for him that you want to be sure that everything is ready for him.

Your horse will probably adjust well to his new situation, but if he is used to being turned out with buddies, it's a good idea to arrange to have one for him. Horses on the horizon may keep him quiet and calm, or they may make him want to jump out of the enclosure and go find them. It depends on how desperate he is for company.

Fence height is a matter that affects the budget. Unfortunately, the safest fencing — tall, sturdy, as horseproof as possible, and with "give" to it in case of a horse-fence collision — is also the most costly. The best horse fencing is generally diamond-mesh or V-mesh wire, 5 or 5½ feet high, with a board on top. This will keep most horses safely inside. Stallion fencing is often higher — 6 to 8 feet. Some people get by for years with 4-foot fencing, but it's unlikely to keep a horse in if he sees a reason to leave.

If your wire mesh fence is V-style, you've got horse fencing. If the openings are two-inch rectangles, then you have fencing that, with a top board and perhaps an electric wire if the fence is well under 5 feet, should be suitable for adult horses (foal hooves *will* fit through that size opening, however). If the openings are four-inch squares or larger, they will easily accommodate adult hooves, and you'll want to replace this fencing with something safer. Check whether the fence is woven or welded wire; if it's woven, work with it. If it's welded wire, plan to replace it, piece by piece, as you can afford it, and definitely put an electric wire on the inside top portion to keep the horses away from the fence itself.

You'll probably want to replace the chain-link fence, too; it's not particularly useful or safe for horses, and 4 feet is very low. Again, you can probably put an electric wire on the inside top of the fence, which will help keep the horses away from that section of fence until you can replace it.

Making your property horse-safe takes thought, money, and time. But it's well worth it.

Call your county extension agent and ask him to come out and inspect the pasture with you. If there are dangerous plants growing there, find out now — and find out how to get rid of them. If you have thorn bushes, they may need to be pulled up and/or burned; your extension agent will be able to advise you. He'll also be able to suggest grasses that are good for horse pasture and that will grow in your area, so that you'll know how to reseed the pasture when the time comes.

If possible, you might want to go on boarding your horse elsewhere until you have your electric wire installed and your pastures in shape. Don't forget that you'll need to walk every inch of that pasture; there always seems to be a forgotten wire, piece of glass, old metal post, or broken piece of fence somewhere. You'll want to find that before your horse does, as horses seem to have a magnetic attraction for things that can hurt them.

Bringing a Young Horse Home

Q About three months ago, some very generous friends gave me a two-and-a-half-year-old black-and-white tobiano Paint gelding. He has lived at the same home with two other geldings all his life. I have a couple of concerns about moving Dancer to our home.

Dancer has impeccable ground manners; he yields to very minimal pressure both away and toward you, and he also accepts a saddle well. We recently tried to put weight in the stirrup, and Dancer began to buck out of fear and not understanding what we were asking from him. At this point, my husband and I decided to take him to a trainer who has studied with Ray Hunt and has a good grasp on the difference between respect and fear.

We will move Dancer from the only home he has ever known to the trainer's, and then we will be moving him to our home. He will be the only horse in our pasture, with two yearling calves (he has been around longhorn cattle at his present home). Will the calves give him the comfort of a "herd" when we move him here, and how can I help these moves between his present home, the trainer's, and our home be as stress-free as possible for all of us?

I have spent a minimum of 30 minutes a day with him for the last three months working on ground manners, grooming, and so forth. I also intend to visit with him every day that he is in training, as the trainer is very close by.

A   Your plan is a good one. Your young horse will be better off if he is started by a trainer, especially if the trainer moves slowly and remembers that this is still a very young horse that is not yet ready for under-saddle work.

Whenever possible, spend time with your horse and the trainer at the trainer's. Don't just visit with your horse (although that is a good idea too!), but spend time observing his training. Watch, listen, and learn, so that eventually, when the horse is ready, the trainer will work with both of you. This is important. Your horse is being taught a new language, and when he comes home to you, the two of you will communicate better if you have learned the same language from the same trainer.

I'm sure that Dancer will miss his buddies, but at least with two calves around he'll have companionship of some sort! It's definitely better than nothing. Horses need other horses, but they can be kept with calves or a goat; the important thing is that they shouldn't be kept alone.

Once he's moved to the trainer's and has gotten used to that, it won't be quite as strange for him to move home with you. The first move is the most confusing. You will be feeding him the same feed and treating him and working with him just as you did when he was at the trainer's, and he will know you, so there will be some continuity. It may even work *for* you, as he may see you as his security — the only one he knows in this new place.

Given a choice, most horses will accept cattle as pasture companions.

Bear in mind that he will miss the other horses, though, and that he may act wild for a while. It's normal. Just be very careful with him, and for safety's sake, you might want to wear your ASTM/SEI-approved helmet whenever you are handling him, not just when you ride.

If he does get a bit wild at first, you'll need to understand that he's confused and disoriented and that, to a horse, all changes in environment are potentially threatening. This is all thanks to millions of years of evolution; the Gene Police tossed all of the brave, calm horses out of the gene pool umpteen years ago. The ones that lived long enough to reproduce were the ones that thought they saw something scary and ran away. The sensitive, observant, nervous ones lived and bred, and we're riding their descendants today.

There's not much you can do about the stress, other than to get Dancer used to doing different things in different places, and let him enjoy whatever he does. When you bring him to your place from the trainer's, you may be in for a week or two of Dancer running the fence and looking for other horses and making faces at the calves. Then he may well settle in and become a calm and rational horse. Ask your trainer for some tips on managing Dancer at home, and ask whether the trainer would be willing to come to your home occasionally and work with you and Dancer there. If your trainer is good, and if you stay with your plan and learn to work with your horse, everything should go quite well. You'll know how well it's gone when Dancer has been under saddle for six months and still comes running up to you when he sees you with tack. Keep him happy, keep him secure, let him know what the rules are, don't punish him for being a horse, and you'll do just fine.

Young Horse in New Surroundings

Q I brought my new, young (almost three years old) filly home and put her in the pasture with my old mare. They are good friends now. In fact, they may be too close! I have a limited amount of time to ride, so I usually see the horses every other day and ride three times a week. The problem is that my filly is a complete pill about leaving the other mare. When I take her out to ride, she screams and yells, pitches fits, and isn't any fun to ride. The old mare doesn't care; she just goes on grazing. If I take the old mare out, she is calm while the young mare runs alongside the fence, screaming and carrying on.

Before I bought her, my filly lived in a field with some other horses, and she didn't carry on like this. My neighbor says that if I put the old mare in his field for a couple of weeks, the young mare will calm down and learn to depend on me instead. Will that work? His fence isn't very safe, but my old mare is quiet. Also, will the young mare start depending on me so quickly? I need to be able to work her more. She hadn't been handled much before I bought her, and she was just barely broke for riding.

A Your filly is only half-grown; she's still a baby in many ways. She obviously depends on your older mare for companionship and security. Your older mare is quite secure and not dependent on the younger one. That's why the filly is the only one to make a huge fuss when they're separated. She's upset and insecure.

The good news is that you should be able to change the way your young mare behaves, since the behavior isn't yet an iron habit. The bad news is that you won't be able to do this on a three-times-a-week basis; you'll need to spend much more time with her, at least for a while. This may be what you do with your vacation time this year.

Since the filly had so little handling before you bought her, it's probably safe to assume that she has never learned to bond with and rely on humans. Helping her learn this is now your job. You'll need to teach her to feel comfortable and secure when she's with you, so that she won't feel insecure and alone when the two of you are together.

Horses naturally feel secure with one another and depend on one another for company, security, and even survival.

Horses naturally feel secure with one another and depend on one another for company, security, and even survival. The herd means safety, so other horses mean safety. Humans do not automatically mean safety, but a well-handled young horse can learn to be comfortable and secure around humans, even when there are no other horses around. In fact, that's the basis for early handling and for most forms of training.

Your neighbor is right: It will be easier for you to help your young mare learn to rely on you if she sees you as her primary companion. If you feel that your old mare will be safe behind his fence, moving her for a few weeks could help.

But you'll need to be quite sure that she'll be safe, and you'll also need to be sure that your own fences are high, tight, and solid.

You'll need to spend a good deal of time with your young mare and work with her several times a week. You don't know how she was handled, but you do know that she hasn't bonded with a human yet. To ride her, take her away from home — go somewhere new, where she will feel dependent on you.

New Horse Adjusting to New Home

Q I purchased a five-year-old Missouri Fox Trotter mare about two weeks ago, and she was a dream when I rode her at her home. She was also perfection when she first arrived here, while her trainer was still around. Since then, she's extremely insecure, and I feel that's because she was at her previous home since she was eight months old. She doesn't know me or her surroundings very well. When my daughter and I go out on the trail, if my daughter's gelding passes her, she has a fit. She bounces from front legs to back legs, sort of like a canter in place. I feel she's testing the waters for rearing.

Now I'm thinking she needs some time to settle in and bond with me. Then she needs to learn to accept parting from the gelding in baby steps — just a few strides at a time. I figure she doesn't really know me from Adam, and she really has no good reason to want to please me or trust me yet. Currently, all her attention is on her surroundings and the other horses, not on me. Today, I took her in the round pen to do basic inside and outside turns, which are all based on attention to me. Then we proceeded to eat lunch together. I think this is the type of thing we need for now, instead of demanding she let my gelding canter past her and get herself worked into a tizzy. But under no circumstances do I want her to think she can do whatever she pleases, and a horse that can't be separated from others is pretty worthless.

Is my thinking on the right track? I know it can take quite a while for a horse to adjust to her new home. I don't want to push her too hard too fast. Do you think I should just proceed slowly, a little at a time, and let her develop trust in me? Or is there another way I should proceed?

A Your instincts are excellent and your plan is right on target. It will take your mare some time to adjust to her new home. As a general rule, I

Because she has a companion, this horse feels secure enough to lie down for a nap.

would give her at least one week — if not one month — for each year that she lived in her old home to become accustomed to her new surroundings, pasture, companions, humans, feed, and daily routine. Her whole life has changed! Horses that have been very actively shown or that have changed hands (and barns) many times are often much more quick to adjust to a new place. Just relax, be very clear and calm with the mare, and she'll come around. It sounds as though she's found a wonderful home.

It's normal for her to be high-headed and inattentive while she's taking in all the changes. Her attention will be on her surroundings for several weeks. This is absolutely normal, and you shouldn't worry about it or feel that she doesn't like you because she's ignoring you. She's just being a horse — a prey animal that relies on sensitivity and speed as a warning and defense system.

Do you remember how it felt when you were a child and spent your first night in another house? Every stair creak, every loose floorboard, every fan, every brush of a branch against a window made your heart pound simply because you weren't used to the noises and couldn't identify them. It's quite similar for a horse in a new place. This nervousness is compounded by the nature of the horse, which is very sensitive and very attentive, enabling a horse to notice all the changes and strange sounds, smells, and sights and to be prepared to run away from anything that could possibly be harmful. For a prey animal, *anything* means, well, *everything*. Eventually, your mare will learn what the new sounds and smells and sights are, and the more relaxed she feels, the more confident she will get, and the more attention she will be able to pay to you.

You mention that she doesn't know you — think about this. She will learn to know you through her daily time with you, and she will learn to trust and like you through your treatment of her. Be calm and confident when you handle her, treat her gently, move slowly, and talk to her in a low voice. Again, think back to when you were a child. If you were in a strange place, everyone you knew was gone, and you were frightened and needed reassurance, would you accept comfort from a strange adult? What if that strange adult made sudden, jerky movements and yelled? Put yourself in your horse's place and realize that your behavior is the only way you have to convey your intentions to her. She's a horse, after all; you have to show her what you're about. Telling her that she's come to a lovely home and you love her won't make an impression on her, but handling her kindly and consistently will. Your handling methods sound ideal; just keep on spending quality time and quantity time with her.

Once your mare has settled in — and this, as I said, could take several weeks or several months — take her for rides in a familiar area, maybe even her own pasture at first, or down a nearby wide trail. Don't believe anything you've been told about her training and experiences — let her tell you what she knows and what she's comfortable with. Many well-meaning horse owners get into trouble by assuming that their horses know things that they do not. Assume that she knows nothing, and teach her everything. If she already knows something, that's fine; you can "teach" it to her very quickly. If she doesn't know it, you'll be glad you took the time.

Introducing an Old Horse to a New Home

Q I am seeking advice on the best way to introduce a previously boarded 20-year-old mare to her new home (ours). The barn is currently under construction, and we expect her to move in within a month or so. We have six dogs who have never seen a horse.

Also, do you have any knowledge of, or experience with, miniature horses? I am wondering about a stablemate for our horse. I have heard that goats and horses are good companions.

A Congratulations on getting your mare onto your own property; you must be very excited about that. The single most important factor will be your fencing — horse-safe fencing is a must. Any horse moved to a new facility will probably be nervous, worried, and missing her friends for the first few weeks, and you want everything to be as safe as possible so that an anxious horse running the fence line can't injure herself.

Even if she runs the fence line, though, turnout is essential! More is better, and pasture is ideal. A mare of 20 years will be much healthier if she spends most of her time outdoors and can walk about freely and graze. If the arrangements at her current barn involve less turnout time, find out whether you can arrange to increase her turnout for the last week or so. If you need to turn her out in a halter for some reason, be sure to buy a safety halter with a breakaway leather crownpiece.

If she'll be spending any time in a stall, be sure that the stall is safe, with no sharp edges, no doors that open inward, and no protruding nails or hinges, and comfortable (large and airy, with lots of light and deep bedding). Use the bedding that she's used to, at least in the beginning, both for the sake of continuity and for her health. If she's always been bedded on shavings or rice hulls and you fill her stall with straw, she may eat the bedding! The stall will be new and unfamiliar to her at first, but it will help if you put her in it briefly, then lead her out of it, walk her around, and put her back in it briefly, then repeat the process five or six times. Repetition is very reassuring to a horse, because at some point when she goes into the stall, she will relax a little and think, "Oh yes, I've been here before."

Introduce any feed changes at her boarding barn in the weeks before she moves; for a week or two, mix her new hay and grain with her old hay and grain, adding a little more of the new and a little less of the old every day. The feed should no longer be new and different when she arrives at her new home. The stress of moving can change a horse's eating and drinking patterns and upset a horse's digestive system, and you don't want to add to that stress by changing her feed at the same time.

Your dogs should be kept in their run until the mare is accustomed to her new home. Then you can introduce them to her, one at a time, on leads. If they are well trained and will come, go, and "down-stay" when told, they should be fine off the lead. If they aren't, it would be a good idea to train them before your mare comes home, even if this means boarding her for another month or two.

Horses and dogs can become good friends if they are properly introduced.

Otherwise, someone may get hurt. Some horses are understandably terrified of groups of dogs and will destroy a fence and injure themselves in their attempt to escape what they see as a pack of predators. Some horses have previous experience with dogs, are not fond of them, and will kick or bite them if the dogs get too near their legs. It's safer for everyone if the dogs are well mannered.

Horses do need companions; they are social animals and don't do as well if they are alone. Depending on your situation, you might want to adopt a second horse or some other animal to be a companion for your mare. Miniature horses are small, but they are still horses and have to be treated like horses. You have to go to a lot of trouble to keep minis; a tiny halter is a onetime expenditure, true, but there are other things to be considered. For example, you may need to modify your fencing and the height of mangers and water troughs. Minis still need salt blocks, shots, worming, and regular hoof trimming, just like big horses, and it doesn't cost less because they're smaller — it can actually cost *more*.

Getting a farrier to come out to a barn for only two horses can be difficult, getting him to come out for one horse is almost guaranteed to be difficult, and getting him to come out to trim one horse and a mini can be impossible, because farriers have to get down on their knees to trim the hooves of miniature horses. Some farriers simply don't want to do this. This is something that you might want to discuss with your farrier in advance of any purchase, and it's also something you might want to discuss with your vet.

In fact, you might ask your vet about finding a companion animal for your horse; he may well know of another horse, perhaps a retired one, that would enjoy sharing your horse's pasture. There are any number of ways to find horses looking for homes; a lot depends on whether you want an animal that can be ridden or will just be a friend for your horse.

Whatever type of companion you get, introduce it gradually and over a fence or from the next stall until both animals are more curious than fearful. And don't introduce a new companion immediately — your mare is going to have quite enough to cope with after moving to a new home and then meeting six dogs.

Don't despair if it takes your mare quite some time to adjust to her new home. If she has moved every year or so since she was a young horse, it will take her a relatively short time to make the adjustment. But if she has lived at only a few barns and has spent quite a few years at the last one, give her time to adjust to her new surroundings and situation. Give her the time she needs to adjust, be patient, spend extra time with her, and show her that her new home is a very nice place to be.

Is My Horse Sleep-Deprived?

Q My new horse seems to be fitting in well at home with my other three horses. They normally share a big pasture during the day, and I put them in stalls at night. For the last few months since he came here, I have had to reverse this schedule and turn them out at night, as it is very sunny and hot in the daytime and there is no shade in my pasture. This seems to be working out, but I am worried that my new horse is not getting enough sleep. Whenever I go into the barn during the day, the others are awake, but he always seems to be asleep and then wakes up when I come into the barn. Is my turnout schedule disturbing his

The yawning horse may be sleepy, bored, or just very relaxed.

sleep pattern, or is there something else wrong? He did not do this during the first month; he was always very alert in the daytime, even though they were already on the night turnout schedule. Also, why is it that I never catch all of the horses sleeping at once? One of them is always awake (not always the same one, though).

A Your new horse is napping during the day. Horses don't sleep very much — typically four hours out of twenty-four — and they don't get all their sleep at once. Sleep in the form of short naps is normal for a horse.

In a herd, horses take turns "standing guard" so that the rest of the herd can graze and nap. Even in a small, domestic herd, this still holds true. If you spent a day or two just watching your horses constantly, you would see that there is always one horse on guard.

Horses that are physically separated from other horses or that are new to a group of horses and don't yet know exactly where they fit in tend to sleep less than regular herd members. As soon as the new additions become part of the herd — or even find a single buddy — they begin to nap more, because they now have someone to stand guard over them.

If your new horse was a little bit sleep-deprived during his first month in his new home, he's obviously catching up now that he trusts your other horses to stand guard while he naps. It sounds as though he's fitting into his new home very well.

CHAPTER 23

There's Always
More to Learn

THERE'S ALWAYS MORE TO LEARN, and good horsemen never stop learning. The study of horsemanship requires at least one full lifetime, and the subjects that touch on horses, riding, and horsemanship are limitless. Horse and human anatomy, physiology, psychology, and biomechanics, horse management, the art of riding, the history and practice of horsemanship — even if you include the study of tack and equipment, you'll still have barely scratched the surface of the subject. True horsemen find this exhilarating. There is so much to learn, and in such depth, that a true interest in horsemanship guarantees that you will never stop using your brain, you will never stop developing your intuition, and you will never be bored.

Problem-Solving: Alone or with Help?

Q I guess you'd probably call me a cowboy. I've spent most of my life on horseback on the family ranch on land that was originally purchased by my great-grandfather. We're lucky: Our kids seem like they want to keep running the ranch, so they're always ready for a discussion about horses.

Over the years, there have been just a few horses that I couldn't work with. Most of the time I can get things done with horses without too much trouble. One of my kids is also good with horses. He's 18 and pretty much thinks he can ride anything and train anything, and he doesn't always pay a whole lot of attention to his old dad, who says that sometimes you need to back off and hand the horse over to a professional. I'm proud of him, but I'm getting more cautious in my old age, and when I was his age I made a lot of mistakes and broke a lot of bones that I now wish I hadn't. I know he has to make his own mistakes — we all do — but I'd just as soon he didn't get too busted up in the process.

> *I want my son to work through the problems he can work through, but I don't want him risking his neck.*

I want to know how *you* make up your mind if somebody needs to work through their horse problem by himself or if he needs to get professional help. I don't think there's any shame in bringing in a pro — heck, we do it all the time with vets and farriers. I guess I've always just done one or the other without really thinking about it; I just sort of get a feeling that either the problem is something I can handle or it's something I need help on. But now that I'm trying to explain this to my son, I need to be able to tell him something more than, "I just get a feeling." I want him to learn to work through the problems he can work through, but I don't want him risking his neck taking on a problem he isn't equipped to handle.

A You're asking about a decision-making process, and more than that, you're asking about brain mapping! Not an easy question to answer, but I'll have a go.

There's a lot that goes into any decision: conscious thought; unconscious thought; everything you've ever learned about horses, riding, training, and humans; everything you know and believe about training; your basic attitude toward horses and humans and learning; and probably some things I haven't even thought of. You don't run through all these things on a conscious level, but they're in your head, and they inform everything you do.

That's why a good trainer or teacher has to be informed *and* aware. Being informed will equip you with good general information and principles to follow, and awareness will help you notice every tiny detail about a specific horse and a specific human and their interaction in a specific situation. Lacking the information, the awareness isn't very useful. You might notice that a horse has his ears back and is waving his head, but if you didn't understand that this body language is threat behavior, you could get hurt.

You might notice that a horse isn't eating, and, in fact, is rolling around in his stall, but if you didn't understand colic, you might just go back to the house and think, "Silly horse, playing instead of eating breakfast!" Or you might see a horse pin his ears back and shift away when the rider starts to mount, and think, "That horse doesn't like that rider," instead of wondering about how well the saddle fits the horse.

Intuition is a good thing to have, and it's something that you can develop over time. It's not a magical gift from the Intuition Fairy. It can be learned and practiced and practiced some more, and the more you use your intuition, the better and faster and more accurate it will become. It's nothing more and nothing less than the ability to take in a lot of information very quickly, shift it around, process it, filter it, find a pattern in it, and come up with one or more possible answers. Intuition also isn't foolproof, but it's useful. The important thing to remember is that even intuition is based on information — lots of it — and the ideas you get don't come out of the clear blue sky. They come from inside your own mind, and what you get out of your mind depends on what you've put into it over the years.

At clinics and lectures, whenever I'm answering questions, I try to get as much information as possible from the questioner, because sometimes the initial question isn't the one that really needs answering. For example, "How can I make my horse keep his mouth closed?" isn't a useful question, but "What's making my horse open his mouth, and what can I do to change the situation so that the horse is comfortable and doesn't want to open his mouth?" is a very good question. It's also what the questioner really wants and needs to know.

Since so many problems and horse behaviors are actually reactions to the actions or lack of actions of a rider or a handler, I've learned to go under and around and through the actual question and try to deal with the real issues behind it.

As for when I might say, "Do it yourself" and when I would say, "Call a professional," it depends on the situation, the circumstances, the horse, and the knowledge, abilities, and attitude of the human. Most problems exist on a sort of sliding scale. If someone says to me: "My four-year-old is just learning to go out on trails, and whenever we leave the property, as soon as he realizes that he's alone, he stops for a minute and gets a little light in front. I'm worried that he might actually rear one of these days, so how do I prevent that?" then I have a *lot* of information about that person's attitude and knowledge, and I have a good amount of information about the horse. In these cases, I'll typically say, "Here's what you can do."

On the other hand, if someone says to me: "I just bought a horse and I always thought I wanted a horse, but this one is scaring me. I've only had him two months and he has a real attitude problem; he rears whenever he doesn't want to obey. Lately he's been rearing up so high he's fallen over backward. I managed to get out of the way just in time, but I'm scared he'll crush me one of these days. How do I make him stop and get his mind right?" then I also have quite a lot of information about that person's attitude and knowledge and abilities and a good amount of information about the horse. I have enough information overall to know that this is an extremely dangerous situation that is rapidly getting out of control, and it's time to bring in someone who can help.

What will do your son the most good, now and forever, will be learning to ask himself, Is this the best thing for the horse? He must answer that question honestly. If he does that, his ego won't be on the line. It won't be all about him, it'll be all about the horse.

What will do your son the most good, now and forever, will be learning to ask himself, Is this the best thing for the horse? He must answer that question honestly. If he does that, he'll handle things himself some of the time and call in the professionals when he needs them, and his ego won't be on the line either way. It won't be all about *him;* it'll be all about the horse.

When you're 18, it's hard to learn to put your ego aside, but that's what horsemen do, and it sounds to me as though you've raised a horseman. Realizing that what you're doing with a horse is about the horse, not the trainer, is quite an achievement, but it's worth making the daily effort to do what's right. As your son gets older and accumulates thoughtful, considered experience (that's the kind where 20 years of experience is 20 years of different experience, not the same year's experience repeated 20 times), he'll be in a position to follow not only in your footsteps but also in those of trainers like Bill and Tom Dorrance, Ray Hunt, Mark Rashid, and Harry Whitney — good horsemen all. Horsemanship combines knowledge, understanding, respect, affection, skills, and experience. It doesn't require special talents — just a lifetime of dedication. The learning never stops, and you can continue to improve as long as you live. The more you understand about horse behavior, the better horseman you will be.

Resources

Now that you have an idea of what's involved in developing your horse-handling abilities and your intuition, here are some resources that will help you continue your horse-related education, even if you never leave your home.

On-line Resources
Dr. Jessica Jahiel's Holistic Horsemanship: www.jessicajahiel.com
Dr. Jessica Jahiel's HORSE-SENSE e-mail newsletter and archives: www.horse-sense.org

Some other extremely useful Web sites for advice and information about horses:
Gincy Bucklin: www.xpos.com/ofonemind/gincy.htm
Cherry Hill: www.horsekeeping.com
Rick Lamb: www.thehorseshow.com
   Radio program about horses, interviews archived and available online

Books
Ainslie, Tom, and Bonnie Ledbetter. *The Body Language of Horses.* William Morrow & Co., New York, NY, 1980.
Berger, Joel. *Wild Horses of the Great Basin.* University of Chicago Press, Chicago, IL, 1986.
Blake, Henry. *Talking With Horses.* Trafalgar Square Publishing, North Pomfret, VT, 1992.
_____. *Thinking With Horses.* Trafalgar Square Publishing, North Pomfret, VT, 1993.
Bucklin, Gincy. *What Your Horse Wants You to Know.* Wiley Europe, 2003.
Dorrance, Tom. *True Unity.* Quill Driver Books, Sanger, CA, 1994.

Hill, Cherry. *The Formative Years.* Breakthrough Publications, Ossining, NY, 1998.

____. *Making, Not Breaking.* Breakthrough Publications, Ossining, NY, 1992.

____. *Horse Handling and Grooming.* Workman Publishing Company, New York, NY, 1997.

Hunt, Ray. *Think Harmony with Horses.* Quill Driver Books, Sanger, CA, 1991.

Jahiel, Jessica. *Bits and Saddles,* Storey Country Wisdom Bulletin, Storey Publishing, North Adams, MA, 2001.

Kiley-Worthington, Marthe. *The Behaviour of Horses.* J. A. Allen & Co., Ltd., London, England, 1999.

Kurland, Alexandra. *Clicker Training for Your Horse.* Sunshine Books, Waltham, MA, 1999.

Langley, Garda. *Understanding Horses.* Trafalgar Square Publishing, North Pomfret, VT, 1990.

McCall, Jim, Dr. *Influencing Horse Behavior.* Alpine Publications, Loveland, CO, 1988.

McCall, Jim, Dr., and Lynda McCall. *Horses Behavin' Badly.* Half Halt Press, Boonsboro, MD, 1997.

McDonnell, Sue. *Understanding Horse Behavior.* Eclipse Press, Lexington, KY, 1999.

Miller, Robert. *Imprint Training.* The Lyons Press, Guilford, DE, 1992.

Rashid, Mark. *Considering the Horse.* Johnson Books, Boulder, CO, 1993.

____. *A Good Horse is Never a Bad Color.* Johnson Books, Boulder, CO, 1996.

____. *Horses Never Lie.* Johnson Books, Boulder, CO, 2000.

Rashid, Mark and Harry Whitney. *Life Lessons from a Ranch Horse.* Johnson Books, Boulder, CO, 2003.

Schafer, Michael. *The Language of the Horse.* Arco Publishing, New York, NY, 1974.

Skipper, Lesley. *Inside Your Horse's Mind.* J. A. Allen & Co., Ltd., London, England, 1999.

Waring, George H. *Horse Behavior,* 2nd ed. Noyes Publications / William Andrew Publishing, Norwich, NY, 2003.

INDEX

Page numbers in *italic* indicate illustrations.